going back

MONICA JACKSON

Dedicated

to my grandchildren:

Laura, Jessica, and Matthew

Acknowledgement

I should like to acknowledge with unending gratitude the help given me in the preparation of this manuscript by my beloved husband, Bob.

introduction

This book is about what it was like to grow up in a well-loved place, to be exiled from it for twenty years, and then to revisit it in the role of an allegedly unbiased observer.

I was born and brought up in the south Indian hills. My parents and grandparents were coffee planters, and the plantation of Honnametti on the Biligirirangan range was my territorial base until I was over thirty. Although my husband and I lived in other parts of India after our marriage, Honnametti remained our refuge until we left India in 1953, and our children were the fourth generation of my family to think of it as home.

When our children's education was completed, it was time to make good the ragged gaps in my own. I graduated from Cambridge at the age of fifty with a first degree in archaeology and anthropology, and then went on to take an M.Phil. in social anthropology and a PhD. in demographic anthropology at the University of Edinburgh. It made sense to do the fieldwork for these studies in a region with which I was familiar, and it was therefore undertaken in a taluk of Mysore district in the state of Karnataka. The taluk contains and is bounded by the Biligirirangan hills, which are relatively easy of access from its administrative and market town, which is also a railhead.

My previous links with the area provided a foundation of background information which mercifully eased that first sticky period when I wondered what on earth I was doing there and what on earth to do next. Not only was I furnished with a ready-made entrée into the local social networks but also with a unique opportunity to observe the effects of social change over the past quarter-century. To put it another way, my chief qualification for doing research in that particular part of the world was a matter of nurture.

My second research project arose out of my earlier study of caste and kinship in the area. It was a population study which sought to determine the effects of caste cultures on fertility. This meant going beyond the traditional methods of participant observation employed by generations of anthropologists and carrying out a questionnaire survey. My early reservations, based on a general distrust of the questionnaire form as a clumsy method of obtaining information, faded as I began to realise that many of the respondents regarded the interviews as a rare opportunity to air their views and pour out their domestic grievances to unbiased but sympathetic listeners.

This was especially true of the women. What they had to say confirmed my growing conviction that all the efforts of India's family planning campaign would fail to solve its population problem unless a radical improvement in the status of India's women gave them the self-confidence and independence they need to gain and retain control over their own fertility.

Between 1974 and 1981 I lived in Kollepet for varying periods of time, once for a year and never for less than four months. Apart from an initial sojourn with a typical high-caste Hindu joint family in the taluk town, I lived in a mud-walled and palm-thatched shack on the fringe of a mixed-caste village which I will call Lokkanhalli. The room-with-verandah which I rented there was my operational centre for nearly eight years. Along with its other advantages, it was a base from which I could visit and re-visit my dear wild uplands.

Malinowski's classic injunction to anthropologists to come down from the verandah is hardly applicable, taken at face value, to south India, where every hut, however humble, has its verandah as a focus of activity. Living alone and cooking for myself on the cow-dunged floor of my own verandah, I received a constant stream of visitors of both sexes and all ages, castes and classes. Nor was participant observation by any means neglected. On the contrary, it was omnipresent and unavoidable, and there were times when I could have done without it. Wherever I went, shopping, working, visiting people's houses or other villages, going to the temple, attending ceremonies, travelling on buses, I was involved subjectively as well as observing (I hope) objectively. Furthermore, I was in turn observed, discussed and no doubt classified. But it was not long before I was also accepted as an interesting cuckoo in the taluk's cultural nest.

The goodwill earned by my parents which, twenty years on, led to this tolerance of my presence was summed up on one occasion by a pillar of Kollepet society in a welcoming address. "We will not call her a visitor. She belongs here and is one of us." It was a generous compliment but, conscious as I was of the honour and advantages of being offered, so to speak, the freedom of Kollepet taluk, I was often aware of the advantages of not in fact belonging there, and of the positive value for an anthropologist of this ambiguous position. On the one hand people were able to 'place' me. On the other, as a well-disposed stranger with no local axe to grind, I was regarded as an ideal recipient of gossip and grumble, anecdote and shrewd comment, which afforded me many an insight into the usages of caste and class and the way in which individuals manipulated traditional codes and concepts as best they could to suit their personal requirements. One thing which always struck me in the days when I laboured studiously through the approved ethnographic monographs was the effortless way in which the authors managed to converse with the locals, apparently without the help of interpreters. How could I ever compete with my meagre store of residual Kannada, I wondered anxiously, when I realised I was committed to Kollepet. The surprising discovery of an academic lady from Karnataka in Edinburgh led to language lessons with her.

"But you can't say it like that," she exclaimed in dismay as I dredged up forgotten phrases. "It's incorrect." What she really meant was that it was uncouth. Armed, therefore, with a few carefully memorised flowers of refined speech, I tried them on my first hosts in Kollepet. They fell about with mirth. "You can't say it like that," they cried. "Only poets and pandits talk like that." I tried them on the villagers. "We only speak Kannada," they replied. In the end I found that my original Kannada patois slowly came back and was understood perfectly by the villagers, who talked that way anyhow. In time a compromise was also effected with the more educated, although their Indian English, even in its pidgin form, was always a good deal more fluent than my laborious efforts at polite Kannada diction. In short, although I learned to grasp the gist of even good Kannada, I mostly spoke Indian English with the more educated unless I had a companion to interpret. But I got along fine with my peasant friends in their own language. I would like to stress here that the following chapters are meant to be illustrative of my experiences rather than exhaustive. Finding the task of distilling the experiences of many years quite beyond me, I have chosen to present a series of remembered incidents in the form of flashbacks to portray my family's life in India in the past. For the rest I have taken from my diaries a representative five days or so in village and town, and a few weeks in the hills, to exemplify the kind of ongoing drama (to lapse into jargon) in which I was involved in the course of my research, plus my personal reactions to living in the village and to revisiting my old haunts in the hills.

It remains to me now to acknowledge a few debts to those with whom I have latterly had dealings in India.

The presence in Bangalore of Laeeq Futehally, my alter ego of many years, whose parents and mine had been old friends and who knew Honnametti in its former glory, was a great comfort. She and her husband Zafar put up patiently with the traumas of my retreats from the field to the refuge of their house (usually in the throes of some indisposition), and were sparing in their reproof. The same is true of my fictive 'aunt' Ivy Muthanna, who nurtured, chided and aided me. That hospitable pair of family friends, de Wet and Joubert Van Ingen, never failed to offer bath, bed and a stiff gin as a panacea for the neuroses and crises of fieldwork. Living in Mysore, less than fifty miles from Kollepet, they were called upon quite often over the years for asylum. I am also beholden to the staff of Honnametti, Kartikerri and Attikan estates for their kindness and interest in my family affairs; to Sri K.S. Vaidyanathan for the shelter of Attikan bungalow; to my friendly Kollepet landlord; to gentle Dr. Jaya; and to all those other friends in the town, villages and forest settlements of the taluk whose forbearance was so often imposed upon by my silly questions.

For various reasons I have changed the names of taluk, town and village, along with those of all the characters I mention in the first five chapters. But I have been unable to bring myself to change any names, whether of people or places, in the hills. I know this seems illogical, but for the purposes of this book I think it is the right way to do it.

One final point: The stout volumes which comprise my academic findings currently lurk in the vaults of Edinburgh University and may be consulted there by anyone driven by a fanatical urge to do so. Meanwhile, those looking for weighty scholarship in the following pages have got the wrong book. This one isn't really about anthropology at all. It's about a love affair between a person and a place.

the divided village

Something fell out of the thatch and flopped on the top of the mosquito net. Suddenly awake, inwardly groaning bloody-hell-what-now, I reached for the torch at once and shone it upward. The battery was too low for the dim light to reveal more than a few small bulges in the cotton cloth stretched overhead. None of them moved. Most of them were caused, I knew, by the usual bits of palm-leaf and defunct beetles I had to shake off from time to time, but there were other possibilities. I left the torch on for comfort (it needed a new battery anyway to reduce the risk of treading on a snake if I had to make one of my reluctant sorties to the latrine round the back of the hut) and lay in my sheet sleeping bag speculating on these possibilities.

Not a snake (though a cobra had once glided into the room through the door in daylight), because the bulges now revealed were not big enough. It could be a big cockroach. I hate cockroaches: they always seem to be lurking in a sinister manner or rushing about hysterically. It could be a big centipede, of which I was truly scared because of its poisonous bite. Or, worse, it could be a big scorpion. Well now, what else could that flop portend? Most likely a baby rat. The roof-tree of the shack was literally a tree, a long palm-trunk resting on forked wooden posts, running beneath the apex of the sloping thatched roof and supporting it. The rats which used this central beam as a highway and forum in their comings and goings from their homes in the thatch clearly regarded it as their private domain, and I myself tended as a rule to regard them as the people upstairs. Noisy perhaps, but otherwise not much of a nuisance. It was true that during the night recently a huge rat had squatted on the beam above my bed and peed. It's urine had gone straight through the mosquito net and sprayed me and the sleeping bag. Scrambling indignantly from under the net, regardless of what insect or reptile life my bare feet might encounter, I had shone the torch on the monster and squirted insect spray at it to dislodge it. It had moved off unhurriedly, waited till I was back in bed, returned to the same spot, and peed on me again. But apart from this somewhat bizarre episode, the rats and I usually lived separate lives which did not impinge on the other unless a young one lost its footing on the beam and either fell with a lethal splat on the cow-dunged earthen floor of the hut or bounced on to the top of the mosquito net.

But the rat episode had happened three weeks before. Whatever it was that had disturbed me tonight, I was now wide awake and prey to the midnight sound effects of rural Kollepet taluk. A night-watchman's transistor blasted film music from the field behind the hut, which currently bore a flourishing crop of the millet jwara awaiting harvest. A wedding feast broadcasted through hired loudspeakers, the theme-song of a different film, while from the temporary cinema recently erected between my village of Lokkanhalli and the taluk town, the soundtrack of yet another epic was all too clearly audible. The cinema was, I knew, nearly a mile away to the south. Judging from the direction of the lively din, the wedding was being celebrated in the next village, a mile away to the north. Against this: background of musical decibels, the barking of various pi-dogs failed to drown the distant howling of a pack of jackals. And, effortlessly submerging the rest, the screech of a lorry's windhorn assaulted the ears as it hurtled down the road a hundred yards away. I rolled over and put my head under the pillow.

In spite of the unpromising ambience, sleep came at last, not to be dispelled until the dawn chorus began with the first clunking notes of the 'coppersmith', the crimson-breasted barbet and an early hawk-cuckoo, better (and bitterly) known as the 'brainfever bird', starting to practise its repetitive rising scale. Somewhere in the room the friendly clicking of a gecko, the fat little lizard with suction feet which explores the walls of Indian houses devouring flies, signalled a cheerful start to a new day. In the pale ray of light which filtered through the wooden shutter of my small glassless window, my watch indicated 5 am. My neighbours would be up and about any minute, and if I was to make a visit to the latrine in privacy it was time to creep from under that protective net.

It seemed as well to check first on whatever had fallen out of the thatch on to the top of the mosquito net, and would have fallen on me had it not been for that indispensable shield. The mosquito net was tied with string to the rough-hewn poles which gave lateral support to the thatched roof and, thus suspended above the bed, was tucked in at the bottom under the mattress to form a cage of fine cotton mesh. It was the only possession which I regarded as absolutely essential to my sanity and survival in village India. Fetching the wooden stool from the verandah I stood on it and peered at the top of the net. The night-comer was still there, manifesting itself as a large black lump which I thought at first was a hefty frog crouching on the cloth. Something about its immobility made me peer at it suspiciously and give the net a shake. The lump unfolded and revealed itself as a great black scorpion, scuttling towards me with curving claws and upreared sting. I jumped off the stool with a yelp, ran outside and grabbed a long stick from a pile of brush-wood my neighbours had gathered for fuel. Returning at a gallop, desperate to intercept the unwelcome intruder before it could conceal itself to emerge once more at night, I remounted the stool, knocked the scorpion to the floor and hit the poor brute with a ferocity born of terror. A scorpion that size has a heavily armoured carapace, and by the time I had killed it I was l shaking with a mixture of revulsion and guilt. The atavistic horror inspired by the creature was slow to recede, although I reminded myself that humans are more dangerous than scorpions. After all, I had killed it while it had probably not contemplated killing me unless I sat or trod on it.

The short trip outside through the dewy grass to the latrine and wash-place made me feel better and padding back in pyjamas and flip-flop chappals, I looked around appreciatively. This was the best part of the day. The mud-walled building thatched with rice straw over coconut-palm leaves faced east. In front of it, across a strip of sparse grass, was a big deep round well, flanked by a small concrete outhouse which contained the engine for the electric pump which brought clean water up from far below. From the upper walls of the well shrubs sprouted, with the funnel nests of weaver birds dangling from their branches. To the right and left were rows of young coconut palms. Beyond the well the smallholding was bounded by a hedge of prickly-pear cactus and spiky aloes which separated it from the road, a narrow ribbon of metalled surface fringed by two broad strips of deep dust. Both sides of the road were also fringed with old banyans. Once they had been huge sheltering trees shading the whole road, planted by a past maharajah who, unlike many of his contemporaries, strove for a contented populace as well as for a beautiful State. Now they were reduced to maimed and pollarded stumps by villagers seeking increasingly elusive firewood and fodder for their beasts as the pressure of population on the land increased.

On the far side of the road fields of sugarcane and the millets ragi and jwara stretched to the shores of two reservoirs or 'tanks', Dod Kere and Chik Kere (Big Lake and Little Lake). Below the bunds, the high banks which dammed the waters on their northern side, the irrigated and valuable 'wet lands' grew rice and bananas as well as sugarcane, graceful areca palms and the pan trees which supply the leaves for pān chewing. Ownership of the coveted 'wet lands' ensured financial stability and even wealth for the fortunate proprietors; and though the Land Ceiling laws placed a limit of ten acres for each individual land-owner, there were various and convenient ways of getting around such restrictions. Beyond these rich fields and plantations the 'dry lands' began again, to merge in their turn with the scrub jungle which stretched away to the foot of the hills, blue with distance, which formed a great wall along the eastern horizon. These were the Biligirirangan hills, the White Hills of Rangan, where once I had lived. They held my longing gaze as if they were the promised land.

I was back now, ducking under the edge of the thatch to enter my portion of the long building. The middle bit was a storeroom and the other end housed my neighbours. My part of the house was open to the front, a kind of verandah, which contained my little desk and stool; two cane chairs; a rickety wooden table; a small kerosene stove about the size and shape of a large Primus; some cooking pots; and a metal cupboard which kept rats, ants and cockroaches out of my foodstuffs. This was in fact my living room. The bedroom opening off it contained a very hard, solid wooden bed on which lay a thin flock mattress and a sheet sleeping bag. Over this hung the tucked-in mosquito net. Apart from the bed and net there was another metal cupboard for clothing and a set of wooden shelves on which stood washing things and a plastic basin. A towel and a short cotton dressing-gown hung over a pole supported by two wires hanging from the roof. I entered and lifted the dressing-gown, wincing as a fat cockroach dropped from its folds and scurried off, and donned it after a shake to dislodge any further domestic hangers-on. Next I opened the wooden shutter. Then I returned to the verandah to brew my morning tea on the stove, a simple kerosene burner which engendered a lot of black smoke and coated my pans with soot. Seated in the comfortable old cane chair rather than the modern metal one, the seat of which was made of a slippery plastic raffia which gradually slid one off it, I sipped the first cup of the day and wished this innocent hour before sunrise could go on indefinitely. But within a few minutes the business of the day had overtaken it as Siddha, the father of the neighbouring family who lived at the other end of the mud-walled building we shared, came out of his verandah, a grey-haired bony figure fully dressed today in shirt and shorts and pushing his bicycle instead of making his usual trip to the well outlet in his brief dhoti for a wash. We exchanged salutes. "Yelli hogitaree, Siddhappa?" (Where are you going, father Siddha?) I asked. He replied that his employer, my landlord, had told him to get off to the village early to make sure that the gumpu or team of female labourers would turn up that morning to pick the flowers in the onion field. "Sulpa matches takambani, Appa" (Then please bring me a few matches). "Serre serre," (All right) he replied and departed.

I sat looking at the silhouette of the hills and planning the day ahead, but my peace was once more disturbed by four almost simultaneous occurrences. The sun rose above the hills, sending a ray of warm light under the thatch; the first of the daytime lorries screamed down the road asserting its macho right to the central metal strip by a continuous blast of its windhorn; the huge blue creatures which resembled fat hornets and spent the daylight hours obsessively drilling holes in the poles supporting the verandah thatch started buzzing in to begin work; and Mahadevi, Siddha's eleven-year-old daughter, came in smiling shyly and picked up my plastic buckets. Normally Siddha kindly filled them for me when he went to turn on the pump, but in his absence Mahadevi had obviously been told to take over. She was much too small to be allowed to attempt the job. To the accompaniment of her protests, we filled the buckets together at the water outlet and staggered back with them one at a time, liberally splashed. Mahadevi retired with my hot-water pot to put it on her mother's wood fire, returning immediately with a grass broom almost as big as herself and disappeared into my sleeping quarter. Sighing, I sat down again to await the completion of this chore, to which she appeared to attach an almost ritual significance. I hated her sweeping out the room, which I could do much better myself and which achieved little but raising a cloud of dust to settle on my soap and toothbrush. But it was regarded by her and her parents as a justification for the five rupees I gave her every week, which went into their savings for her wedding, and so there was nothing for it but to acquiesce.

In due course she reappeared, driving before her with the broom a reluctant frog which she had rudely evicted from a cool corner. This too was a daily occurrence. She shooed the frog outside and round the corner of the building. As soon as she went away the frog came back inside, hopping purposefully across the verandah towards the open bedroom door.

By this time the sun was getting hot. A resolute column of large black ants were marching in to cross the smoothly cow-dunged floor of the verandah on some mysterious mission of their own; and the two-way traffic of the hornets had intensified. While they flew in quite normally they had an eccentric way of going out, casting themselves in a Kamikaze dive to the floor, which they hit with a loud crack before ricocheting off under the overhang of the thatch into the sunlight beyond. Occasionally they ricocheted off me if I was sitting there, and this I did not much care for, although I had been assured that they were harmless, unlike the true hornets, sinister yellow things like nuclear missiles, which also flew in quite frequently.

It was time to start the working day. Behind the closed door and window of my bedroom I laid down my straw mat, went through my boring routine of yoga exercises, came out carrying my day-clothes, picked up the pot of warm water deposited in the verandah by Siddha's wife Rangi, and heaved it round to my bathplace at the end of the building. The bathplace was roofless, its mud walls about five feet high protecting the user's modesty but affording no protection against the weather. It was divided into two spaces by an inner wall separating the latrine from the bath area. When I first came to the smallholding, the latrine was a hole in the earth and the bath area a stone slab for keeping one's feet off the earth. The daily dousing of bathwater this patch received made it one of the most fertile spots in Karnataka, and it grew a knee-deep crop of green grass. Later, my landlord had the floor cemented and a kind of cesspool built under the latrine, which meant I had to keep a bucket of water and a beaker there for flushing it. Apart from that, conditions were unchanged. It was still full of ants in assorted sizes which bit fiercely when discommoded, and during the monsoons I took many an involuntary shower in addition to sloshing water over myself in the bath area or when answering the urgent calls of nature which were such a feature of my frequent attacks of gastro-enteritis.

After the bath, breakfast consisted of two little local bananas, each about four inches long and a Coorg orange, as big as a Jaffa but with a skin as easily removed as that of a tangerine. Then, with the stool drawn up to the desk, work began on checking the questionnaire forms collected from my four interviewers the day before. The first interruption was caused by Siddha's return, alone. "Aren't the women coming?" I asked, reimbursing him for the matches. He shrugged and spat eloquently. Exploited though the female agricultural labourers of the taluk were, being paid at that time half the wage of the males for the same type and duration of work, they did have some redress. When they formed a gumpu they derived a certain collective power from the situation and were thus enabled to play off one landowner against another and so extract better wages. In this situation they were quite unscrupulous, though justifiably so, about defaulting on prior arrangements. Siddha was in the anomalous position of having a foot in both camps. As the landowner's sole employee-cum-farm manager, it was his business to organise hired labour to do the maximum of work for the minimum of pay. At least, that was the view of his employer. On the other hand Siddha, like the hired workers, was a Harijan, low-caste and poor, with a wife who from time to time laboured on the lands of others. If he had owned the land himself it would have been a different matter but he did not and therefore wasn't about to break his heart over the defection of the gumpu. But he did want to keep his job.

Shortly after nine o'clock Govinda Rajan, owner of the six-acre tote (farm) and the dwelling I shared with Siddha and his family, arrived on his scooter, immaculately clad as usual in sports shirt, well-pressed terylene trousers and dark glasses. We hardly had time to exchange greetings before he realised that the gumpu was not to be seen, and the shouting-match with Siddha began. Returning to the forms I minded my own business with discreet ostentation until, worn out with recrimination, G.R. turned away and ducked under the thatch overhang to enter the verandah. "Those damn women," he complained, mopping his forehead with a nice clean handkerchief and collapsing moodily into the raffia chair. While I finished my checking Siddha entered in dignified silence, selected a mamuti (hoe) from the storeroom which separated our residences, and stalked off through the palms to the fields, his back radiating a sense of injury.

"Listen, Govind," I said, shoving the forms into a drawer. "I've had an idea. I'll help you pick off the flowers. If we start now, you and Siddha and I could get it all done in a few hours."

He looked appalled. "I can't do that," he said.

"Why not?"

"Because it would be beneath my dignity." He looked ready to cry.

"All right. I'll do it with Siddha then."

"Siddha has to start digging up the ground nuts today. Besides, whatever you may do in your own country, it would look very bad if I was seen to let you do that work here. People would talk."

"But what about your onion crop?"

"I suppose another day or two won't do it much harm," he muttered, trying to make the best of it.

In that case, I suggested, hoping to cheer him up, he might as well make the most of a day off. Why didn't we go to visit his brother's farm, the one he'd been wanting to show me, beyond Dod Kere? This did cheer him up. We agreed that he would return to Kollepet, the taluk town where he lived, and leave a message at the house where my interviewers rented rooms, telling them to meet me later than had been previously arranged. He would then come back in the afternoon and we would walk to the other farm together. I offered him some tea or coffee, which he hastily refused, accepting instead a glass of mango squash. In traditional south India tea leaves or coffee powder are boiled up with milk and quantities of sugar to make a thick, sweet, strong leverage which bears no resemblance to the watery Western brew which I persisted in producing and which my visitors found almost undrinkable, though they were usually too polite to say so.

As soon as G.R. had left to give further instructions to Siddha prior to departing for his joint family household in the town, I braced myself to change into stronger sandals, don dark glasses and headscarf, gather up notebook and ballpoint, and set off, not without a sigh, to make a family-composition survey in the nearby village.

Although G.R.'s smallholding was not far from either main road or village, it was sufficiently distant and screened by palms and hedges to make it a relative haven of peace and privacy. Once through the rickety bamboo gate and out on the road I was fair game for one and all. When I first came to undertake fieldwork in the taluk, one of my worst trials was the unwelcome company of small boys who followed me, shouting, giggling, and trying out their common stock of south Indian English with maddeningly repeated cries of "Whaaat is the time? Whaaat is your name?" As the seasons rolled on most of the Lokkenhalli urchins came to know me quite well, many of them having been brought or sent by their parents to my quarters from time to time with cuts or sores to be treated with disinfectant, ointment, plasters, and a handful of sweets. They had had the tables turned on them with my enquiries of "Nimma Izcsaru yemi?" (What is your name?), as I strove to distinguish between the little Baswas, Rangas, Nanjas and Jownas, as well as the somewhat more coy Baswis, Rangis, Nanjis and Jownis. As a result most of them had abandoned catcalls in favour of the proud display of healed wounds and the greeting, "Amma, Amma, do you remember me? My toe (or knee, or shin) is better now." Their beaming smiles were heartwarming, no doubt, but there was a catch. My unsought image as Lady Bountiful had misled the local populace into regarding me as a free and limitless source of the much prized patti, or elastoplast dressings. And this came expensive, to say nothing of the inconvenience of constantly having to dig out a patti along with a sweetie for some little dear to take home for a Granny's alleged injury. Fortunately, I was usually away from the farm for much of the day.

Today I was swiftly surrounded, a reluctant Pied Piper, by a mob of children. It was not long before they grasped exactly what I was doing as I went nervously from door to door explaining my purpose and reassuring the women that I had no official axe to grind. "Ikadi, ikadi," (this way) those in the vanguard cried. "You haven't done this street yet." By the time I was half-way through they had practically taken over the investigation and were introducing me to the householders. "Don't worry, she only wants to know....etc." The advantage of moving around in the centre of a local posse rapidly dawned on me. With a horde of children jostling round me, people accepted me much more readily but at the same time the more inquisitive householders were less inclined to invite me in for coffee and a brisk session of counter-interrogation.

In the end only one person begged me so hard to enter that I could not refuse her. She shut the door smartly in the eager juvenile faces and, to my surprise, offered her hospitality in halting English. She was a tall, graceful woman, obviously literate since she held a book in her hand and, remembering that we were now in the Ganigar or oil-presser quarter, I realised that she must be the Brahman woman I had heard about. Her brother was a bus-driver who had one day brought home one of his mates, a Ganigar by caste. The young Brahman daughter of the house had fallen in love with this man of comparatively low caste and had eventually eloped with him. Her Brahman parents, while sufficiently neo-liberal to have allowed their son to bring into their house a fairly low-caste person and their daughter to meet him, had found this cross-caste marriage too much to accept. They ostracised her from that time on and now she lived a lonely life in a community to which she did not belong, more educated than and differently brought up from the other women of the quarter. Today she talked and listened avidly, plying her guest with coffee to keep her longer. When I left she entreated me to come again. I asked her to come and visit me at the smallholding and she said she would, but I suspected that she would not. She had made her one great bid for freedom, but she did not seem like the kind of person constitutionally capable of taking on the whole system, and well-brought-up young women of high caste from orthodox families do not go out unaccompanied by their menfolk.

By the end of this visit half my juvenile escort had lost interest and drifted off, while the rest had begun to flag, as had I. In fact, the Ganigar and Kumbar Shetti (potters) quarters in the village were the last on the morning's schedule, the Harijans having already endured a previous visitation. The village revealed the close parallels between the structures of caste and class in rural India which, while by no means as concordant as they were in the past, still tend to coincide fairly well. At the northern end, where today's investigation had started, there were wide spaces, shaded here and there by huge trees, pipul, tamarind and banyan, under which cattle rested, chewing cud peacefully. The streets were relatively wide, permitting the progress (though not the passing) of bullock carts, and the houses which lined them were the traditional village dwellings of the well-to-do. They had railed verandahs and tiled roofs which sloped downward in the middle like a funnel to permit rainwater to run into a shallow reservoir in the central room and to allow light to penetrate the cool dimness within. The rooms surrounding this central space were illuminated by small barred glassless windows supplied with wooden shutters to protect the privacy of the household's females. In these comparatively posh houses lived the Lingayats and Brahmans. The majority were Lingayats, members of the largest and most important caste in the state, and certainly dominant in this area.

The southerly part of the village housed the Kumbar Shettis, Ganigars, and other 'clean' low castes (in contrast to the 'untouchable' Harijans, who had a separate quarter adjoining the village). Here the 'streets' were no more than narrow, smelly alleys, each with its central drain, a shallow runnel of filthy water, buzzing with flies, recipient of the garbage thrown out of the close-packed huts. The mud-walled dwellings roofed with palm thatch each had a back room, part kitchen, part sleeping quarters for the females, with a front verandah which was the domain of the males. Crowded as the huts were with the families who lived in them, even more space was taken up by the local cottage industry, the breeding of silkworms in large round frames of intricately woven palm leaves. Around the gutters the smaller children played, with snotty noses and fly-plagued eyes, frequently left with older siblings while their mothers and grandmothers went to work in the fields or factories. In the past they would have been left for even longer, as the women would have had to walk a mile each way to Chik Kere to fetch water. In those days, Lokkanhalli men had difficulty in finding wives since parents in the town or surrounding villages did not wish to subject their daughters to a lifetime of hard labour. Today there are several standpipes in the village, around which the low-caste wives stand gossiping (since they are free to go about unaccompanied) and the families of Lokkanhalli men can look beyond the village for spouses for their sons.

That they still do not look far was confirmed by a survey I did, which showed that most wives came from within easy walking distance of the village. Frequent visits to and by their natal families thus presented no problem. This attests to the south Indian predilection for marriages between cross-cousins (children of mother's brothers or father's sisters) as well as between a man and his elder sister's daughter, who is categorised by the kinship system as a terminological cross-cousin. Marriage within the kutumba, the bilateral family, is still preferred in south India, in contrast to the very different kinship system of north India. The northern system is much harder on the women, contributing as it does to their separation from their natal kin, their uncertain position in their marital households which is only resolved by the bearing of sons, and the low esteem in which they are held.

By the time I walked out of the village I had developed the inevitable stress headache which never failed to ensue after a bout of door-to-door interviewing. A shy person myself, and one who values privacy, I always felt guilty about invading the privacy of others and sympathetic towards those who refused or postponed interviews. On the other hand my sympathy with these was nothing compared to my gratitude to the majority who were ready and willing to impart information, even though it often meant imparting a great deal of information about myself in return.

Across the road a group of Helluva women gathered round their standpipe waved at me amid shrieks and giggles. Waving back, I turned firmly away towards home. One had to be feeling very strong and preferably, to have some moral support when visiting the Helluva quarter which, like that of the Harijans, formed a sort of suburb to the main village. The Helluvas are a caste of beggar-bards. In the past the men wandered from village to village singing traditional ballads based on the Hindu epics and Puranas. Now they sing songs from films, clubbing together to send a few of their number to the cinema to learn the words and tunes. When they are at home they get drunk on home-brewed liquor, the only people I know of in the area with a drink problem. The women, left to themselves for most of the time, cut grass and gather herbs to sell. They are all pretty uninhibited, and on the one occasion I had ventured reluctantly into their quarter in the interests of research, my companion, a Kollepet stalwart, had been so nervous that we had come away somewhat short of data on their community's birth rate and family planning arrangements, to say nothing of their ambiguous place in the local caste system.

Along with the others on the road, I made my way down the middle to avoid trudging through the thick dust impregnated with human and animal ordure on the unpaved portions on either side. This central strip was thronged shortly after sunrise and before sunset by herds of cattle and flocks of sheep and goats, raising clouds of dust. At midday only bullock carts, bicycles, pedestrians and the odd dog, buffalo or sacred bull competed for its amenities, to be driven off into the dust every few minutes by a shrieking brownish whirlwind which disclosed itself in passing to be yet another truck driven by yet another driver with foot strenuously applied to accelerator, hand apparently glued to windhorn and no time for such trivialities as brakes, rear-view mirror or rules of the road. From time to time two of these titans, travelling in opposite directions, approached each other at speed and engaged in a battle of wills which ended at the last moment in a wild swerve into the dust of the 'soft shoulder', scattering pedestrians and other livestock like fallen leaves.

It all made for unrestful walking, and I took refuge in nostalgic recollections of the old days when we drove along this road on our way from the hills to Mysore before the era of the juggernauts, indeed before there was much other motorised traffic on the road at all. Even then everyone, including ourselves, kept to the crown of the road. We did so to avoid the razor-sharp cast bullock shoes which lurked in the soft dust at the sides and caused punctures. But at least we drove with less verve and flamboyance.

In those days we passed through Kollepet on our way to more salubrious places, only stopping briefly to talk business with our local agent, Sri K.V. Reddy, an enormously fat man, who would come out to greet us on the verandah of his office-cum-store in his spotless dhoti and well-pressed shirt, a scarf hanging over his shoulder. He and my parents had an excellent symbiotic relationship, and they would discuss at length arrangements to be made with contractors; goods to be ordered from Coimbatore and Mysore; prices; transport; petrol supplies; the state of the crops; the road to the hills; and everyone's health. Meanwhile my sister Sheila and I, when we were children, sat holding our breath as long as we could because of the stench of the open drain in front of the shop. We were a fussy pair in those days, but no fussier than Mr. Reddy. Once he got rid of us he always took a bath immediately, his son told me half a century later, because he had shaken hands with polluting persons who may have eaten beef. Although, as our handling agent, he was aware that we did not eat beef on the estate, there was no guarantee that as Europeans we did not eat it elsewhere. Thus in his eyes we were untouchables, albeit ones to be touched from time to time as an occupational hazard of the calling of middlemen.

Mr. Reddy was a living embodiment of the caste system at work. He and the other members of his community in the taluk (who were all more or less related, as it was one of the smaller castes of Kollepet), were practising the traditional torn of social climbing through the system. Once the acquisition of some wealth has been achieved — the essential requisite for an upward shift the trappings of a ritually 'pure' or Brahmanic lifestyle are adopted, such as vegetarianism, refusal to accept cooked food from members of castes deemed to be lower in the ranking scale, the avoidance of other polluting activities and objects, and restriction of the women.

This is not to say that all Brahmans are rich. Some are poor. But they are born Brahmans. Other castes have to prove to the local society their right to wear the sacred thread of the 'twice-born' by ostentatiously distancing themselves from any connection with a polluting occupation, and this takes money. The source of the money, of course, may well have been the original polluting occupation, such as dealing in liquor or leather. This is why it may take several generations for a local caste to rise in the hierarchy, and along the way it may mean dropping any relations who have the misfortune to be forced to earn their living in unacceptable ways.

So, if the caste system was alive and well and living in Kollepet in Mr. Reddy's day, what about now? Have things changed? Well, in Kollepet they (the relatively educated, at least) say that class is beginning to supersede caste. The model for class ranking and social climbing is a 'modern' or Westernised lifestyle, and the chief status symbol of Westernisation is first and foremost an (English) education. Education is equated with prestige, especially if combined with either inherited wealth, a thriving self-made business, or the secure financial status arrived at through a Government post or a job in one of the nationalised industries or the armed forces. The new elite hope to join Western-type assocations like the Rotary and tennis clubs, while scions of traditional joint-family corporate households who have done well on their own tend to break away and buy or build a modern house.

But the old elite, while less visible, are still powerful, and it's probably true to say that the caste system still flourishes, especially as a general means of classification, though its rules for advancement may have diversified.

It strikes me as ironic that, living in a pristine world of towering forests and rocky hillsides, abundant wildlife and exuberant flora, where if you went on foot further than a local walk you took along a rifle for protection against the more uncertain tempered animals, such as the ubiquitous sloth bear, it was the countryside beyond the wilderness which seemed, when I was young, the essence of mystery and excitement. The graceful areca, coconut and date palms; the vivid emerald of the batta (rice growing in the paddy fields); the craggy little conical hills rising abruptly from the plain and often crowned with a crumbling shrine to a local deity; the sandy nullas; the great banyan trees with roots hanging from their branches that sheltered throngs of rhesus macaque monkeys and shadowed the road like green clouds; all were the ingredients of adventure seen from a car driving from our jungle-fastness towards the beckoning cities of Mysore and Bangalore or the sophisticated hill stations of the Nilgiri range. Now, palms and paddy fields were all too familiar to me, the few monkeys remaining in the stunted banyans, perpetually harassed by stone-throwing boys, the commonplace of the walk from the village to the taluk town. Now I lifted up my eyes longingly to the hills as I trudged through the dust of the road in the midday heat. If I had grown up with a bird's-eye view of the Indian scene, fortune's wheel now presented me with a worm's-eye view that was salutary, engrossing and singularly appropriate.

My family's connection with the hills began in the nineteenth century with my grandfather Randolph Morris, an adventurous refugee from Perthshire with an entrepreneurial eye. A coffee planter in the Nilgiri hills of Tamil Nadu, he was first attracted to the Biligirirangan hills by their reputation, that of an elephant-infested terra incognita. He set up an exploratory expedition which followed narrow game paths and hacked a way through the heavy deciduous forest of the lower slopes to emerge into a hidden arcadia, the rolling grasslands, rock cliffs and evergreen forests of the higher reaches.

Grandfather Morris lost his heart there and then to the White Hills of Rangan (so called on account of a prominent white cliff in their western foothills). He had no difficulty in acquiring the land from the Forest Department, as everyone thought he was daft to think of settling in such an inaccessible wilderness, inhabited only by a seminomadic aboriginal tribe and swarms of wild animals. But in 1888 he began to open up the first of five coffee estates and by 1891 had begun to build a road into the interior and was joined by his stalwart wife. In 1894 their second son, my father Randolph (Ralph for short), was born in the little house they had built of the local stone, which they called Attikan, the house of the wild fig grove.

My grandfather died in 1918. Ralph succeeded him as uncrowned king of the hills: hunter, naturalist and friend of the Sholiga people, the hill tribe. A year later he married Heather Kinloch, eldest of the four beautiful daughters of a Scottish planter then living in the Nilgiris, who was himself a naturalist, ornithologist and an authority on snakes.

My parents planted Honnametti, their own estate, and built a long verandahed bungalow, which my mother surrounded by landscaped gardens, near the summit of one of the high hills in the central spine of the Biligirirangan range. My sisters and I grew up at Honnametti; my own children spent much of their early life there, and the range remained the geographical focus of my life until first my husband and I, and then my parents, left India in the early 1950s. More than twenty years later I returned to the area as an anthropologist and revisited the hills. Now I was back again, officially engaged this time on a population study which, by grace of their recent inclusion within the boundaries of the taluk, would take me up to the hills once more.

doing it yourself

Entering the gate of the tote and ducking under the cornice of the thatch into the cool shade of the verandah was always a kind of homecoming. After the regular drill of filling a basin from the bucket and washing hands, face and feet, it was time to eat. It was too hot to think of anything but a few biscuits and fruit, this time a large slice of a papaya someone had given me which was rapidly becoming over-ripe. In the process of spooning it up while reading through the morning's notes I became aware of being watched, and glanced round. Yes, a strange woman stood with Siddha's wife Rangi in a corner of the shade outside the neighbours' dwelling, waiting politely until my meal was over. With a small puff of breathy resignation I rinsed and dried the plate and dutifully prepared to receive the visitor, reflecting on the curious mixture of loneliness and lack of privacy which is the anthropologist's lot.

"Yarn, Amma? Yen beku?" (Who are you mother? What is it you want?)

The woman came forward shyly and stopped outside in the sun. Her sari was ragged and dirty and her uncombed hair carelessly knotted. She was very thin.

"Walegi lnmm'. Kulukeli" (Please come in and sit down).

She entered, stood staring about her for a moment, and then muttered, "Give me some medicine."

"Are you ill? What is the trouble?"

She shook her head, hesitated, and then spoke rapidly. "I am pregnant. I don't want the child. If I have another I will die. Give me some medicine."

"Have you tried murungakai?" I asked. The juice of the murunga or drumstick tree is perhaps the best-known local abortifacient, and some women find it effective.

"Yes. It didn't work. But you can give me medicine."

"Mother, I have no medicine of that sort."

"How many children have you had?" she asked abruptly.

"Two, but..." "You see? Only two. You must know about some medicine. I have had six, though one died. I am so tired. If I have this child I will die soon, and then who will look after my other poor children?" she began to weep.

I got up and put my arm round her. "Sit, sit. Let me bring you some food and drink." She squatted reluctantly, still crying, while I fetched bananas and biscuits and mixed milk powder, sugar and coffee to boil up together for the strong sweet milky drink which I was normally too tired or too idle to supply to my grander and healthier guests. The biscuits and fruit she accepted, but knotted them into a fold of her sari to take away, as well as the sweets for the children I produced as an afterthought. Then, as she sipped cautiously from the coffee mug clasped in both hands, I squatted down beside her.

"Now. How long have you known about this pregnancy, and how old are you, and how old is your youngest child?"

"Not long. Only a few weeks. I don't know my exact age. About forty, perhaps." She paused to reckon. "I think the child is about five."

Looking at her with anxious speculation, I considered. She appeared to be middle-aged, and it struck me that she could be missing a period at the onset of her menopause. But I wasn't about to hazard a guess.

"Look," I said. "All I can give you is advice. I will send you first to a woman doctor friend in the town. If she says you are pregnant she will give you a letter to the family planning clinic at the hospital. Tell her and them what you have told me. I think perhaps you may not be pregnant, but if you are I think they will terminate it for you on the doctor's recommendation because of your ill-health. And if you ask for it they will give you a tubectomy at the same time and you will not have to fear pregnancy again. Have you istanentaveru — friends and relatives — to look after your children for a short time?"

"My eldest daughter will do that," she began, and then broke down in tears. "But my husband will be angry. The operation will make me too weak to work."

"You will also be too weak to work if you bear another child in your condition," I pointed out. "If you rest after the operation it will not harm you. Give me your husband's name and tell me where you live. I will ask the family planning workers to speak to him. Have you relations of your own you could go to for a time after the operation?"

"My brother in Hadaranhalli." She was cheering up a little.

"Good. Now, Amma, I will write you a letter to take to my doctor friend, who is a kind lady. She will not charge you anything this time." My gynaecologist friend only charged poor women a rupee or two, but in this case I decided to ask her to debit the fee to me instead. In view of the emotional and moral connotations of abortion, I tended to send women who came to me with this problem to her before directing them to the Primary Health Centre. She was full of good sense and a dedicated professional. If the women were obviously physically drained or determined to have an abortion she would recommend one, considering the claims of worn out or desperate women and of their living children before those of the embryo, unless it was too far advanced. The alternatives so often resorted to, some back-street female abortionist who would insert a pointed stick or apply powdered chillies to the cervix to produce a spasm of the uterus, was too appalling to contemplate and indeed frequently led to death after severe suffering.

A free sterilisation service for both sexes is available at Primary Health Centres (hospitals in towns) in India, and this is by far the most common form of birth control in general use today. The majority of the operations are the tubectomies performed on women. Vasectomy for the men, though a far less serious operation, tends to be associated in their minds with castration and is therefore, needless to say, much less popular. There is also a widespread fear among both sexes that both types of operation will cause prolonged weakness and thus affect the earning capacity of the acceptor, as it may well do if the patient returns to work too soon. But my own survey of three hundred married couples produced little evidence to confirm that this was a common occurrence. In fact, while it revealed a surprisingly large percentage of sterilisations, at least among the better off, it also revealed a general satisfaction with the results, expressed in such terms as: "We could not afford to feed another child and now we don't have to worry any more."

So I wrote a note for my latest would-be client to take to the gynaecologist, and gave her some more coffee. Over this, she began to relax and to tell me of her hopes that her eldest daughter would marry her younger brother, who was living with his elder sibling in Hadaranhalli, and thus reinforce the ties with her natal family. She went off in better spirits, but left me with the usual residue of anger over the despair of such women, guilt over my own good fortune and depression over the moral dilemma of the anthropologist. How was it possible to equate compassion with objectivity? I decided, not for the first time, that I was a biased anthropologist.

The old adage 'Man he works from sun to sun, but women's work is never done' fits the case of the poor working woman in India with grim accuracy. In south India she may be better off than her unfortunate sisters in the north, and she may have more freedom (including the freedom to divorce a bad husband) than the restricted wives in orthodox high-caste families. But she is nevertheless not only a slave to poverty but to the male view of what constitutes the division of labour between the sexes. She gets up before dawn to relieve herself with modesty in the fields before the men get up. She then fetches water, lights the fire, prepares food, feeds her husband first, then the children and lastly herself. These chores completed she sets off for a day's manual labour (for which, to nobody's surprise, she gets half the male wage for the same hours and mostly the same type of work). On her return, while her husband rests or goes to smoke and gossip with his friends, she collects fuel, fetches water, cooks the evening meal, feeds husband, then children and then herself on what is left. After which she cleans the pots and, if it is not yet dark, grinds tomorrow's grain before she sleeps. For much of this time she is either pregnant or lactating. Her marriage is normally consummated within a month or so of her reaching puberty, and on average she has her first child round the age of fifteen or sixteen. Each one is born under conditions so appalling that it is a wonder that mother and child survive. One or more of her children are likely to die, either from malnutrition or gastro-enteritis. They are all likely to suffer from worms and scabies and to have frequent bouts of dysentery. Lengthy lactation, sometimes up to four years, may protect her from conception as long as she breast-feeds frequently. If she happens to have a husband who cares for her, periods of sexual abstinence will ensure a wider spacing of pregnancies. But all too often the husband insists on his 'rights' while refusing to take precautions. Or she may fear to deny him in case he goes off with another woman. The use of locally known abortifacients is quite common but apparently not very reliable. The end result appears to be a chronic and self-perpetuating state of anaemia. This vicious circle not only leads to lowered resistance and an early death (life-expectancy statistics show that men in India tend to live longer than women, while the reverse is the case in the West) but affects the children's welfare, since an exhausted mother cannot give her children the care and attention they require. The popular sophistry that women are the weaker sex turns out to be a self-fulfilling prophecy.

When my mother began running Honnametti estate she discovered that although the women labourers had to prepare the family's evening meal at the end of the day while the men were free to relax, when the crop was picked it was the men who had their bags of coffee beans weighed first while the women had to wait. She insisted that the women's harvest of beans should be weighed first. The men were furious at having to wait and were on the verge of mutiny until she pointed out that under the new dispensation they would get their supper earlier. Impressed by this argument the men acquiesced. But when I returned to the estate twenty years after my parents left, the men's loads were once more being weighed first. The thought of this absurd inequity depressed me even more until I remembered that at least recent legislation had ensured that female plantation labourers should receive equal wages with the men. There is nothing like economic parity as a generator of independence and perhaps, I thought, the estate women would soon begin to demand justice in other spheres. I envied my mother's opportunity to make constructive use of her convictions.

By now it was too late to have the rest in the privacy of the inner room I had promised myself. But there was time for a quick cup of nice weak unsweetened tea to be brewed and drunk with a slice of lime while getting on with report-writing before the landlord arrived.

All too soon he turned up, refreshed and bathed after his siesta and carrying a small cloth bag which contained, he said, screws and washers to anchor the tar-cloth roof of the engine-house he had built by the well on the plot of land we were to visit. He refused my gnat's-piss tea, having enjoyed the richer brew provided at his own house before he left, so I changed my sandals for canvas shoes and we set off on foot.

Our route took us across the road and down a lane which led towards the 'tanks' or reservoirs, between hedges of prickly pear and flowering lantana. Behind the hedges were fields of sugarcane and of ragi, staple diet of the majority in the taluk who could not afford to eat rice, and in fact a good deal more nourishing than rice. There were also fields of mulberries for feeding the silkworms which were bred as a cash crop by so many of the village women in their houses. At a corner of the lane, in a grove of splendid pipul trees was a little temple, painted in vivid blues and yellows, dedicated to the goddess Parvati, consort of the high god Siva and, as an aspect of the high goddess Durga as well as of Mysore's local goddess Chamundi, an important deity in her own right.

Opposite the temple was a cluster of shacks inhabited by a large family of landless Harijans. In the earlier days of my fieldwork my pleasure in walking alone by the lakes had been somewhat eroded by having to run the gauntlet of the stares, giggles and juvenile shouts of this unusually (for Karnataka) rude and aggressive group of people. But one day a woman had turned up at my quarters on the tote with a baby girl about a year old covered all over with the worst case of scabies I had ever seen. She would not be persuaded to take the baby to the hospital. It was too far and too tiring for her to walk there carrying the heavy child. Besides she could not spare the time, as she had to go to work. Eventually I gave her a cake of soap and my big tube of scabies ointment and told her to wash the baby twice a day before applying the ointment. It seemed unlikely that such a simple remedy would make much difference to so bad a case. But to my astonishment the next time I walked past the huts a woman ran out holding a baby and smiling. "Come and see. Come and see." It was the same mother and child, but the baby's skin was now miraculously clear and smooth. Convinced since then of my benign intentions and cherishing a wholly unjustified belief in my efficacy as a physician, the group henceforth hailed me with friendly greetings, as they did today.

At the point where the lane adjoined the end of the bund or dam, we turned off to walk along the top of the raised earthwork. On our right as we walked were the two reservoirs, now beginning to shrink in the dry weather. On our left lay the rice fields of the fertile wetlands, interspersed with thick groves of trees: mangoes, coconuts, the beautiful areca nut palms, betel trees, banana groves and a few date palms and feathery casuarina trees. Before us rose the rampart of the hills, looking much nearer now. We could see where, in the foothills, the temple dedicated to the local deity Ranga perched above the cliff of gleaming whiteish rock which gave the range its name.

People were working in the fields on our left, mostly women transplanting rice. In one field a young man worked alone, ankle-deep in mud and water. My landlord exchanged salutes with him and turned to me. "See that young fellow? He's the son of a rich Lingayat landowner, just graduated from agricultural college, and yet he is not ashamed to be seen working like a labourer." His voice expressed both admiration and approbation.

To probe further was irresistible, however tactless. "If a high-caste person like a Lingayat doesn't mind being seen working in his own fields, why should you mind?"

"That's different," he muttered, looking confused.

He was right. It was different, and the question was rather unkindly designed to elicit his rationalisation of the situation. But as he was either unwilling or unable to engage in an analysis of it and began to talk of other things as we walked on, I did not pursue the subject. The fact was that the actions of the Lingayat landowner's son would be based on confidence in the security of his position. A member of the caste which claimed equality in terms of ritual purity with Brahmans (a claim which in their Lingayat-dominated region was accepted to some extent by the other non-Brahman castes), well-educated and wealthy as well, the young man had clearly opted for Westernisation and thus out of the hierarchy of caste. Furthermore, Lingayat Gowdas, a farming- sub-division of the caste, in any case feel less discredited by manual labour than the Brahmans or those castes striving to rise in the hierarchy by emulating Brahman orthodoxy in their own way of life. My companion was a member of a community some of whose members were busy taking the orthodox route in their efforts to scale the social ladder while others opted for that of Westernisation. But the majority of them were often unsure as to which path they should follow, and my companion belonged to this third category, poised uncomfortably between the old and the new ways in a kind of transitional limbo. He was a nice man on the horns of a dilemma. The idea that an educated person is not expected to carry heavy objects or do any kind of manual work and the fact that nearly every Indian who can afford it employs as many servants as possible, are indications of deep-rooted attitudes. Certainly in Kollepet the idea of the indignity of labour is manifested in many ways. Most people who can afford it are born delegators, passing orders downward from one level to another until the work eventually gets done by those who, by virtue of the fact that they are uneducated, underpaid and often undernourished, are the least capable of carrying it out successfully. The existence of this syndrome may explain why a lower caste, however much it Brahmanises its other customs, cannot rise in the hierarchy until it is economically viable.

My landlord's attitude towards the young Lingayat in the field was therefore that of one who is impressed by the free and easy ways of a person of high standing but feels too insecure about his own social status to emulate them, and clings for safety to more traditionally superior behaviours.

Since at present these values exist alongside traditional ideas which place a premium on an orthodox lifestyle, the local citizens are faced with two separate routes for advancement. Socially insecure people do not hesitate to switch from one to the other as the occasion arises, and are not particularly disturbed by any inconsistency they may betray in doing so as they try to move forward on two fronts simultaneously.

An example of this dual approach is that of a young Harijan doctor who had achieved his position through hard work, intelligence and judicious use of Government grants and scholarships for 'scheduled castes'. He was busy consolidating it in Kollepet, where he had a post in the state medical service, on the one hand through membership of the elite clubs which accepted him on the basis of his 'class' position and modern social graces, and on the other by restricting his wife and denying that his jati allowed divorce and remarriage to women. He had not yet discovered that the relatively Westernised men to whose peer-group he hoped to belong and who were happy to accept him on the grounds of his education, income and job, looked down on him for his adoption of an orthodoxy which they were busy putting behind them. They were, in fact, sorry for his wife.

As we walked along the flat top of the bund, we began to meet the occasional homing bullock cart driven by men, groups of women carrying bundles of firewood or piles of damp garments washed in the kere, and the vanguard of a steady stream of flocks and herds driven by children who also carried bundles of fuel. Women and children have to walk further and further today to gather fuel as the scrub jungle recedes in the face of the pressure of the population 'explosion'. The children now wanted to get home, and the cattle did too, advancing en masse at a sharp trot. "Akadi, akadi" (Keep to that side), shouted the children if we looked like standing our ground. The sheer weight of numbers drove us down the banks towards the water, which was probably less of a hardship than having to inhale the clouds of choking dust raised by the droves, to which the young herders seemed immune. But in spite of such minor hazards it was a pleasant walk. The files of homecoming animals and villagers, silhouetted against and mirrored by the blue waters, their shadows lengthening in the slanting golden light of late afternoon formed graceful compositions which linger in the archives of memory to epitomise the south Indian scene.

Eventually we turned off along a path which ran northward, leaving the bund behind. Following it, we arrived in time at a rather derelict stretch of untended fields near the boundary of which we came upon a large and well-built well. This was our journey's end, a piece of truly debatable land. My companion's brother had been left this plot as a separate parcel from the joint family inheritance. Uninterested in managing it himself, he had employed a man to work the smallholding for him. This character, inspired by legislation designed to give long-term tenant farmers the right to possess the land they farmed, had laid claim to these fields himself. The owner and his family based their case before the Land Tribunal on the premise that the man was not a tenant but a paid employee. The litigation had been going on throughout my years of fieldwork in the taluk and for all I know, may still be going on. The owner was apparently content to deal with the lawyers and the Tribunal, an activity to which he seemed to attach an importance which he did not extend to the land itself. His brother, my friend, was on the contrary concerned about the land which was suffering from lack of irrigation. He was anxious to fit the well with an electric pump, but first the roof of the pump house had to be secured. He directed me to stand inside and push the bolts through the requisite holes while he climbed a ladder on to the roof to screw on the nuts.

Unfortunately I was too small to reach the roof, even standing on a stone brought in from the field.

"It's no good," I panted. "We'll have to change places."

He came down the ladder looking downcast. "We might as well go home," he said.

"But you can reach it easily. You do the bolts and I'll go up and do the nuts."

"You can't do that," he cried, aghast.

"Why not?" Remembering his anxiety of the morning I looked about. Not a soul in sight. "Don't worry, nobody will see us"

"But you might fall."

As a dedicated mountaineer I was incensed by this aspersion on my climbing ability. "I'm not going home until we've fixed the roof," I snapped, mounting the ladder. "Your prejudices are losing you money, my friend."

Confronted with this fait accompli he entered the hut, found he could insert the bolts without difficulty and set to work. We made an excellent team and the task was quickly finished. He came out, saw me squatting smugly on high wearing an 'I-told-you-so expression', and began to laugh.

"I don't know what people would say if they saw you."

"What they ought to say," I observed, descending, "is that you should accept free labour when you are offered it. That sort of thing doesn't happen often."

We walked back together in high good humour at the success of our mission. Once on the bund facing west our eyes were filled with the sunset. Against the scarlet background, the palms were silhouetted like black cut-outs pasted on red paper while the still water of the lakes reflected back its refulgence in a flamboyant double image. The sun was going down behind the rocky temple-crowned hill that overlooked Lokkanhalli village and its rays formed an aura around the little eminence, investing it with grandeur and mystery. The flocks and herds had gone home and while the ubiquitous crows were still conducting their evening debate as they circled to their rest, our own voices were stilled by the splendour of the scene until it began to be swallowed up by the brief Indian dusk. By the time we reached the tote it was dark and we had to shine our torches at our feet to avoid treading on a snake.

The kerosene lamp shining in the verandah showed that the interviewers had arrived and unrolled the straw mat I used for seating visitors. The landlord took a chair outside, sat down and called upon Siddha. The rest of us sat in a circle on the mat while the four young people handed me their questionnaire forms and reported on the interviews each pair had done that day. Four married couples had been interviewed. The interviewers were all in form. Manjula fussed, complained and demanded cold drinks. She also expanded on the reports of the others, commented wryly on the foibles of the respondents and made sensible suggestions. Although life for her (and, it must be admitted, with her) seemed to progress from crisis to crisis, she was the most intelligent of them all as well as the most conscientious. Not only was she able but she possessed considerable courage which, poor soul, she needed. Her husband Jagan was nothing like as bright or reliable, though he was an improvement on young Rajan, the most immature and idle of the four, who had to be chased, lectured and otherwise exhorted all the time but whom I still employed because of his good-natured cheerfulness. The last of the four was little Ramani, the only one from Kollepet itself, a quiet and self-possessed young lady with a sense of humour. She was a Brahman, only daughter of an impoverished but liberal widowed father who had somehow managed to send her to university, though at home they lived very frugally in a thatched shack. She had a degree in sociology and an M.A. in folklore.

Rajan also had a higher degree. Once, more than usually exasperated by some ineptitude, I rashly wondered aloud in his absence how he had ever managed to obtain it. "But didn't you know?" asked Jagan with a pitying smile. "He has influential relations." The cynicism was a measure of the disillusion of these young graduates. Sometimes I would overhear them discussing their chances of getting another job when their temporary employment with me came to an end. They seemed to know the exact size of the bribe required to obtain every type of permanent and official post, and it certainly put a new construction on the phrase 'the rate for the job'.

Manjula and Jagan, graduates of Bangalore university, were Lingayats, or passed as such in the taluk. She was truly a member of the caste, but he was a Brahman. They had committed a grave indiscretion in the eyes of orthodox lower-middle-class people in India by making a cross-caste 'love-marriage', and were terribly afraid of the strictures of that dread instrument of verbal flagellation, 'society'. The questionnaire forms filled in by the interviewers constantly reiterated this pervasive fear which ruled the lives of the respondents. 'People will talk'; 'Society would not approve'; 'What will people say?' 'Society' (at least in rural and small-town India) does in fact disapprove of cross-caste marriage unless it is made by those members of the elite who have managed to repudiate the caste hierarchy and risen to the top of its class equivalent. Then, like my friend's reaction to the rich young landowner working in his own field, 'society' is no more than pleasurably titillated, and even applauds. This type of marriage among the élite is regarded not so much as shocking as fascinating, even if faintly perverse. Most people (in conversation with anthropologists, that is) agree that in the future the practice is likely to spread to all castes, and that this will bring about the end of the caste system, which would not be a bad thing. In the meantime one shakes one's head and gossips about it if it rears its head among one's ordinary acquaintanceship, and is truly appalled if it occurs among the circle of one's own family. Unless, of course, one's relative marries someone much higher up the ritual and the economic scale. There is also a tendency to be impressed on the rare occasions one comes across it if it is a success, and to exclaim "What else can you expect?" if it is a failure.

The interviewers called me 'Auntie', a title commonly used by south Indians who speak some English in addressing elderly female friends. And I was fond of them all in an auntly way, gratitude for their good humour and willingness under what were often very trying conditions triumphing over irritation at their inability to recognise and question inconsistency in the replies of their respondents. Neither exhortation nor precept (I accompanied them on all their earlier interviews and still did so frequently), cured them of this, though they did improve, especially Manjula, as time went on. I finally decided it was due to what appears to be a feature of south Indian culture, the apparent ability of people to hold two dichotomous opinions at the same time without allowing this state of affairs to disturb them in the least. This plurality of attitudes has been remarked upon by the anthropologist John Caldwell for another part of Karnataka and by Sheryl Daniel for the neighbouring state of Tamil Nadu where, she says, a man may refer in the course of the same conversation to the superiority of husbands, the superiority of wives and the equality of the sexes without noticing any inconsistency in his remarks.

After we had gone through the previous day's questionnaires again, sorting out their more cryptic interpretations of replies and comments by respondents, and discussing the refusals and postponements, we reviewed plans for the next day. We were currently interviewing couples belonging to high castes other than Lingayats, and a factory manager had agreed to be interviewed but had postponed it until I was able to be present and to have tea with him and his wife after the interview. Working their way along a suburban street the four had made appointments for the following morning. It was arranged that Manjula and Jagan should then come with me in the afternoon while Ramani and Rajan caught up with another postponement. My morning, after the mandatory checking of the latest forms, would be taken up by a visit to the bazaar and a midday meal with a joint family of my acquaintance.

The conference over and soft drinks consumed to the accompaniment of laughter over the day's misadventures, the interviewers set off to walk back to the town by torchlight and starlight. Siddha and Govinda Raian entered, the former bearing an ominously light but bulky-looking sack. I eyed it suspiciously. "If those are ground-nuts for your family, Govind, I hope you're not thinking of putting them under my bed again?" The last time this had happened, what seemed like the entire rodent population of the village had converged in my room. Those which were not fighting and screeching to get at the nuts under my bed were tearing up and down the beam above, shrieking abuse. To spend a night as the middle of a kind of rat sandwich was not my idea of a good time, and I had been dead against my room being used for storage ever since.

"No, no," he replied hastily. "I'll take the bag home on the back of my scooter." Directing Siddha to tie the sack to the pillion, he settled down again in the chair. I gave him a lemon squash, fetched a knife and chopping board, and began to chop onions, tomatoes and thin little green badnaikai, the local aubergines, for my supper, which consisted most evenings of a kind of ratatouille, this being the quickest and easiest dish to cook in semi-darkness on one kerosene burner.

"We've nearly finished this group of castes, so we'll be going to the hills next week for a month, to interview the low-caste estate workers there, and the Sholiga tribe."

"Take your money with you, then. Don't leave any valuables here while you are away, and padlock your door when you go." He tended to veer between deep distrust of the local populace and a possibly equally misguided confidence in their collective probity. When I had first rented these quarters and moved in, he had alarmed me by bringing a shotgun and ammunition and placing them in a corner of the room, pointing out that there was only a little wooden latch on the door and that people would automatically assume that I was rich. I wasn't at all keen on the idea of confronting an attacker with a shotgun. I might be tempted to fire it. I was even less keen when I subsequently peered down its grimy and pitted barrels. Having been brought up with guns and the necessity of cleaning them, nothing would have induced me to risk using this one. Fortunately, he turned up a day or two later and removed the weapon saying, "My mother says nobody is going to harm you here. They all know who you are." His mother was quite right. Nobody ever did.

"Your money will be safe enough on the estate," he went on. "They all know you are your father's daughter."

"My parents' daughter."

"Yes, yes, of course. Your mother was a very good lady. I have heard how she would intercede with your father when he was angry with wrongdoers.”

This seemed an unlikely story, though I did not argue the point. As one old estate worker had expressed it to me a few months previously: “It was quite easy to get around the Dorai. He gave us no trouble at all. But the Doraisani! Aiyō!”

We said goodnight, and I was left to check a form or two while the vegetables cooked, to eat the sloppy stew without much interest, being now bored with the lack of variety in this diet, and to heat a pan of water for washing up. This was done in a little plastic basin while squatting on the cow-dung floor, working surface for all my kitchen chores. The lamp attracted swarms of flying ants which filled the air, fell into the basin, and crawled drunkenly over chairs and table, floor and me. Huge stag beetles zoomed about, crashing into walls and furniture and tumbling stunned on to the floor. The high whine of mosquitoes and the itching as they bit voraciously through the layer of hastily applied repellent cream suddenly became intolerable, as it generally did at about nine o'clock every night. Siddha, Rangi and the children were silent and probably already asleep. It was time, after last ablutions, to retire under the blessed sanctuary of the net. And so to bed.

But not immediately to sleep. The day's events had engendered a series of vivid images of my parents, and I lay awake thinking about them. The old estate worker was right. My mother had been a fairly formidable character, whose fragile appearance was deceptive. Competent, hardworking, never idle, she measured up to her own exacting standards and expected her family and employees to do likewise. The house, smelling of polish, woodsmoke and flowers, had sparkled with cleanliness. The acres of garden she created and supervised with love and vigilance repaid her liberally with a harvest of lilies and roses, larkspur and canna, phlox, pansies, mignonette and gerberas. If, in the house, she had to make concessions to my father's interests which were contrary to her own tastes, the garden was an extension of her persona and the main outlet for her creativity. Her beloved dairy herd provided lavish supplies of milk from which she made cream, butter and ghee. Their steading was neighboured by about half an acre of chicken run in which wyandottes and white leghorns ranged contentedly. There were terraced beds which gave us strawberries for six months of the year, a prolific vegetable garden, and an orchard in which Eastern and Western fruit trees co-existed successfully. It was due to her efforts and imagination that we were more or less self-sufficient for food.

An old family friend, the ornithologist Salim Ali, writes in his autobiography of his first visit to Honnametti "...in the heart of more or less primaeval tiger and elephant-infested jungle". It was memorable, he said, for the insight it offered into the demands of life in such an isolated place: "Unrelenting hard work, dedication to a lonely jungle life cut off from social contacts and amenities, self-sufficiency as jack of all trades, carpenter, mason, plumber, motor mechanic and general handyman... Heather had all that it takes...which included a working knowledge of medicine...and a general concern for the welfare of the labourers and their families."

She had a gift for diagnosis. Consulted when the estate mechanic failed to solve some technological problem, she was usually quick to discover the cause of the trouble. She prescribed for and treated the ailments of family, employees and domestic animals. She might be called upon to attend a difficult birth in the labour village, sew up a cow's torn udder or treat a daughter with bacillary dysentery. In her time she nursed employees suffering from smallpox, bubonic plague and rabies, as well as more common ills such as hepatitis, malaria, broken limbs and infected wounds. She might be called out at any time, and she always went.

Basically she was a perfectionist. Fanatically tidy herself, she could not bear dirt and disorder, dealing summarily with such conditions when she came across them. But if all this portrays a priggish paragon, I have misrepresented her. She had been brought up to an eccentric lifestyle. Her father, Angus Kinloch, had had a passion for snakes, being prone to carry about venomous specimens in his pockets, and had kept a tame python in his bathroom. He was also keen on falconry and nurtured a black eagle which he had trained. When the eagle, released for a flight, was due to come home, Heather and her sisters had to retreat indoors to discourage it from making an affectionate crash landing on their unprotected heads. Besides these pets the household harboured a full-grown sloth bear which wandered about the garden terrorising unwary visitors. Both Heather's parents were unconventional for their time, and perhaps this accounted for the fact that she grew up to be an innovator, a natural rebel, and a crypto-feminist. But she was also shy and reserved, on the surface undemonstrative. She was gentle and compassionate with animals and besotted with babies. She also possessed innate grace and elegance and could exert enormous charm. She was well loved. The influence of my mother on me was profound. I spent much of my life trying to live up to her and failing to do so.

My father was another multi-dimensional soul. His hopes of reading zoology at Oxford had been abandoned when he returned to India to help his ailing father and then his widowed mother, and he settled instead for growing coffee in a zoologist's paradise. It has to be admitted that his wife was the better planter of the two. This was largely because he spent a great deal of his time either in the jungle observing the behaviour of wild animals and learning from his friends in the hill tribe, or sitting in his office writing scholarly articles on fauna and flora for the journal of the Bombay Natural History Society. But how is this vague, good-natured fellow, the kind of person who walks into lamp-posts, of whom a friend once said, "Ralph is the only person I know who arrives not hours but weeks late for dinner," to be reconciled with the macho evidence of the sporting trophies which hung on the walls of Honnametti? They had nothing to do with Heather, who could see no merit in shooting for sport. (She also disapproved of trophies on walls, but had to compromise by restricting them to specific areas of the house.)

The fact is that Ralph was an old-fashioned hunter-naturalist. Completely fearless, he hunted on foot except when he sat up in a tree at night over the corpses of cattle killed by felines, and his close encounters with peril were legendary among those who knew — or knew of — him.

In those days the hills, and the scrub-jungle of the plateau country from which they rose, swarmed with wildlife. The inhabitants of the hamlets, scattered like islands in the sea of forest round the foot of the hills, were constantly harried by marauding elephants, tigers and panthers, and were in the habit of sending him urgent requests to rid them of some persistent raider. He seldom refused and often risked his life in this way, but it must be said that this dedication beyond the call of duty owed something to the fact that he got so much fun out of it.

As his fame spread he was much in demand as mentor and guide in 'his' jungles by wildlife photographers, collectors for museums, and by people, mostly Indian Civil Service and army officers on leave or rich Americans, who wanted to do big-game hunting. These visitors had to observe the strict sporting rules by which he himself abided. Never, never, for instance, shoot at a water-hole or from a car. Never shoot the young of animals, or indeed the females, except in self-defence or if the latter were known marauders. Always drop everything else to follow up a wounded beast for the coup-de-grace.

In later years my father became a devoted conservationist, though he still maintained that controlled shooting by those concerned for wildlife and the environment was an aid to conservation because they went into the jungle and saw what was going on. Events seem to have proved him right. The forests that surrounded us were full of animals and retained their ecological balance until my parents left. Within twenty years, in spite of being designated a wildlife sanctuary, the area has lost most of its wildlife to indiscriminate poachers. Only the elephant, the sloth bear and the wild pig survive in any numbers.

Portrait of my father? There's more. He was brave and adventurous, but mildly deprecating in manner. He was patient, until he blew his top. He was very funny, often iconoclastic, and devoutly religious. His absent-mindedness was a standing joke with family and friends. One of these, Humphrey Trevelyan, wrote in his book, The India We Left, "You took an elephant rifle in the car, drove up...on a private road, backed round the unfenced hairpin bends, and emerged through the coffee on to a glorious hilltop overlooking a great sweep of forest. The monarch of it all was Ralph Morris, as much at home in the forest as the villagers who lived in it. He was a brilliant shot, tireless, without nerves, liable to fall asleep in the middle of a word or driving on a dangerous hillside, late on the grand scale."

One story which my father was never allowed to forget epitomises his particular brand of distrait sangfroid. He was a great one for falling asleep at any time. On this occasion he had dozed off on a machan (improvised platform in a tree) where he was sitting over a tiger's kill with a house-guest. When his companion, tense with excitement but obeying his instruction to keep perfectly still, cautiously raised her eyes to the stars, she noticed with alarm something long and hairy dangling from the branch above. "What's that?" she whispered, nudging him awake. He looked up. "A panther's tail," he replied and fell asleep again. Her anguished yell unnerved the panther, which had climbed the tree to see if the coast was clear to dine illicitly on the tiger's kill and was indeed sitting on the branch above them. It leaped off the branch and departed in a huff. The tiger, disturbed, wisely kept away, and. Ralph, complaining about the commotion, went back to sleep.

He was an engaging man who endeared himself to everyone, including his employees on the estate and his cronies in the tribe. But he was rather alarming to live with.

Shifting cautiously from time to time on the flimsy mattress to avoid bruising hips on the unyielding planks of the wooden bed, I lay ruminating affectionately on the disparate personalities of my progenitors. It seemed a bit hard, I thought, that I should have inherited shyness and the genetic potentiality for walking into lamp-posts rather than my mother's efficiency and my father's calm indifference to danger. But then, if I had fallen heir to the latter attributes I would be someone else and not me, wouldn't I? And if I were someone else I'd probably have had the sense not to be here on this uncomfortable couch. So all this heart-searching was really irrelevant, wasn't it? At which point I fell asleep.

a day in town

Rightly or wrongly, I deemed the stretching and flexing of muscles entailed in the routine of morning exercises to be essential for the upkeep of morale, if not for fitness, however tedious they might be. This twenty-minute prelude to the working day required privacy, and the closure and fastening of door and window to the inner room sufficed, I hoped, to indicate to visitors that privacy was desired. In most cases it did. But there were exceptions, and one of them turned up the following morning.

Knocking at a door is unknown in rural south India. People stand outside and call upon the occupant to appear. Thus at 7.30 am. a plaintive yet implacably repeated cry of "Amma, Amma," interrupted a peaceful shoulderstand and nearly dislocated my spine as I sprang fretfully to my feet. The summoner had applied an inquisitive eye to a crack in the window-shutter and I knew exactly who she was and why she had come.

As my parents' child, I had found myself caught in a web of expectations on my return to the taluk which no longer could be fulfilled. There was no way in which I could afford to support retired employees of Honnametti estate, though I did what I could, obtaining, for instance, insulin for one with old-age diabetes, providing in other cases blankets, sandals, umbrellas and contributions towards the weddings of their grandchildren. The informal system of reciprocity involving hereditary relationships and various conventions of customary rewards between landowning patrons and their service 'clientele' which had existed in the old days, were long gone in Kollepet taluk. It is true that each well-to-do family still has its own priest, washerman-or-woman, and sweeper, whose links with the family have until recently tended to be hereditary. But the traditional structured relationship which had existed between my family and their employees, the kind which tends to survive as the result of expectations about the performance of recognised roles, had irretrievably broken down on my parents' final departure from India.

In the view of a number of veterans, however, charity was a fair substitute, and there were some who thought they had discovered in me a widow's cruse. Of these by far the most persistent was one old lady, she who was clamouring outside my door this morning.

As soon as I appeared on the verandah she flung herself on her knees and clasped my feet in a theatrical gesture of supplication for the benefit of my neighbours and anyone else who might be around, in this case the vanguard of the recalcitrant gumpu, who had just turned up and now stopped to stare, fascinated. Grabbing the doorpost to maintain balance in the face of this flying tackle I returned her greeting with regrettable testiness. "Namaste, Baswi. What are you doing here so early?"

She rose to her feet and began to scold in a penetrating voice. "I came from my village on the early bus. It is a long time since you visited us. Why have you forgotten me? I never forget your parents who took such good care of us."

Old, small and unkempt though she looked, artfully clad in a torn and dirty sari, though I had given her several new ones, her powerful personality still made her a commanding figure. In my youth her husband, a cheerful character called Devera Gudda, much beloved by us children as a truly funny man, had polished floors, cut and carried firewood, and generally made himself useful around the house or on the coffee plantation. As the leader or maistry of a group of workers recruited by himself from his own and neighbouring hamlets, he lived in one of the workers' houses on the estate with Baswi, then a very pretty woman who as a side-line carried on a thriving trade as the estate prostitute. In spite of this the marriage seemed a happy and stable one. When I returned a quarter-century later I learned that dear Devera Gudda had died and Baswi and her sister were living in their village where they had inherited his plot of land.

The village was one in the hinterland at the foot of the hills from which so many employees of Honnametti had been drawn over the years. When I arrived there in pursuit of rural Harijan genealogies Baswi had pushed her way to the front of the crowd to embrace me, be embraced, and to claim my full attention. She and her sister were living in a room with its own hearth in a cousin's house. The cousins did not seem very pleased with this arrangement, which was not surprising since Baswi was such a bossy lady. She introduced her sister as Devera Gudda's first wife, but whether the marriage was thus a case of sororal polygyny — which sometimes occurs in the low castes — or of concubinage never became clear. In any case the sisters seemed to get on very well together and shared such profit as they made from their fields. That there were no children for the old ladies to turn to in their declining years might well have been due to V.D. contracted and passed on in the course of Baswi's frolicsome past.

Be that as it may, Baswi was convinced that I owed her a living and since we were both relics of colonialism, perhaps she had a point. Others, while less vociferous, felt the same. As long as I stayed in Kollepet taluk they would keep on trying, and I would respond to the best of my ability, driven by a confused mixture of guilt, nostalgia and affection, both for my parents and for these old acquaintances from my past. Unfortunately my response was not always good enough for them. On one occasion, in the course of a door-to-door survey I was conducting in the 'lines', the labour village at Honnametti, an elderly man shouted accusingly from his doorway, "You deserve to pay us five rupees for every question you ask, the way your parents went away and left us, their children, to this lot." As one or two of 'this lot', the present estate manager and staff, were there in person, the situation could have been embarrassing. Luckily the crowd of bystanders decided it was very funny and my lame rebuttal was drowned in mirth. However, today Baswi was satisfied to receive what she had come for: a promised pair of blankets, plus money to pay for the ploughing of her land and to tuck away as a nest-egg, plus a tin of instant coffee, a bag of sugar, and a bottle of cooking oil. A man somewhat younger than her now approached smiling, hands folded in a namaskara. It was Chama, who had once helped to look after our cows. We had nicknamed him 'Charming Chama' on account of his radiant smile, but he signally failed in his cow-herding duties, having pushed the herd bull to its death over a cliff because, he said, it was dangerous and might attack him. Thus he had departed under a cloud many years ago. Now, on the strength of our acquaintance in that dim past when my sister Sheila and I were little, he too expected financial recognition and indeed received some on the strength of that remembered smile. After which he picked up Baswi's bundle, placed it on her head (men in their circle do not carry loads for women of equal or lower rank) and the pair went off with an air of honour satisfied.

All this had left little time in which to check yesterday's forms, but they had to be done while the interviewers' recollection of those particular interviews was still fresh. Breakfast banana in one hand and pen in the other, notes were made of questions to be raised and the fat questionnaire forms relegated one by one to the pile in the tin cupboard which represented the caste-group currently under survey. A little boy turned up demanding a patti for his akka, his elder sister. Couldn't she come herself? No, she was busy. What was wrong with her? A sore on her ankle. He left with a large elastoplast dressing, a squeeze of antiseptic cream wrapped in a bit of paper to go underneath it, a toffee for himself and my profound hope that this circuitous method of obtaining relief would prove successful.

The last form completed, it was time to go. Change into best cotton trousers, long overblouse and newer sandals. Put ballpoint and notebook into shoulderbag, collect cameras, headscarf and dark glasses. Interesting how when I was a child a pith topi was considered by Westerners and indeed by many Indians as essential for protection against the midday sun, whereas nobody nowadays wears topis, but dark glasses are de rigeur instead, not only for foreigners but also for those Indians who can afford them. Wave farewell to Rangi and Mahadevi, washing saris at the well outlet while the youngest child played with mud-pies at their feet.

Walking up the road I thought about my neighbours. Siddha was an admirable man, upright, high-principled and very intelligent. Fluent in Kannada, Tamil and Urdu, he was nonetheless illiterate, having had to earn his living from early childhood. Their eldest son was also bright and Siddha had been determined that he should have the education his father lacked. The sacrifices contingent upon very poor people sending a child to school in India are considerable. Not only does the family lose his or her contribution to their pooled income, but books, writing materials and decent clothing have to be provided. These sacrifices they accepted, and the boy did well, obtaining a scholarship to the secondary school. But he had not inherited his father's moral fibre — or perhaps his father had never been subjected to such temptations at his age. He found himself in a peer-group of lads dedicated to the recreations of the urban teenager in Kollepet: the cinema, coffee-houses and gambling. These pleasures required cash which the others had and he had not. He took to demanding money with menaces from his mother, and then to stealing. Resounding rows with his father occurred more and more often, and eventually the police caught up with him. Siddha removed him from the school and for a time he had no option but to work as a casual labourer. After a few years Siddha's employer, my landlord, got him a job as a peon, a kind of office boy.

Siddha, disillusioned with education ("It only makes poor people want things they can't afford"), lost all ambition to raise the status of his other children. His eldest daughter Jowni, a pretty girl of stalwart character, took first place in his affections, and her affairs became paramount. He announced to me one day that Jowni was to be married to a cross-cousin, his wife's brother's son (a preferred form of union in south India), invited me to the wedding, and requested a contribution to her wedding jewellery. "Isn't she rather young?" I asked. "Young?" Siddha's eyebrows rose in astonishment. "But she's twelve years old."

And so Jowni was married, and after she reached puberty went off to her young cousin-husband's family household. The marriage was not a success. Visiting her parents, she complained that she disliked the boy and his mother, who both bullied her. In the North, or among orthodox high-caste families in the South, she might have been condemned to a lifetime of misery. But divorce is acceptable and indeed institutionalised among low castes in the South, and one day she walked out and walked home to her parents, who took her in and arranged with the caste panchayat (council) for a divorce. A year or two later a young man of the same 'untouchable' (Harijan) caste who had met her working in the fields and fallen in love with her, approached her parents to ask for her hand. She reciprocated his feelings, a kuduvali or secondary marriage was arranged, the young couple settled down happily, and before she was seventeen Jowni was the mother and Siddha and Rangi the devoted grandparents of a baby girl.

Siddha and Rangi's next two children seemed to be fatalistically accepted rather than arousing stronger emotions in their parents' breasts. The little boy was sent to work for a neighbouring farmer at the age of eight. Illegal, but who in Kollepet apart from the élite knows or cares much about recent legislation except when it suits them to do so? Mahadevi became the family drudge at about the same age. When, eight years after the birth of her last child, Rangi became pregnant again she was so convinced that she was past childbearing that she went to the doctor believing she had a tumour in her swelling stomach. The child turned out to be another girl. In the North a fifth unwanted child that turned out to be a girl would have been regarded by villagers as a disaster and quite likely allowed to die from neglect. This being the South, the whole family was besotted with her and she was outrageously spoilt, even supplanting Jowni in her father's favour.

Although Siddha and Rangi had lived in poverty all their lives, their present position in the smallholding was a sinecure compared with the lifestyle of the average landless 'untouchables' in the taluk, who mostly lived in overcrowded squalor. Their end of our joint dwelling consisted of a neat and clean inner room containing the cooking hearth, where Rangi and the girls slept and an outer room or verandah where Siddha and the boys slept. They had the whole compound in front of the building and around the well where the children could play in safety and relative cleanliness, good water from the well within easy reach, and plenty of space in which to grow their own vegetables, keep a hen or two, and sometimes graze a neighbour's cow or buffalo in exchange for its milk or the next calf. The climate was never cold, and though hot enough at times it was seldom intolerably so, which meant that not much expenditure on clothes and bedding was necessary, and none at all on heating. The job was not well paid but it was secure, as Siddha was known and respected as an honest and conscientious man, and if they did not get a free share of the crops grown by the landlord they at least paid a reduced price. On the whole things could have been a lot worse for them, and indeed had been so in the past.

Musing on my neighbours' affairs took me along the main road and through the village; past the threshing ground; past the turning to the temple of Mariamma, the village goddess; past the temporary cinema, a fire-trap built of woven palm leaves; past the blacksmith's house, outside which he was clamping an iron tyre to a big wooden cart-wheel; and on between thorn-hedged fields of ragi and mulberries. Here and there the battered banyans gave way to a big shady neem or tamarind tree, someone's private property and therefore protected. The road ran gently uphill here, passing a house or two and a small new sugar factory before reaching the pillars of the toll gateway at the beginning of the town. Here on the left was the little Protestant church set in the garden of the Morris orphanage, originally sponsored by my father and his brother. Beyond it was the magistrates' court and the travellers' bungalow (the Government rest-house found all over India). On the right beyond the shade of banyans, in better shape possibly due to the proximity of the law, the maidan began, an open stretch of recreation ground. No doubt at one time it had been grassy, the equivalent of a park or village green. Now it was a stretch of red beaten earth, playground of children and of pathetic pi-dogs with appalling skin diseases whose sufferings wrung my heart.

On the maidan were the State schools: girls' primary, boys' primary; girls' secondary, boys' secondary. There was also a private primary school elsewhere in the town run by Catholic nuns and patronised by the elite. A co-educational high school too, and a college entitled to offer Mysore University degrees. Both these latter were Lingayat foundations and patronised as well by those of other castes who could afford the fees. It was cheaper and easier for many people to send their offspring to the college rather than send them to Mysore for their higher education, particularly in the case of girls whose parents tended to prefer to educate them locally so as to keep an eye on them and their virginity.

The road took a wide bend round the maidan and pedestrians coming to or from the town usually took a short cut across it, getting dusty feet but saving time. As I began to turn off the road a male voice behind me said "Good morning" in English. It belonged to a youngish acquaintance, clad in the well-laundered shirt and well-pressed terylene slacks of the Kollepet man-about-town, who now dismounted from his bicycle to talk. He was a son of a high-caste family, cultured by Kollepet standards, but unemployed and likely to remain so, since so many available jobs had turned out to be either beneath his dignity or to entail longer hours and more effort than he was prepared to bestow on them. He said he wanted some advice, so we sat down together on the stone coping of a culvert bridging a dried watercourse while he spoke of his loneliness, his family's lack of understanding and his own lack of friends and confidantes. To whom could he turn in this narrow provincial town? Cut off from and deprived of the society of intelligent companions among whom he might have found soul-mates he felt he was rotting away in this backwater. Sympathising with his predicament, the product of both nature and nurture, I gave it some consideration before pointing out the obvious solution: that he could start with confiding in his wife. He looked puzzled.

"But what could I talk to her about? There's only films. Or love." "Well, the things you've been telling me just now, for instance. Then you would have a friend and confidante here after all, wouldn't you? She told me only the other day that she wished you would talk to her sometimes." He pondered over this for a moment with a worried frown and then shook his head regretfully. "No, I can't do that. You see, our wives have to worship us as god. How can they do that if we treat them as equals?" His beautiful wife, coming from an urban and more sophisticated background, pined for the freedom of her pre-marital state. She was as lonely and at least as intelligent as he was, but while she was anxious to break with tradition and gain an ally by establishing a relationship other than sexual with her husband, he was trapped by his need to retain his dominant role.

"It must be tough, being a god," I remarked.

He laughed uncomfortably. "Well, of course I know we're not gods really. It's just...well, it's just our custom."

"I know. But many people nowadays have turned their back on that custom and seem very happy. Look at your brother."

His brother had declined to have a girl chosen for him by his family, declaring that he wanted an educated wife who would be a companion for him. He had subsequently married a graduate. In spite of the disapproval of his relatives, who claimed that university life could only corrupt young women and teach them 'loose morals', the marriage had turned out to be a successful one, although it had resulted in the couple leaving the joint family household and settling in Bangalore.

He shrugged. "I am not like my brother."

In mutual unspoken agreement that we had reached a transactional cul-de-sac we rose, exchanged polite farewells, and continued on our chosen ways, he to enter the magistrates' court to engage in yet another bout of litigation which sometimes seemed to me to be the favourite pastime of upper-crust Kollepet males, and I to cross the maidan to enter the town. His problem was one which epitomises what seems to be a deep-seated fear among men which is not confined to India: that the emancipation of women implies in the loss of male 'superiority' a further loss of personal identity.

Kollepet is a fairly typical south Indian rural-based market town. Because it possesses neither large focal industries, notable ancient monuments, interesting architecture, nor natural scenic charm, very few foreigners apart from our family have had occasion to visit it in the past and fewer do so today. In fact, the visit of a foreigner is still an event which draws a crowd and is discussed all over town. There is no hotel, only the travellers' bungalow and a lodging house in a back street. The hospital, schools and college, banks, cinemas, and some of the larger and newer shops, and the houses and places of work of officials and richer citizens are supplied with electricity, but according to the latest census, less than a fifth of all the town households have electricity laid on. Most dwellings and smaller shops are still lit by kerosene lanterns. Very few buildings have water laid on — most of the richer houses have their own wells and the rest use street standpipes. Only one hundred and eighty-three households out of the five thousand three hundred odd have any kind of water-closet plumbing and sewage disposal in their case is by cesspit or septic tank. For the rest, open sewers line the streets throughout the town and are crossed by stone slabs to reach shops, offices and dwellings. Food shops hang over these drains while myriads of flies divide their attention between the drains and the uncovered wares, vying with the cockroaches for their share of the goods. The general public relieves itself directly into these sewers or in the back alleys of the town, except for those who live near enough to the outskirts to use the margins of the main road and the neighbouring fields.

The streets of Kollepet are unpaved and potholed, the shops open-fronted, many of them wooden stalls, and pedestrians, bicycles, bullock carts, buses, lorries, cows, goats, starving dogs and the occasional car jostle for priority and right of way, keeping firmly to the crown of the street. As dusk falls the legions of flies give way to those of mosquitoes, while rats, cockroaches and scorpions come out to go about their business. But in the midst of these uninviting features the most striking characteristic of the place is the liveliness, jocundity and generosity of its inhabitants and the personal cleanliness achieved in the face of so many impediments. Nor is life in Kollepet ever dull. On the contrary it overflows with interest, variety and colour.

Down the main road of the town, and then left into the square, is a kind of mini-maidan of beaten earth crossed with paths and embellished with a few dusty palms. Ahead is the devastana, the temple, an architecturally uninteresting edifice built in the last century and containing shrines to the high god Shiva, his consort Parvati, and to Chamundi, family goddess of the princely lineage of Mysore, who is also an aspect of the demon-slayer Durga, India's exemplification of the universal mother-goddess.

The square is rather a boring place as a rule, the people in it usually on their way to some other part of the town. The temple is rather uninteresting too, except at festival times such as Mahashivaratri, the Great Night of Shiva, when households go en famille to leave offerings at all the little shrines of the manifestations of Shiva that encircle the inner courtyard. Then it comes alive as the focus of a social occasion. Another such occasion which fills the square with a cheerful throng in holiday mood is the temple jatre (fair), when the images of Shiva and Parvati (who is another aspect of the mother goddess) are brought from their main shrines, enthroned in the huge heavy wooden temple chariot and hauled round the town in procession by local Hindu men of all castes. On this day of the devastana festival the whole of the Hindu Kollepet, dressed up in his or her best, is en fête and rubs shoulders good-humouredly. Normally dogged by a claustrophobic fear of crowds, I found the festive mood so exhilarating that I lost my silly inhibitions and entered happily into the carnival. Friends and strangers met in laughing, jostling company kept reiterating eagerly, "Do you like it? Are you enjoying yourself?" To which there was really no need to reply as, grinning all over my face and scurrying about with a camera, I was plainly having a lot of fun.

But today the square was just a featureless open space to be traversed and I was crossing it with my thoughts far away, when a smallish elderly stranger accosted me politely in English.

"Excuse me, Madam," he said. "May I ask you a question?"

"Oh. Good morning. Yes, of course."

"Would you mind me telling what you are doing in this awful place?”

"Well, I'm working here just now. Do you really think it's awful?”

"Madam, I live in the Nilgiris and I have had to come here for the first time on business. I have found the accommodation poor, there are no decent eating-houses and the place is hot and dirty. In fact this is the worst town I have ever visited.” He paused, bent his grey head towards me and added in a confidential tone, “I can tell you are British. What I can't understand is how you can bear to stay here.”

His vehemence was such that I couldn't help laughing. “Sometimes I feel the same. But you know, most of the people here are very nice and friendly.”

“I am glad you have found them so,” he said doubtfully. “For myself, I am relieved to be leaving and I do not wish to return. Thank you, Madam, for your kind attention. I have to catch my bus now. May I shake your hand?”

We clasped hands heartily and replacing on his head a battered khaki topi, he turned and trotted off towards the bus station.

Watching him go I discovered to my discomfiture that he had somehow tapped the bottomless well of cowardice that lurks within me, and longed for a moment to accompany him to the cool eucalyptus-scented heights of the Nilgiri hills. But this would never do. Call yourself an anthropologist, my girl? You ought to be ashamed of yourself. Thus admonished, the craven inner woman stopped screaming to get out and slunk back into hiding, temporarily overruled by a sterner ego.

These cogitations took me across the square, past the administrative offices of the taluk, and the morning's objective was reached. Bazaar street, the core of the town. Dirty, stinking, disease-ridden no doubt, but throbbing with life and crammed with all the goods and merchandise sought by the people of the taluk. There were sweet stalls with piles of brightly coloured confections, buzzing with flies; huge piles of portly brass and aluminium cooking pots; stalls bulging with cotton flock mattresses and pillows covered in brightly printed materials; food shops crawling with cockroaches;

tailors sitting at their machines. There were Aladdin's-cave stalls brilliant with bunches and cylinders of gorgeous glass bangles...How I remembered the excitement when we were children and a bangle-seller occasionally made his way to the hills where we lived. His wares were so beautiful en masse, and so fragile. He was so skilled at manipulating the bones of the hand to slide them on to a narrow wrist. Deluded by their glitter we bought them by the dozen, but like balloons or flowers they soon broke and were thrown away.

In the bazaar the flower stalls bore mounds of sweet-smelling garlands made of jasmine, tuberoses or kannakamba, for presentation or for women to wind in their hair. Non-Westernised Indians do not go in for flower arrangements in vases, since beautifying their homes is not a priority. Their talents in the floral decoration line lie in the making of garlands and the embellishment of pandals, temporary arches or canopies put up for weddings and other festive occasions. In south India it is the charming custom for women to wear flower garlands wound round their chignons or to tuck a few blooms into them. Bending over a barrow to inhale the sweet fresh scent and to buy for a few paise a delicate circlet of jasmine to wear as a necklace, l was reminded of the previous Christmas Day, when I had gone to the morning service at the little church near the orphanage. It was a day of sparkling sunlight, and all the windows of the church were open. Sitting on the floor on the women's side of the aisle, I watched the butterflies flutter in to hover around and settle on the wreaths and sprays of fresh blossom in the women's hair. Flowers, butterflies and sunshine in church combined with the familiar Christmas carols sung in Kannada to make something idyllic of the occasion. Today's hunting-ground was the sari shops. Less silk and gold here than in the fabulous sari emporia of the cities and more of the hind-wearing, deeply-dyed cotton or the rather sleazy nylon, but still a joy to browse around. I wanted an outfit for Mahadevi, the long full skirt and overblouse worn by young girls in the South before they are promoted to saris. Her present everyday outfit was torn and faded with much bashing on stones in the wash. She didn't have much fun, poor lamb, and deserved a treat. I went into a shop and looked round, remembering my last visit there, which was with Jowni, Mahadevi's elder sister. We were choosing a sari for me to buy her as a wedding present. She knew exactly what she wanted. It had to be the colour of kannakamba flowers, a rich shade of apricot. The shopowner, a high-caste Hindu, was torn between his obligation to a friend who had recommended his shop to me, his desire to please a foreigner with good customer-potential, and his disgust at having to serve an 'untouchable' girl. Using the term for addressing small children, accepted if insulting usage from 'twice-born' superiors to low-caste inferiors, he plucked at random one sari after another from his shelves and flung them disdainfully on the counter, saying, "Take this one, kusu." Jowni stood her ground with dignity and courage, turning to me to point out those saris nearest to the colour she desired. My role of go between involved supporting Jowni and persuading the shopkeeper to dig out more saris and stop trying to force on her ones which did not fulfill her criterion. The story had a happy ending. A sari of exactly the right colour was noticed under a pile of others, reluctantly pulled out and displayed, approved and bought. Patience and determination on Jowni's part had prevailed over prejudices, and we departed in triumph.

The transaction today was brief. With the girl's outfit wrapped in newspaper and tucked into my shoulder bag, I had time to buy some chilli buns or 'breadu' from the baker, averting my thoughts from the probable condition of the dark kitchen behind the counter. Roti is the traditional Kannada word for bread, but everyone in Kollepet used for the leavened variety, the English word 'bread' with the common Kannada suffix of 'u'. Many English words have become naturalised in this way where the indigenous term seems less appropriate. I remember watching a game of tennis on the town's one court, patronised by the élite, where interrogative cries of "outa?" when the ball went over the back line were answered by affirmative cries of "outu".

After the bread, the vegetable market, where thin green badnikai, purple onions and misshapen but delicious tomatoes could be bought for the equivalent of a penny or two and shovelled loose into the shopping bag from a heap on the planks of the stall. I also bought limes to go with a papaya I had purchased from an old woman sitting in the street who was selling them by the slice and was surprised but pleased to dispose of a whole one. Now rather heavily laden and brushing off with difficulty offers by small boys to carry my bag for a consideration, I sought the house of the joint family with whom I had been invited to share the midday meal.

The entrance was on a busy road, the usual stone slabs bridging the noisome drain and a couple of steps leading to a narrow door in an anonymous looking high wall. From the door a passage led into a pleasant open courtyard with oleanders and hibiscus bushes around the entrance giving the effect of a garden. But most of the courtyard had a floor-surface of smooth shiny red chenam or polished plaster. Here children played, washing hung, red chillies, ground-nuts or other foodstuffs were spread out to dry, and the women sat, cleaning or pounding grain. The household buildings surrounded it on four sides. The business part was in front. On one side was the kitchen and eating annexe plus two bedrooms; on the other, two rooms for the guests and the household well. At the back the house was two-storeyed. On the ground floor was a kind of central hall, unfurnished except for the hanging cradle of any member of the family currently in the infant stage. At night the. young unmarrieds and the children spread out their bed rolls there and it became a communal dormitory. Next to it was a small sitting room for receiving guests, with cane chairs and a radio. Behind this was the puja or prayer room, a kind of family chapel. On the floor above were more bedrooms, each belonging to one of the married brothers and his wife. Apart from this concession to marital privacy the life of the household was communal, although male and female affairs did not impinge much on each other. The kitchen verandah extended into the cowshed, where a buffalo and a cow or two chewed cud peacefully. Off the cowshed was the bathplace and two latrines.

The household was fairly typical of the old and traditional elite of the town, high-caste Hindus who had achieved financial success without too many concessions to Westernisation, and still lived in the joint family tradition. This particular one was, however, in a state of transition, the sons having attended university and the children of both sexes the private primary school, the high school, and in the case of a couple of older ones, the local college.

There was no attempt at interior decoration apart from the traditional rangoli (intricate designs drawn on the floor with a white powder poured from the hand by the women, mostly outside doorways, which have a ritual significance). The floors, where people sat, were swept regularly by a woman-servant, but the rest of the house was rather dusty and cobwebby, with crumbling plaster and peeling paintwork. Photographs of the family's married couples, and those of the deceased decked with dusty garlands, hung high up on the wall. Besides these a few calendar lithographs of favourite deities had been tacked up rather haphazardly. Apart from the radio and a ceiling fan in the sitting room and a single dangling electric bulb in each room there were no modern appliances. No need for them either, with a band of wives and as many living-out servants as required to do the work — indeed, in the case of the wives, with nothing else to do but the work.

Seated on a cane chair in the little guest 'parlour', conversing with some difficulty against the high-decibel competition of the radio with a couple of the sons and a wife or two who drifted in with cups of sweet milky coffee for the husbands and guest, I learned with some relief that the widowed mother, a formidable matriarch with a disapproving eye, was away visiting one of her several married daughters. As the producers of many sons she had fulfilled the principal requirement of a high-caste Hindu woman and — having had a hard time herself when she came as a bride into this house — now made sure that her daughters-in-law were properly restricted and subjugated in accordance with the tenets of high-caste orthodoxy.

All the same this was a south Indian family and the lot of the daughters-in-law differed from that of women in the North. Restricted to house and courtyard though they were on account of their high caste and the traditional outlook of the mother and some of the sons, they were not in purdah. They talked freely and unveiled to male friends and relations visiting the house or met on their occasional chaperoned sallies to the devastana or cinema or on visits to relatives. The married daughters returned frequently to the house and stayed for long privileged visits after the accompanying spouse had returned alone to his home base. The wives went home at least once a year and remained there until their husbands came to fetch them back.

Further liberalisations were creeping in. The wives were all at least literate in Kannada and their daughters would all be literate in English as well. A major catalyst for change in his household had been the recent marriage of a family member to a girl whose scientific qualifications had led to very remunerative employment and an income higher than that of any other member of the family. Since she managed to combine her relatively independent position with tactful behaviour towards her in-laws, she was held in esteem by them all and her own success as an autonomous breadwinner was having a cumulative effect in eroding traditional shibboleths. Thus the intelligent eldest unmarried girl of the branch of the family I was now visiting was to have been married off as soon as her last unmarried aunt and uncle (who were about her age) had been found suitable spouses: But the example of the prospering newcomer had inspired her parents to think again and her father now talked of her obtaining a higher degree in the hope of making a career in computer science.

When the meal was pronounced ready I asked if I might wash my hands. The bathroom, opening off the cowshed, had its drawbacks. Used daily by anything from seventeen to twenty-four people, it still harboured dust, cobwebs, large spiders, mosquitoes and sometimes swarms of red ants which bit fiercely. It was also extremely dark. The indifference of the well-off orthodox lower-middle-class in India to the state of their accommodation never ceased to amaze me, in the same way that Americans used to be amazed by the lack of central heating and adequate plumbing in British stately homes. I once remarked somewhat tactlessly to a scion of one such household of the old élite that a windowsill in their kitchen which was crumbling to rubble could do with re-plastering. "Oh," he replied dismissively, "We don't waste money on things like that."

Having washed by means of pouring cold water over my hands from a beaker dipped in a big brass cauldron — hot water was heated separately in a sort of primitive copper vessel, fuelled from below by a fire of sticks and dried sugarcane fibre — I joined the household gathering in the eating-room off the kitchen. We removed our sandals to enter, since this was an adjunct of the ritually pure kitchen. My presence there was another symbol of change. In the father's time no foreigner would have been allowed in here, only Indians of high caste and therefore of the requisite ritual purity. Even when the mother was there I was entertained in solitary-splendour in the little 'parlour'. Today the brothers and I sat on stool around the long table, while the chattering children sat on the floor along one wall. The wives served and would eat later. As a foreigner I was treated as an honorary man. A Westernised Indian woman would have received the same treatment, an example of the Hindu tolerance of the traditions of others (with the notable exception of beef eating). As we ate with the fingers of our right hands one of the brothers, seeing me struggling to tear one-handed a tough chapatti, looked at me with a conniving grin. "Go on," he said. "Use your left hand. We all do when Amma is away." This was yet another indication of social change. The left hand, only employed for polluting tasks, should never be employed for eating, giving, receiving or greeting — unless joined with the right in the last two cases.

After our meal the men began to drift off for their siesta and the women were able to sit down and eat. The dirty plates were put out on the verandah floor where, covered with flies, they awaited the arrival of the part-time maidservant. She would scour them with cold water and wood-ash. A few years ago a small pi-dog loosely attached to the household used to lick the plates before they were washed. Since he wandered off into the streets every day, no doubt sharing snacks of garbage and ordure with his companions among the legions of ownerless strays in the town, and since bodily leavings are regarded as ritually polluting to the high castes, I once remarked on this. "Oh, the plates get washed," was the indifferent reply. Well, yes, they did, after a fashion, but anthropologically speaking it was an interesting point since they were not subject to cleansing with any ritually pure substance, such as cow-dung. On my return a year after this subject came up, the little dog was missing. It had died, I was told, of rabies. The child who had last touched the poor little creature before the disease was diagnosed was given anti-rabies injections, but the rest of the family did not bother.

It was now time for the older children of the household to go back to school, while the women took themselves off with the little ones for the afternoon's rest. Thanking them all for their friendly hospitality and refusing with resolute politeness an offer to await my interviewers in the guest parlour (which harboured a particularly insatiable breed of small grey mosquitoes apparently adjusted to daylight as well as nocturnal feeding), I went to sit on the step outside the street door. It was a good vantage point, in spite of the ripe odours emanating from the drain, from which to watch the world go by and exchange greetings with acquaintances among the passers-by. The arrival of my four young assistants, fresh, smiling and handsome, was nicely timed for the moment when this occupation began to pall. They seemed just then to embody the pathetic hopefulness of puppies and I felt like hugging each one of them in gratitude for being such good company. Since this would have been the signal for the instant gathering of an appreciative crowd, I desisted and took a photograph of them instead. The crowd gathered anyway, pushing to get into the photograph and striking self-conscious poses. The camera was a polaroid, which entailed a great deal of on-the-spot dishing out of likenesses to one and all. When we eventually turned away down the road we were followed for some time by plaintive cries of "Photo, photo" from optimistic urchins who had turned up too late for the bonanza.

Looking back over my shoulder at the drab and dusty expanse of the square, with the temple in the background, I remembered how it had quickened with life and laughter at the devastana festival, the one day in the year, I thought, when town and taluk seems to forget about segmentation. The spectacle of Kollepet citizens en fête at the festival conveys a strong sense not only of community but of homogeneity. Here are the inhabitants of a linguistic region, subject to the same national and state laws and to the tyrannies of the same climatic and other environmental hazards, brought up in the same general tradition, technological methods and local lore, living according to the same calendrical cycle, both ritual and agricultural, using the same idioms, propitiating the same local deities, and possessing in common a number of collective beliefs and values. That this impression of homogeneity is an illusion and that the social body of the taluk population more closely perceived turns out to be as disjoined as a jigsaw puzzle is hardly surprising in view of the fact that it is a caste society. Take a step away from it, I told myself, and it's a picture. Look closely, and what you see is a web of separate communities. Closer still, a shifting mass of struggling individuals. And when you come as close as that, you're looking at Everyman.

relative values

We walked together along the main road through the town, passing the surgery, with waiting room open to the street, of a doctor friend, and the shop of the chemist who owned a refrigerator for his drugs and allowed me to keep my butter there during the hot weather. As we continued on our way, the bigger shops and houses built of cement or plastered and colour washed brick, gave way to small mud and plaster dwellings and wooden stalls selling betel nuts, pān leaves, single cigarettes and bidis, the rolled tobacco leaves tied with red thread which are far more pungent than the average cigarette and much cheaper. At a point where a subsidiary road turned to the right we separated, Rajan and Ramani setting off to one interview while Manjula, Jagan and I turned down the side road to visit the silk mill.

To reach our goal we had to traverse the Upuliga quarter of the town. The Upuliga caste is one of the largest in the taluk. They share a common 'low caste' culture with the Harijans, although Upuligas are a 'clean' low caste since they do not eat beef or undertake such polluting work as the removal of faeces or the bodies of dead animals and are thus not categorised as 'untouchables'. Uppu means salt in Kannada, and their traditional caste occupation was the making and selling of saltpetre. Today they specialise in all sorts of heavy labour, where the women work sturdily alongside the men. Most Upuligas are illiterate and poor but because the silk mill is situated at the end of the Upuliga street, virtually all those employed at the machines are Upuliga women, many of whom earn more than their husbands, and they are extremely independent. In fact most Upuliga women are pretty tough and a Kollepet worthy once remarked to me with something like awe, "They don't even fear the police." The whole community in the town has a fearsome reputation for quarrelling and aggression and one of their ejmanaveru or community leaders complained to me that his position was no sinecure since it involved the arbitration of disputes in the course of which he was liable to be beaten up by both sides. When I repeated this to the present manager of Honnametti, where a large proportion of the labourers are Upuligas, he said, "I can well believe that. Here on the hills the women seem to spend all their spare time beating their husbands."

All the same I liked the Upuligas. On the estate at least they reserved their truculence for intra-caste squabbles and they seemed to treat everyone with a kind of forthright directness which made for easy communication. As we ran the gauntlet of stares and uninhibited critical comment from passers-by and roadside loiterers, I was reminded of an interview I'd had with a young man of the caste. After submitting amiably for a while to cross-questioning about the marital and kinship norms of his community, he turned the tables on me with a brisk, "Well, you've had your turn. Now it's mine. There's a lot I want to know about the customs of your people." Whereupon he began interrogating me in some depth as to the truth of the tales he had heard about young women in the West consorting freely with young men without scandal and even having sexual relations before marriage without bringing disgrace upon their families or incurring the lasting opprobrium of 'society'. This was something a good many of Kollepet's jeunesse were dying to know more about, but mostly did not like to ask, and certainly none had dared to ask so freely.

In contrast to their predisposition to conflict, Upuligas tend to be devout, to get readily possessed by their caste deity, Muntaswami, at his festival, and to specialise in ritual dancing and fire-walking. The sister of my bluff young interlocutor, an illiterate and unassuming girl in everyday life, was also a seer, possessed, it was claimed, by a local goddess known as Adi-Shakti. Roughly translated, Adi-Shakti means primal female energy, and certainly in her trances the girl projected a formidable and rather frightening presence.

As we went along the main street of the quarter we passed the shrine of Adi-Shakti and the shed behind it where the young seer held her seances. Two or three years ago a friend and I had been taken there by a devotee of the seer and had squatted at the back of the crowded shed to watch and listen as she dealt with those who approached her with offerings to lay them, along with their problems, before her. Impressed by her powerful persona, we were somewhat alarmed when she suddenly called upon "those who are here to observe without belief" to come before her. The people around us nudged us, whispering "Go on, she means you," and sheepishly clutching our propitiatory offerings of limes and flowers we moved forward and sat down in the open space before her. After chiding us briefly for approaching the session in the wrong spirit she suddenly pointed at me, seated cross-legged and rather scared before her, and cried out in that uncannily powerful voice, "You. You are troubled. You have been sad for a long time." I can think of no way she could have known the things she told me then except by paranormal means. Her utterances were just oracular enough to avoid giving away my private affairs to the silent crowd of devotees but they affected me so profoundly that I sat there weeping openly. Her tone altered. "Don't be afraid," she said almost gently. "A change is coming. It will all turn out well very soon." We went away from the shed subdued, impressed, and in my case absurdly hopeful. She was right too. In a few months time the cause of my grief was dispelled and all turned out well enough.

There was nothing sceptical about the reception Manjula and Jagan accorded this story. The occult, in the form of diviners and seers, ghosts and witchcraft, spirits and spirit possession, along with the activities of local deities, is an integral part of the everyday life of all but the most sophisticated in India. After all, as even the sceptical West is now beginning to admit, the paranormal does manifest itself as part of everyday life.

Anyway, their fascinated questions occupied the rest of the walk until we arrived at the factory compound. Here villagers carrying baskets of fluffy yellow cocoons on their heads were milling around the weighing shed. We were greeted by the manager, shown around the works where women sat at the machines deftly spinning off the sticky floss and transforming it into creamy-yellow silk yarn, and then led to his house.

The house was in a grove of trees, mangoes and gulmohurs. It was quite old and rather dark but a pleasantly cool place in the heat of the day. The manager and his wife were fairly 'modern' in outlook and had expended considerable effort to make it more convenient and comfortable. Having listened for a while to Manjula's conscientious interviewing of the lady I joined Jagan and the husband. After a couple of initial scoldings in the early days of the survey, Manjula had got the message and always tried to clarify the answers in her forms, but Jagan still needed supervisory prodding from time to time to keep him up to the mark.

When the interviews were over came the payoff: we must stay to tea. I was still rather full of rice, sambhar and chapatti but drank the tea gratefully and nibbled at delicious gram and chilli vaddays and rich sweetmeats, Mysore pak and lozenge-shaped bits of halva, while Manjula and Jagan tucked in with enthusiasm. The two children, a girl and a boy, joined us and were introduced. They were both bright, it seemed, and the parents had career ambitions for them both. "Girls must be able to stand on their own feet today," the father said, adding shrewdly, "Graduate status for both sexes is the minimum requirement for success in modern India."

"When it comes to finding a husband for your daughter," I asked, reluctantly reverting to the role of investigator, "which would you look for first, property or education?"

He looked at me pityingly. "But today education is property."

We still had another interview to do, once more combined with a social occasion, before we could go home. This one was at the house of a banker's family, who lived on a road leading out of the town which was fast becoming an enclave of the new élite.

The houses springing up along the road were modern brick or concrete villas, plastered and colour-washed, nothing like as suitable for the climate as the old high-ceilinged ones with tiled roofs, but painstakingly set off with lawns and flowerbeds. The gardens were planted with flowering trees and shrubs, such as those which add grace to residential areas in Mysore and Bangalore: bougainvillea, hibiscus and oleander; pink cassia, jacaranda and gulmohur. Inside were bathrooms with Western-style water-closets, kitchens with refrigerators, sitting rooms with ceiling fans, sofas, chairs, rugs and display shelves. Some of the more sophisticated even had fresh flowers in vases, though many were content to stick a few plastic flowers in a handy receptacle as evidence of their awareness of the value of decor, and then leave them to gather dust. On the whole, however, the houses of the new élite were kept clean and well tended by their house-proud owners, whatever snobbish reservations one might have about their taste. It was the outward sign of the inward difference between them and the old élite: the difference between the 'modern' outlook and traditional orthodoxy or, to put it another way, between ideals of secular hygiene and ritual purity.

The banker and his wife had an emancipated daughter now studying medicine in Bangalore. When she was still at Kollepet high school she had epitomised the privileged and Westernised — at least in Kollepet terms — youth of the town. She was the proud possessor of hi-fi equipment, but also played the veena and gave recitals at the annual Ganesha festival. Within the limits of Kollepet standards of respectability she had a good deal of freedom, being permitted, for instance, to engage in amateur theatricals with friends of both sexes. But, unlike her peers in the big cities of Mysore and Bangalore, she wore saris rather than T-shirts and jeans outdoors and did not go out alone with boys.

After the interviews we drank yet more tea, toyed politely with excellent idlis (steamed rice cakes eaten with chutney) and discussed the implications for women of social change in south India. That the effects of female education are cumulative (a fact which subsequent analysis of my survey data confirmed) was exemplified by this family. The wife's mother had had secondary school education; the wife herself was a graduate but had never been allowed to have a career outside the home; but the daughter was expected to combine marriage with a career and had been given the same educational opportunities enjoyed by the son. "Education for women is essential," the father said thoughtfully, "because the entire family depends on the mother." Nodding agreement over the tea cups 1 was nevertheless reminded of the indignant defence of the illiterate wife by an equally illiterate Harijan labourer we had interviewed: "A mother doesn't have to have that kind of education to know how to bring up her children to be good people." He was another thoughtful man.

By the time we had reiterated our thanks and farewells it was time to go home. It would be dark by seven and it was about an hour's walk to the smallholding. Manjula and Jagan were tired. They had done three interviews that day, whereas two was usually the maximum. I was suffering from a surfeit of civilities. So 1 thankfully stuffed the completed questionnaire forms into my shoulder-bag and we walked together towards the main road. Before we reached it we passed two houses, one traditional and one modern, with whose owners I was acquainted. The last thing we needed was any further hospitality, and there was a marked tendency to scurry on my part as we passed by the gates.

68

The first house was an old one in the traditional style, grey on the outside. and equally dingy within. It belonged to a Brahman astrologer, a portly gentleman who made a comfortable living casting the horoscopes so vital to the arranged marriages of the orthodox high castes. In view of the importance attached to the horoscopes by families trying to marry off their young, I was always astonished by the gleeful tales I heard about the fraudulent 'cooking' of them which was resorted to if necessary by the very people who appeared to believe in them so devoutly and were so zealous in their employment. The astrologer seemed to be perpetually torn between the tenets of scriptural orthodoxy and the common sense manipulation of local rules and customs in which he, like everyone else, was involved in everyday life. For instance, when I was trying to discover his views on the restriction of women he gave me the orthodox line. "The female is the equivalent of the earthernware pot, which is porous and thus not easily cleaned. If polluted it must be thrown away. The male, on the other hand, is like a brass pot. If polluted it can be scrubbed and retained." This is the symbolism used in the Dharmashastras. Reflecting that this view is probably at the root at the universal double standards of morality relating to women and men, I nevertheless felt I must point out to him that his own womenfolk seemed a pretty independent lot. To which he replied with a dismissive laugh. On another occasion, when he learned that l was studying the incidence of preferential marriage to kin in the area, he sternly cited the dictates of the law-giver Manu, as well as the ancient Mitakshara marriage law still ritually valid in north India, to prove that close-kin marriage was both sinful and unlucky. "So your wife was not related to you before your marriage?" I asked, all innocence. "Ah well," he said with his loud jolly laugh. "I have to admit that I married my father's sister's daughter, my brother married our elder sister's daughter, and my own daughter married her mother's younger brother." With him, precept and practice were poles apart. I liked him, though this evening we all hoped to escape his notice. When I first returned to Kollepet after an absence of nearly twenty-five years, it was to study the Kollepet version of caste and the 'Dravidian' kinship system of south India. Now, although my current research project was into the effects of caste cultures on fertility, questions of kinship and marriage were still relevant to my study.

To put it briefly, in Hindu north India marriage between relatives is not allowed and is regarded as incestuous. In Hindu south India it is preferred, and the language of kinship reflects this preference. In the ideology of north Indian marriage the family of the husband are regarded as perpetually superior to that of the wife. This means that they can never marry one of their girls into the wife's family as the ranking situation of the families concerned would then be reversed. Thus in the North, in-laws are widely dispersed, only caste-members who are totally unrelated are considered as possible spouses, and the bride is almost completely separated from her kin forever.

In south India, with a few exceptions, it is the other way about. Marriages are ideally between equals. They have to be, because marriage to the children of the father's sister and the mother's brother, as well as that of a girl to her mother's younger brother, is pre-supposed by the kinship vocabulary, and is in fact very common in the South.

Why is it only acceptable in Kollepet or elsewhere in the South for a girl to marry her mother's younger brother or a man his elder sister's daughter? It seems to be because the principle of relative age is very important in south India. People address their elder brothers and sisters by the kinship term and owe them respect, while they address their younger siblings by name and expect respect from these juniors. This places elder siblings on a kind of mezzanine floor between generation levels, so that their children fall into the category of cousins.

The inhabitants of Kollepet taluk are not unaware that there are risks inherent in the repeated intermarriage of close kin, and a number of them mentioned to me their reservations about avuncular unions. Some referred to the possibility of adverse genetic effects, expressed in the form of anxious questions such as "Do you think this kind of union produces mad children?" One young Lingayat confided that his parents were trying to persuade him to marry his elder sister's daughter but that he was determined not to, because it was too much like marrying a sister.

But the majority of Kollepet informants approved strongly of marriage to kin. One frequently cited reason was that both spouses are known to both families, who have had the opportunity of observing their characters from childhood. Another constantly and optimistically cited theme was that "the affection is already there".

One Kollepet friend, whose wife was the daughter of one of his classificatory elder sisters, told me that she had declared as a child, "Govind is my favourite Mama (mother's brother) and I'm going to marry him when I grow up. I'll pull his hair until he does." The marriage was manifestly a happy and successful one.

Other people stressed the economic advantages of allowing family resources to be concentrated within the small circle of relatives on both sides. And one impoverished Brahman claimed that marriage to kin served a useful purpose in keeping families without corporate property together. Time and time again informants gave as their primary reason for approving of such unions, "We know our daughters will be happy." The girls remain within the related group and are not lost. The marriages renew the ties of affection between sisters and brothers, ties which are greatly valued in south India and which are consolidated by visits at holidays and festivals, presents, and reciprocal help in times of need. One married woman I knew in Kollepet had sold her gold bracelets, her marriage portion, to contribute towards her brother's college lees. Another was a widow who was still supported by her brother although they had quarrelled and were no longer on speaking terms. He was a bus driver and she always travelled on his bus confident in her knowledge that no brother would ever charge his sister for her seat on a bus.

Sisters and brothers cooperate in arranging marriages for each other and for their children and naturally, if the marriage is between their own children or if a brother marries his elder sister's daughter, the ties are reinforced. Furthermore, when a sister's daughter marries into a joint household the fact that her mother-in-law, that awesome task-mistress, is also her maternal grandmother usually ensures that she is loved and protected.

Other justifications offered me by Kollepet people for these kin marriages were that family peace, unity and cooperation were enhanced, that wedding gifts were not haggled over, that dowry or bridewealth obligations (in those castes where they existed) could be waived, and that horoscopes, in the case of the 'Sanskritised' castes which use them, were not usually necessary as the girl and the boy were regarded as "made for each other".

And lastly, though this advantage was not mentioned to me by Kollepet advocates of the system, the bride is less likely to have to 'prove' herself by bearing sons. Girls married to kin are surrounded by known people and are seldom either lonely or isolated, since the marriages are so often arranged to reinforce existing ties. But, in spite of this fairly general approval, I did discover a sharp division between the higher and lower castes when it came to certain other aspects of marriage which affected women. I began to think of this dividing line as the one which separated the traditionally accepted 'high' and 'low' castes.

What it amounted to was that higher castes (with the exception of the Westernised elite) all forbade in principle the working, or free passage of women outside the home; all forbade divorce; and all forbade the remarriage of widows, but not of widowers. Marriages were always arranged.

In the lower castes the women were expected to earn, and if they did not work outside the household for wages, were still permitted freedom of movement. On the whole they came and went as they wished in village or town, though the economic necessity of working for wages in such castes as the Upuligas or Harijans restricted their lives in the same way as it restricted the lives of the men. Among all these castes, including of course the Sholiga hill tribe, divorce and remarriage after divorce or widowhood were allowed for both sexes. Marriages were arranged among the low castes but the girls had the right of veto, in theory at least. And in the case of the Sholigas, the girls chose their own partners.

All the castes in the taluk had their own micro-cultural kinship customs, which varied in their usage of such institutions as bride-wealth among the low castes, dowry (rare) among high castes, reliance on horoscopes, and so on, but the great divide between the orthodox higher castes and the lower castes was that between those who did not recognise women's right to some autonomy in the institutions of kinship and those who did. I found that the frontiers of caste, kinship and the status of women all met at this ideological chasm.

The last house in this suburban road was a particularly new and elaborate one, with a lot of ornamental wrought iron. It belonged to another Brahman, a self-made young man who was now a wealthy timber contractor. His father had been a small shopkeeper and he had very little schooling because he had to start working at an early age.

As a rather brash nouveau-riche, he had applied for membership of the town's one-court tennis club, stronghold of the new elite, and had been turned down on the grounds that he was "not cultured". So neither his high economic status nor his high ritual rank sufficed to gain acceptance at that time by what passed for high society in Kollepet. The requirement was a 'modern' education and the sophisticated mores that went with it. A few years later I heard that he had been accepted by the club after all, but never did find out how he had achieved this. My feelings about him were mixed and ambivalent. He was a friendly and good-natured lad but I had been gleefully informed that he owed his prosperity to the fact that for years he had been taking out far more than the permitted number of trees from the lower slopes of the Biligirirangan hills, getting away with it by means of judicious dispensation of largesse where it would do most good. I had noticed with distress that large areas of the deciduous jungle had been looking increasingly denuded and that erosion was beginning to set in, and was torn between a desire to report the racket and an unwillingness to sneak on the wretch. The result was that I felt a wave of hostility whenever I saw his pleasant face, and while everyone with any sense must deplore wreckers of the environment, I knew that much of my anger was directed against him as a destroyer of my personal roots.

At the crossroads we turned south and walked together to the end of the town. Here we parted, as Manjula and Jagan had rented rooms in the house of a Lingayat family not far from the maidan, and I went on, unattended but far from solitary. The road was full of sheep and goats, women and men on foot or in bullock carts, men on bicycles and scooters, sometimes with a wife side-saddle on the pillion, all returning to their respective homes at the end of the day and giving way with resigned reluctance to the ubiquitous lorries which charged the rest of the traffic, apparently convinced that nobody in possession of a windhorn could possibly be expected to practise the use of brakes.

By the time I reached the tote the sun was sinking into layers of crimson cloud against which the shrine-crowned hill behind the village and the shaggy palms beyond the thatched roof of my lair showed sharply black. It would be good to wash, to accept gratefully from Siddha a green coconut, and to sit for a while under the stars sipping the cool liquid from the coconut without bothering to prepare a meal. I seemed to have been eating all afternoon.

But these optimistic visions of a peaceful evening in privacy were swiftly dispelled. The first caller was Rangi, who came from her end of the dwelling, tin beaker in hand, to ask for a chocolate drink to cure her headache. Some months before she had come to me for something for a headache and I had given her an aspirin and a cup of 'Boost', a malted chocolate preparation manufactured by Cadbury in India. Since then Rangi's headaches had become a regular event, from which I concluded that, like me, she had developed an addiction to 'Boost', a most consoling beverage. However, this evening she did not retire with her filled beaker but hesitated on the verandah. "Is it true that you are going to the hills soon?"

"Yes. The day after tomorrow."

"I hope you won't be away long." She smiled shyly. "It is very besara (boring, depressing) here when you are away."

Pleased and touched, l beamed at her. "I too am happy in this house with you and your family, Amma." And this was true. It struck me then, as it strikes me now, that the two groups of people with whom I felt most at ease in India were, at one end of the scale, those with whom l shared a common intellectual heritage, including an idiomatic command of the English language with all its nuances, and a number of common interests and pre- dispositions; and, at the other end, the village peasants and the local hill tribe. Dealings with either friends or strangers in the latter category were occasionally complicated, it is true, by expectations on their part raised by my family's long connection with the area. But otherwise there was on both sides a simple acknowledgment of and respect for the other's differing cultural background which made for a direct and straightforward personal relationship. With those classes in between, on the other hand, interpersonal relationships could be very perplexing: a minefield of misunderstandings, of tip-toeing around known prejudices or of stumbling headlong over unexpected ones. And this did not make for restful rapport.

I should add, however, that there were two aspects of my association with these middle groups which could be relied upon. The first was that in any attempt to be More Indian than Thou (a syndrome which afflicts all too many Western social scientists dealing with India), I was sure to be ruining the fun of and even offending certain Kollepet citizens who regarded me as their very own pet foreigner. The second was that trying to be a little friend of all the world was a dead loss. Nobody in Kollepet wanted a friend of all the world. Who does? What everyone wants, especially in Kollepet, is an ally.

Rangi had no sooner departed, beaker of 'Boost' in one hand and Mahadevi's new outfit in the other, when the sound of voices, the rattle of bicycle wheels on stony ground and the flicker of torches heralded the arrival of company. Govinda Rajan, the landlord, bathed, fed and rested, had brought along three other equally well-refreshed friends to call. I knew them all. One was a neighbouring Lingayat smallholder. He and his wife were friendly and hospitable, but Rudrappa was by no means a welcome figure tonight as he loomed up in the starlight, on account of his propensity for staying late. Furthermore, on his last protracted evening visit he had brought with him a bottle of gin, which he asked me to keep for him in my cupboard as he did not want his wife to know that he, a good Lingayat, drank alcohol. I wasn't too keen on being a party to this deceit, especially as I was sorry for his poor lonely wife, but felt it churlish to refuse. And now my heart sank at the thought that a convivial evening might lie ahead. The only consolation was that I might get a chance to discuss with him the way his lineage was intertwined with that of his wife, who was his elder sister's daughter. I had learned from his wife that their forbears on both sides had been indulging in this type of kin union for several generations. Now, if sister's daughter marriage is repeated over several generations it becomes mother's brother's daughter marriage. I don't propose to go into details here, but it can be worked out on paper should anybody wish to do so. Anyway, I had worked out that my Lingayat neighbours' marriage was one of these and that she was both his classificatory elder sister's daughter and his mother's brother's daughter.

The second companion was a local contractor who, starting life as the son of a poor goatherd, one of the ragged barefoot boys of the village, had educated himself to literacy in Kannada, English and Sanskrit, become a highly successful builder and was much respected for his learning, his asceticism and his individual approach to religious philosophy. In his house were the only shelves of books

I ever saw in Kollepet. With him came a third associate of the landlord's, a young man who had been my assistant during my previous period of research in the area. He had just left college then, naive and bouncy as a puppy, strong and athletic but with a rooted objection to lifting a finger or taking a step if he could argue his way out of it or find someone else to do it. But despite the frequent brisk confrontations between us this disposition had brought about, his friendliness was disarming and we never failed to make it up. We had some lively adventures together too, hitching lifts on lorries, scrambling through the windows of buses too full to be entered by the door, exploring the rocky hills behind the village and travelling argumentatively together to outlying hamlets or the big cities.

The one trait these four people had in common was their tendency to sit and sit and talk and talk. Tonight was no exception. Hoping my disinclination was sufficiently disguised I spread out the guest mat, and brought glasses of lime juice and water and the bottle of gin for Rudrappa (and for the landlord who also took an occasional nip of the hard stuff). Thereafter it was a question of smiling wanly where appropriate and furtively scratching the night's crop of mosquito bites on neck, wrists and ankles, which proliferated as the evening wore on. However often this situation repeated itself, I never really discovered how to deal with it.

Eventually Govinda, catching sight of a smothered yawn, became aware on closer inspection that one of his party was less than animated. Rising to his feet he said kindly, "We will leave you to take your rest now." Gratefully summoning the last dregs of energy for the polite version of the correct reply to the Kannada farewell of barutane (I will come back). I waved them off the premises with hypocritical cries of Hog bit banni (Go and come back). And once they were gone there was nothing left to do but clean teeth, wash dust off feet, undress and fall into bed. As so often happened I woke in the small hours and lay listening to the frog and its mates thumping around. Sometimes in the past it had been yet another recurrence of gastro-enteritis or amoebic dysentery which aroused me, and I would lie there knowing that at any minute it would be necessary, dammit, to put on the torch, wriggle from under the net and stagger out to the latrine. At other times an account of these restless nights could read like some exotic Eastern calendar of misfortune: the Month of the Abcessed Tooth, for instance, or the

Month of the Attack of Shingles. This time, however, the wakefulness was pleasurable. One could stretch out luxuriating in not feeling ill while giving constructive thought to the programme of work to be carried out in the hills and the logistics of the move. "Who goes to the hills goes to his mother," says Kipling's lama in Kim. The lama was going home and so was I.

going back

On the morning of our transfer to the hills the verandah resembled a chapter from Exodus. Everything, including the kitchen stove, was going. Among other things the mound of baggage embraced a suitcase of clothing; briefcase with clipboard, notebooks and diaries; typewriter; large box of questionnaire forms; another large box containing enough rice, dal, ragi-flour, biscuits, fruit, tinned butter, milk and cheese, and of course 'Boost', to last a month; cooking utensils; kerosene for the little stove; and a miscellaneous collection of presents such as sandals and umbrellas requested by friends among the tribe and work-force. Only a half-dozen bits of furniture and the mosquito net remained. Oh blessed prospect of four netless weeks! Happiness is a long farewell to mosquitoes.

The Attikan jeep, on its way back from repairs in Mysore, was to take the four interviewers and me, plus our gear, all the way to the estates. It was a great weight off my mind. On the other hand it would also be a great weight on the jeep. I was not keen to be benighted on that ghat road, whose hazards, now as earlier, included the omnipresence of elephants and the impossibility of avoiding their attentions should they choose to object to our proximity. The stony track, one car wide, wound constantly, generally with a vertical bank on one side and a precipice on the other. In theory one reversed quietly round the corner if one met elephants, but they were by no means inobservant; besides, it was unwise to rely too much on the vehicle. The Punjur ghat still lived up to its reputation as a test to destruction of motorised transport.

The driver of the jeep was to stop in Kollepet to take aboard the interviewers, which meant a prolonged coffee break as well. I decided to improve the shining hour by enjoying myself and my chattels to the main road to save time. It might be a dusty wait, but we were destined to dust anyway and there was always something interesting to observe on the road. With the neighbourly help of Siddha and family, the move was accomplished and I settled in the shade on a culvert wall, surrounded by bows and bags as if at a

Victorian picnic.

About a hundred yards to the right some smallholders had spread out their ragi harvest over the crown of the road to get it threshed by the wheels of passing vehicles. This was a comparatively recent ploy, dating no doubt from the time when increasing traffic made it worthwhile. The practice often led to monumental skids, and for a few minutes I watched with ghoulish interest the approach of fast-moving lorries.

A soft cough and a "Good morning" in English recalled my attention. An elderly gentleman in an immaculate dhoti (loin-cloth) dismounted from his bicycle and inspected the pile of baggage with some curiosity. "What are you doing here, Madam Monica, may I ask?" As well he might. He was a charming person, a gentle Brahman businessman and landholder who as a small boy had lived with his uncle, the postmaster, at the Attikan post office on the hills. I made room for him on the wall and he sat down beside me for an exchange of news and views. Within a minute or so one of those instant crowds which are such a feature of the Indian scene had coalesced and arranged itself in a semi-circle around us. Since we spoke in English and they could not follow the conversation, it was not worth hanging about once every drop of visual information as to our goings-on had been absorbed to the accompaniment of shuffling, spitting and comment. Thus the components of the assembly kept shifting, young men and women on their way to the fields or to visit nearby villages, children gnawing pilfered sticks of sugarcane, old people bent on hacking yet more green goatfeed from the butchered banyans, all squatting down for a rest and a good stare. The onlookers did not deter us (you get used to an audience in India) but at one moment Mr. Subba Rao looked up and spotted one of his own employees among them. "Bring some green coconuts," he said. Clearly wishing he had never stopped, the unfortunate minion remounted his bike and pedalled off reluctantly towards a distant coconut grove.

I was impressed. "You own quite a lot of land around here, don't you? A lot of wet land too. You've come a long way, Mr. Subba Rao."

"Yes," he replied absently. "Look at this." Taking a notebook and a ballpoint out of his shirt pocket he scribbled something and handed it to me. To my astonishment it was my father's signature.

"Goodness," I said faintly. "You can't have seen Daddy for about fifty years."

"True. But as a child at Maskall (the site of the post-office on the hills at that time) I learned to write English by copying handwriting on post-office forms." I was even more impressed. The signature was a perfect replica.

"You'd have made a good forger."

"Fortunately that was not necessary."

He began to tell me the story of his early life. As a young man he had been a follower of Gandhi and a freedom-fighter, if one can describe in that way an advocate of Satyagraha or passive resistance. He ended with a sigh as the two coconuts were delivered. "Those months in the prison were the happiest days of my life," he murmured, watching the man slice the top of the big smooth green nuts with an expert stroke of his kathi (sickle) and insert the point with a sharp blow to make a hole. "It was not uncomfortable, except for the bed-bugs, and we were well treated. I shall never forget the comradeship. You see, we were all political prisoners. They put us all together." He sighed again. "But now, all is disillusion. Gandhiji is forgotten and instead we have conflict and corruption."

"It's the same everywhere," I said sadly. To console ourselves we tipped up the nuts and drank. He poured his down his throat in a neat jet while I got the juice all over my chin as usual and had to mop up. An errant thought struck me.

"Can I change the subject and ask you something?"

"Please ask."

Several ethnographers specialising in Indian culture have written erudite papers. on what they claim to be 'the indigenous belief' that the 'bodily substance' or 'blood' of a woman changes at her marriage from that of her father's line to that of her husband's line. I had been canvassing the views of Kollepet people on this phenomenon and had never yet come across anyone who had heard of it. When I asked Subba Rao's opinion he was, to my initial surprise, outraged.

"How can that be? If she changed how could she go on loving her father, mother, sisters and brothers? Girls know they belong to their natal family too."

I remembered then that he was the widowed father of three cherished daughters. His outburst was significant because it underlined a conflict of values noticeable among the higher caste in Kollepet. Daughters and sisters are much loved and petted in their natal families, and when they marry there is a strong sentiment that their love for their parents and siblings should remain unimpaired. At the same time a woman is expected, at least in theory and by her mother-in-law, to adapt to her husband's household and transfer her affections to it. Since it is impossible for a bride to conform to both these ideals she is presented with a paradoxical puzzle which, in the South, is resolved by cross-cousin and sister's daughter marriage. In the latter case the bride's mother-in-law is of course her doting grandmother, which provides the most satisfactory solution to the puzzle.

"Who says this thing?" enquired Subba Rao, still indignant.

"Learned men," I replied with truth. Certainly I'd never seen it suggested by a woman.

"Let us ask these people." He addressed the onlookers in Kannada, "What do you say about this...?"

There was a stunned silence, followed by polite attempts to answer helpfully. Well, a woman knows she should respect her husband's kin. Well, women sometimes grow fat after marriage. Well, a bride's face glows after marriage. Voice from the crowd: "So does a bridegroom's." A burst of laughter broke up the session. Nobody knew what we were talking about, or cared very strongly. So much for 'the indigenous beliefs' as far as Kollepet was concerned. Of course most of these people were members of low castes, though there were a few Lingayats among them, distinguishable by their silver amulets, and low castes don't bother with high falutin rationalisations of female status. Still, Subba Rao, a Brahman, ought to know, and he didn't.

The arrival of the jeep at that moment distracted everyone's attention. Adding my impedimenta to the load already bestowed between the seats, I shook hands with Mr. Subba Rao, waved to the onlookers, who waved cheerfully back, and climbed into the front between the driver and Manjula. She had to sit on the outside, being prone to car-sickness.

We set off and slithered across the carpet of ragi stalks on the road, adding our mite to this novel method of harnessing modern technology, to ease for free the traditional chores of harvest-time. For some miles the landscape remained unchanged: fields of millet, rice, mulberry and sugarcane succeeded each other, interspersed with coconut groves. In our own private dust cloud we rattled hooting through a series of villages, scattering chickens and pi-dogs and doing a bit more threshing from time to time. But gradually, as the road began to wind uphill, the land became drier, the fields poorer and more scattered and thorn thickets more frequent, until we entered the scrub jungle of the Kollepet State Forest.

When my family lived on the hills this jungle had spread like a vast carpet east and west of the range. In fact to the east, the other side of the Nilgiris, the carpet was more like a billowing sea, rolling over a wild hinterland of little hills until it reached another, uninhabited, range, beyond which the Mysore plateau dropped to the burning plains of Tamil Nadu. The scrub was mostly composed of thickets of lantana and 'wait-a-bit' thorn and stunted acacia trees, along with bamboo clumps, with lawns and glades of short grey-green grass winding between and around the thickets. My father called the land to the east 'the tiger country', and certainly in those days it swarmed with the big felines, tiger and panther. Shooting was licensed and controlled and bison, wild pig, deer and antelope, especially the graceful spotted deer or chital, abounded in the glades and along the leafy green nullahs or water-courses. So too did herds of elephants. The elephants were protected and only those solitary males proscribed as 'rogues' following persistent destruction of life and livelihood were in danger of being shot, in which case the danger cut both ways. Of all that teeming wildlife only the pigs, bears and elephants remain in any quantity now that the resident conservationists have left. All shooting is now illegal but, with no one to implement the law, poachers have blazed away unchecked and indiscriminately, and the wildlife is dying out. Moreover, their habitat is shrinking every year.

Anyway, there we were, driving through the scrub at last, and I felt a sudden surge of elation. Although I had gone back to the hills from time to time in the course of my previous fieldwork, it had been long enough ago to establish this as a pilgrimage of rediscovery. The road wound up and through the foothills of the range and the trees grew taller. We passed through patches of cultivation, once tiny hamlets that were now spreading and eating into the natural vegetation like some kind of incurable mange on a hairy dog. Then the forest closed in again until we reached the village of Punjur. At this erstwhile hamlet just off the main Mysore-Coimbatore road along which we had been travelling, Grandfather's road to the hills began. It was now a Forest Department road and a toll gate at the turn-off exacted dues from its users. From here the main road continued southward through the Talamalai Reserved Forest, a tumble of foothills covered with bamboo and scrub and still pretty wild.

My sister Sheila and I had once been taken by our father on a camping exploration of the tiger country, ending at Talamalai village. We were told the story of the Talamalai rogue, a solitary bull which turned out to be. maddened, poor creature, by the pain of a bitten-off tail. (Elephants are known to bite off the tails of tuskers defeated in a fight and this one had clearly lost a battle and left the herd). It had taken to preying on bullock-carts travelling along the main road. Its beat was between Talamalai and the old forest bungalow of Hassanur, just off the road. It would ambush a train of carts, overturn and smash up some of them, kill the bulls by breaking their backs and eat the rice and other grains from the sacks the carts were carrying. It also chased the people with the carts and caught and killed. one of them. Once it waylaid a bus and tried to overturn it. The driver and his mate had crawled under the bus, and as the elephant pushed it along the road they had to keep wriggling along underneath it until the elephant gave up and went away. A Sholiga friend of Ralph, my father, told him that he had seen the rogue chasing another bus, which tore down the road hooting while the elephant pursued it trumpeting. "They were both making the same noise as they went round the corners," added the Sholiga who, not being personally involved, thought it a great joke. Eventually my father went to Hassanur and shot the rogue, at considerable risk to himself. But that's another story.

I once camped with him at Hassanur, whence we explored a cluster of hills, the Murkeres, called after the three little lakes which lay concealed within their thick, prickly folds. We saw no elephants that time, only a solitary old bison bull with a massive head and worn horns. From there we followed the road to Dimbam, a tiny settlement at the top of the spectacular Dimbam ghat, the route we took when we went to the Nilgiris. At the little Dimbam Forest Rest House my father told me how he had once stayed there with a friend with whom he had taken an evening stroll. On their way back he heard a familiar snuffling noise behind them and hurriedly hauled his friend up a steep bank. Along the path came a bear, nose to the ground, in purposeful hound-like pursuit. Although the black sloth bear is a vegetarian, it is probably the most dangerous animal to meet unexpectedly in the south Indian jungle, because it is even more likely than the elephant to attack unprovoked. This very rarely happens with the big felines, even the volatile panther, except for females with cubs and the occasional man-eater. Anyway, in this case the ill-disposed bear was foiled by a hasty detour back to the rest house. Dimbam lies at the very edge of the Mysore plateau. From there the land drops away sharply, two thousand feet to the Tamil Nadu plain, and the road tips over the edge, zig-zagging in twenty-six hairpin bends down the face of the escarpment. In the old days the descent was a hair-raising adventure, to say nothing of the ascent with radiator on the boil. Even today, with stout walls protecting the bends and most of them negotiable without reversing, it is an exciting experience.

In 1920, when I was due to be born, a big storm washed away parts of the Dimbam ghat, to say nothing of our own Punjur ghat. So my parents set off on foot, accompanied by a couple of Sholigas, to walk the hundred miles to the little hill-station of Kotagiri on the Nilgiris, where the birth was due to take place.

Eight months pregnant with her first child, my mother walked through the jungle for days, sleeping on the ground, descending from the Mysore plateau into the deep gorge of the Moyar river which separates the plateau from the Nilgiri range, crossing the flooded Moyar river in a local coracle and climbing seven thousand feet up the Nilgiri heights to Kotagiri, whereafter she spent three days in labour. But women and babies are tough. Mother and child were fine and I have been fixated on walking ever since.

The turn off the main road at Punjur preceded by about half a mile the crossing of the Punjur river, key to any approach to the hills by my grandfather's ghat road. In our day if the river was in flood, you just had to wait on one side or the other till it chose to abate to a fordable depth. This situation remains unchanged. But today the interviewers and I were lucky. After a period without rain the crossing was no more than a water-splash and did not delay us. As we roared up the steep incline on the far side I was reminded of the time my mother had come to the river, having driven from Mysore with my children, to find a bull elephant having a bath near the ford. Drawing up at the brink they watched it sloshing water about and enjoying itself while it ignored them. When the tusker turned away to walk upstream she drove through the ford and up to the village, where she was stopped by people rushing out to wave her down.

"Amma, Amma, didn't you see the rogue?"

"We saw an elephant," my mother agreed with a slight sinking sensation.

"Aiyō, aiyō. That's a very bad elephant. Every time it sees anyone it chases them. It has been attacking carts and killing people, and every day at this time it comes to the river to bathe, so we daren't go down to fetch water."

Not everyone who drives up the ghat has been so lucky, and mortality at the feet and tusks of angry elephants is increasing now that their habitat is becoming more circumscribed every year.

Punjur used to be little more than a Sholiga podu or forest settlement, plus a few fields owned by members of other castes. Now it has grown in size yet regressed to a squalid, smelly village. The driver stopped for a cup of coffee while the interviewers and l fidgeted, surrounded by vociferous swarms of flies and children. We bought a bunch of bananas and shared them morosely between us.

Apart from the river my family's chief connection with Punjur used to be a Sholiga known as Punjur Eera. In his prime he had once saved my mother's life and risked his own by hurling her out of the way of a falling tree. Thereafter he had traded on the incident to the end of his days, turning up whenever he was short of wherewithal, smilingly confident that his needs would be met. My parents called him an old rascal and he had certainly not done so well by my father, who had at one time employed him as his chief tracker. They were once camped at a place called Bailur, at the eastern foot of the hills, and had gone out in the evening to shoot something —partridge, peafowl or jungle fowl — for the pot. My father was carrying a shotgun while Eera carried for him his high-velocity rifle, brought along in case of need. The need arose suddenly as they entered a glade and came upon an elephant which took one look at them and charged. Eera turned and fled, shouting "Shoot, shoot,"while departing at speed with the rifle. My father tried to catch up with him to grab it, but he was going much too fast. So was the elephant, and as my father had no intention of peppering it with bird-shot he had no choice but to dodge behind a clump of bamboo. The elephant followed and for about half an hour they played a grim game of hide-and-seek until the elephant got tired and crashed sulkily off. My father gave it five minutes and then slipped quietly back to the camp, where he was met by the remorseful Eera, torn between relief and shame. You can't blame Sholigas for being terrified of elephants. Seven or eight of my father's friends in the tribe were killed by them and many more had narrow escapes. Sheila and I loved Punjur Eera. He always had some delicious offering tied up in a bit of old loin cloth, such as a bundle of annabis, the little brown mushrooms that grow on rotting logs which only Sholigas seem able to find, or a wild honeycomb clinging to its twig. Sholigas are great climbers of tree and cliff in pursuit of honey and astonishingly impervious to the stings of the fierce wild bees.

The driver's return put an end to this reverie of the past and our spirits rose as the jeep breasted the first hill of the ghat road and the flat lands fell away beneath us. As we drove on we began to leave the lantana and acacia behind, to be replaced by more and more deciduous trees, especially the broad-leaved teak. Higher up we came on a wide clearing where new growth was just beginning to cover the blackened stumps and skeletons of burned-out trees. This marked the spot where a minor forum official, who had been colluding with a contractor on a profit-sharing basis to take out far more than the authorised quantity of timber, had set fire to the jungle in the hope of concealing the pillage when he learned that enquiries were afoot. Fortunately the clearing was being allowed to grow again as an ecologically balanced mixed forest, the Department having at last seen the light and ceased to chop down such growth with abandon, replanting it with the fast-growing eucalyptus beneath which nothing grows and the soil leaches away in the rains.

Higher up still we came to a corner where the road crossed the crest of a spur and for once there was no steep drop on one side. It used to be known in the family as Widdle Corner. Here we would stop to picnic and one could wander off to relieve oneself in comfort and privacy without a risky scramble into the hanging jungle above or below. Today was no exception. We ate our midday meal and went off one by one for a peaceful pee before remounting the faithful jeep and proceeding on our bumpy way over the loose stones and ruts which constituted the surface of the track.

Soon we were in the heart of the deciduous forest, the road winding round the flanks of the hills, with the drop below first on one side and then on the other. The leaves were partly fallen and here and there the brilliant flowers of the flame of the forest and coral trees, or the darker red of the silk cotton tree flared from bare branches. Higher up, still taller trees such as the white cedar, rose above and below us, the spaces between filled with long grass at least six feet high, the elephant grass which grows during the monsoons. If you walk through it you can't see a thing ahead, which can lead to trouble, as many a Sholiga has found on ill-meeting a sloth bear. I remember once being suddenly dragged off a narrow game path through this tall grass by my father and a Sholiga, to crouch with them in breath-held silence while two cow elephants with their calves, followed by the rest of a small herd, walked by along the path within inches of our noses. The Sholiga had heard them coming.

At a point where the gradient levelled off and a rocky outcrop rose above the road on the right, Granny Morris had commemorated her husband's near-fatal encounter with a bison by having a stone 'Baswa', traditional representation of the sacred bull of Shiva, placed on top of the rock. The bison's horn had pierced my grandfather's chest, destroying one lung and though he survived the encounter, it led to his death from pneumonia some years later.

Strangely enough, Grandfather Kinloch also died of injuries inflicted by a wild animal. In his case it was a wild boar which brought his life to a tragic end in 1921.

Over the years the outcrop of rock surmounted by the little stone bull had become a shrine. I don't know whether the deva or spirit of the shrine was supposed to be that of my grandfather, the bison, or an aspect of Shiva himself, and I don't think anybody else does either, but those who find themselves on that road feel it unwise to pass by without a propitiatory offering and prayer. When we reached it the driver stopped the jeep and he and I got out, followed by the four young people. Looking around I found some gloriosa superba, the orange 'glory lily', in flower, and breaking off a few heads I scrambled up in the driver's wake to lay them before the 'Karti Baswa' (bison Baswa, as the local people called it), and direct a few loving thoughts to my progenitors. I never knew my grandfather and scarcely remembered Granny; but the Karti Baswa shrine had been a well-remembered landmark all my life and I found the small ceremony as moving as lighting a candle for someone in a church. Flooded with nostalgia I climbed down sniffling and scrabbling in my pocket for a handkerchief. Everyone patted me consolingly on the shoulder and we drove on.

Round the next bend the road ahead revealed ominous signs that we were not its sole users that afternoon. Large grey-green lumps shaped like cottage loaves steamed gently on the stony surface. They were fresh elephant droppings and scattered among them lay a debris of broken branches, their leaves unfaded, revealing a very recent occupation of the road. "Āne (elephants)," pronounced the driver unnecessarily. "Yes," I said, trying to control a certain quaver in my voice unbefitting the role of Old Jungle Hand. "Better stop." He did so reluctantly, apparently a disciple of the carry-on-regardless-and-hope-for-the-best school. Favouring on my part a policy of arrive-alive, I walked ahead as unobtrusively as possible and peeped round the corner. The trail of leaves led to the edge of the road, which had a trampled look, and a distant crashing below signalled the downhill exodus of a herd. With a sigh of relief I beckoned the jeep on, to remount it considerably more jaunty in mien than heretofore.

The interviewers had been whispering anxiously in the back. They were not at all keen on the prospect of any involuntary session of big game observation and neither was I, since you never quite know what elephants will do. The only times I have met them on the road they either failed to notice or chose to ignore us and we waited politely at a discreet distance until they went away. But others, including my father, have not enjoyed such care-free travel. He once drove round a corner to see the backside of an elephant about thirty yards ahead. He stopped, but kept the engine running. Perhaps this irritated the elephant, as it suddenly whipped around and charged.

Ralph just had time to put the jeep into reverse which lessened the impact as the tusker bunted it, showing every intention of pushing it over the precipice. At this, a strange thing happened. Our dog, who had been asleep on the back seat, suddenly awoke to the fact that something funny was going on, jumped out of the car and started barking. The elephant trumpeted, and the two animals whirled round and round in front of the jeep, chasing each other and making a fearful din until the elephant had enough of it and made off. The dog 'Smoke', a Spaniel-Alsatian cross and normally a shameful coward, hopped back into the jeep with a 'you can carry on now, what would you do without me' expression on his face. But the jeep's radiator was staved in, and man and dog had a long dark wait until my mother, thinking the jeep must have broken down — which in a sense it had — turned up in a rescue vehicle from the estate and towed it home.

Those were the days, I thought regretfully. However dangerous jungle travel may have been, you did have a trusty rifle to fall back upon, and though you may have used it only in case of absolute necessity if your life was at risk due to the attentions of some large quadruped, nevertheless we usually had a rifle with us for safety's sake. And now that we didn't, the increased vulnerability was like a kind of nakedness. All the same I was glad I wasn't expected to enact the role of armed guard to our party, and even gladder that the driver wasn't. The prospect of him let loose with a gun was much more unnerving than that of unfriendly wildlife.

After an uneventful mile or two we began to relax and I told the story of Smoke's finest hour to the jeep's company, omitting my father's ungrateful opinion that his canine champion didn't know elephants were dangerous. The driver capped it with more recent incidents, none designed to reduce the interviewers' alarm, and then added with a giggle, "You've heard the story of Mehta and his wife?" I had heard this deplorable tale several times and whether or not it was true, it lost nothing each time in the gleeful telling. Mehta, a high-caste gentleman temporarily employed on the estate after my parents' time, was driving down the Punjur ghat with his wife when they met an elephant and either drove, or were pushed, off the road. Mehta jumped out as the jeep went over the edge, and hastened back on foot to the estate. "But what happened to your wife?" he was asked. "I didn't stop to look," he replied. "Naturally I had to save myself, and I can always get another wife." A rescue team set off, to find the jeep on a gentle slope not far below the road with the poor lady still sitting in it in a state of shock. I never thought this story all that amusing because I was so sorry for Mrs. Mehta, a nice person by all accounts.

By now we had almost reached Bedaguli, the lowest plantation. Evergreen rain forest should at this altitude have been taking over from the deciduous jungle, but we were passing through a couple of forestry disaster areas. The first was a huge plantation of eucalyptus which had replaced a great swathe hacked out of the original mixed forest. The second was a large area of wasteland where more forest had been destroyed with the object of 'settling' Sholigas. The tribe are essentially hunter-gatherers and agriculture is only a secondary means of subsistence for them. Moreover they are, or were, nomadic practitioners of a primitive slash-and-burn cultivation, moving on when the soil in their tiny plots is exhausted. The result in this case was that having burned off the scrub and planted a crop on this huge acreage once, they lost heart and abandoned it. They had obtained much more food from the jungle when it was still jungle, a Sholiga explained sadly, and now they had to walk much further to find it. A few minutes later we were in the coffee, good crop of 'spike' (blossom buds) showing on the bushes. Coffee needs light shade, which is best provided in gravilias, or silver oaks, tall trees with silvery-green lacy leaves. We drove on up the valley under the silver oaks, with coffee bushes spreading away on our left and the beautiful rainforest beginning on our right. The road became steeper and the valley narrower with the big hills closing in on either hand. Every curve in the road was now familiar. We passed through the margins of the three lower estates before we entered the Attikan coffee. On our left the Attikan pulp-house and then the tiled houses of the Attikan 'lines' or labour village showed briefly through the trees. At last we swung round a final bend to reach Yellehottay, the crest of the watershed between two valleys, the one running south, up which we had driven, which contained the other four plantations, and the one running north which contained Honnametti estate.

Yellehottay, known to our family as Charing Cross because several estate roads intersected there, consists of a flat open space surrounded by Attikan and Honnametti coffee, with a cluster of low buildings: post-office, food store, the Attikan school. and the modest house of the Honnametti manager. Mr. Lakhani came out to meet us, tall, handsome, humorous and sharply intelligent. Both he and Mr. Coates. the kindly Anglo-Indian manager of Kartikerri estate (which had passed to my father's uncle Leonard and now belonged to the company which owned Honnametti), had welcomed me as a representative of our family when I came back nearly a quarter of a century after we had all left, and now welcomed me for myself — I hoped — when I came once more. Well, if they weren't pleased to see me they were putting on a pretty convincing performance. Choosing to be convinced, I felt honoured by their friendship and very grateful for all their help and for their hospitality, both undeserved and unrepayable.

This evening he had arranged for the estate tractor to take the interviewers and their baggage to the lodging he had fixed up for them in the house of one of the field clerks, a cheerful young man they had already met and liked on one of his visits to Kollepet. I was anxious to get settled in the Attikan bungalow while daylight held. There was a generator there, as at the Honnametti bungalow, for electric light, but the caretaker, under orders to conserve fuel, never switched it on until well after dark. So, as soon as the others had disembarked and Mr. Lakhani and I had exchanged civilities, informed ourselves as to the welfare of each other's spouses and offspring, and made plans to meet before long, the driver and I set off again, roaring up the steep road between the ranks of coffee bushes, past the hairpin turn off to the Honnametti bungalow, through the Attikan shola (evergreen woodland) with its old wild fig trees, past the little green pond in the woods, to draw up outside the low stone house.

Baswa the caretaker was there, a simple soul with a friendly smile and the slightly puzzled expression of one who knows there must be some good reason for the way people carry on, even if it is not immediately apparent. Having greeted each other after far too long an interlude, and said goodnight and thank-you to the driver, we carried my suitcase and little cooking stove into the bedroom I had begun to think of as mine, and the box of food into the dining room. It was getting dark, so I dug out candles and by their light unpacked lentils and rice which Baswa would cook for me on the old cast-iron 'Bonnybridge' stove still surviving in the dimly-lit kitchen which was his realm and with which I seldom interfered.

Next door to the dining room was the sitting room, in which he had lit the log fire. How lovely to be back, to sit in the dusk in a comfortable chair and write up diaries by firelight until Baswa comes to switch on the electricity. No mosquitoes, no insects at all, just the chirruping of treefrogs to make me feel at home. When the lights came on I would be able to have a hot bath in the bathroom adjoining my bedroom, and later, after dal and rice, I would lie on a proper mattress under a proper sheet and blanket in a netless bed and sleep through the night in unaccustomed luxury.

Why did I stay at Attikan rather than at Honnametti? For a number of reasons. It was too painfully emotive to stay at Honmametti. I had done so several times in the course of my fieldwork and it never got any better. When I first went back the place seemed full of living ghosts, and I half expected to meet my parents and sisters in every room. Vivid memories of the rooms as they used to be, the furniture, books, pictures, trophies, silver, clean, shining, well-kept and flower-decked, contrasted too painfully with the seedy present. The house was now little more than an office, with a couple of beds for visiting officials and a room set aside for the yearly visit of a director. Not that it was noticeably dirty, but it was no longer a lovingly tended house reflecting the interests and tastes of powerful, if conflicting, personalities. When I first returned there a few years ago a kindly member of the estate staff opened the front door and said to me, "Welcome to your home." I entered, looked round, and disconcerted him by dissolving into tears, embarrassing myself and spoiling everyone's fun. Far from being mine, Honnametti was certainly no longer anybody's home.

Moreover, although it used to be a light and airy house with all windows standing open, Honnametti bungalow was now claustrophobic. Mr. Mehta, he of the encounter with elephants, was a north Indian who detested south Indians and was amply detested back. "Whenever we want to see him he's always in his puja room, praying," the workers complained. For his part he once informed me that south Indians preferred marriage to kin because the men all lusted after their sisters. This was because they were in fact the descendants of demons. "That's a historical fact," he proclaimed indignantly when I started to laugh. "It's in the Ramayana." Anyway, to keep out the local demons and other predators he had every window in the house, including the verandah, encased in a kind of shell of wrought iron, hideous and no doubt hideously expensive, which permanently sealed them shut. Mehta eventually retired unmourned, but the house remained encased.

Attikan, on the other hand, had hardly changed at all. It had been left to Uncle Eric, my father's elder brother, who had been with an engineering firm in Madras. It had housed a series of managers since I was a child and its present state, no better and no worse than in the past, was not only an improvement on that of Honnametti but also invoked no nostalgic comparisons with past splendours.

Reviewing that day's journey I considered the little ritual at the Karti Baswa and decided that it had been so moving because it recalled not only my grandfather, whom I never saw, but a whole lost way of life.

Travel to and from the hills became progressively less hair-raising over the decades as Grandfather's road became less like a riverbed, but life on the estate was — indeed still is — isolated from the affairs of planting communities elsewhere in south India. It was a self-sufficient society into which outsiders, apart from employers' relatives or the occasional forestry official, seldom penetrated except at my parents' invitation. In the eyes of the Sholiga tribe and the villagers who came to live and work on the estate, Ralph and Heather Morris appeared as the central figures of this micro-cosmos.

Their lives were inextricably involved with the lives of the local people, not only the Sholigas with whom they had a special relationship of affection, but also the villagers from the Mysore plateau at the foot of the hills. They ran, in fact, an unofficial social service. This was particularly true of Heather's activities on the estate, although Ralph's services were much in demand for mediation in disputes, employment of relations, advice in coping with officialdom, and of course in dealing with four- legged predators. His reputation in this last context rested locally on his exploits as a hunter of cattle-slaying tigers and homicidal rogue elephants, although he received wider recognition as the world's leading expert on south Indian wildlife.

In retrospect I can see how my parents were pressured by local expectations to play the almost feudal part of the traditional Indian landowner. Living in a place where no Western or 'colonial' system already operated because there were no foreigners on the hills apart from the family, or temporary managers on the four other plantations, they found themselves locked in a relationship which could be stigmatised as paternalistic but fitted the value system of the people among whom they lived. The idiom used was that of kinship. "You are my father and my mother" was a phrase much used by villagers claiming aid or advice. Service families and those who had settled permanently on the estate received, in accordance with traditional Indian usage, gifts of coffee, grain and clothing along with their salaries. At the main Hindu festivals, as well as at Christmas, further presents were expected as a right. On my parents' side the expectation was of dependability.

These expectations were on the whole fulfilled because they were reciprocatory "A reciprocatory role relationship," says the psychologist H.C. Kelman, "can be maintained only if the recipients have mutually shared expectations of one another's behaviour." If people find a relationship mutually satisfactory in fact, they tend to carry on with it. My parents carried out their side of this social contract to the best of their ability, with the result that in time they became a local institution. Today, forty years or so after their departure, reports of their exploits, their generosity and their lifestyle gain steadily in the telling and are repeated with nostalgia by a new generation which never knew them personally. Their transient stewardship has already taken on the characteristics of a golden age legend. At this point further reminiscing was cut short by the coughing of the generator and the light came on. Baswa entered, demanding dal and rice, and shooed me off to have a bath. Reflecting that his relationship with me was not unlike that of his parental generation with my parents, except that he was a good deal bossier, I went off at his bidding, enormously relieved to be back.

the house of the golden footprint

At about 5 a.m. the first light of day crept into the room, heralded by the staccato crow of the south Indian jungle fowl. "Cok-cck-jungle-cok" sounded the burden of his call. There always seemed to be a jungle cock in the shola behind Attikan bungalow to rouse you on a promising morning. The cheerful notes brought me from my bed bouncing with anticipation, to pull on my clothes, and then, feeling the chilly hill air, to add a light wool sweater. A sweater! This was the life. No socks, though, even for cold feet in canvas shoes. So soon after the north-east monsoon there would be leeches in the shola undergrowth, and who needed blood-clotted socks?

Letting myself quietly out of the front door I stopped to take a deep breath and look around. Coming back to the hills always caught me in the solar plexus with a wave of pleasure in the present and nostalgia for the past.

Attikan bungalow had been built facing east, in the lap of a hill, on a shelf of naturally level ground rare in this region of steep slopes. Behind the house the forested hill rose again to its summit. In front, level lawns shaded by a couple of fine cedars and circled by the loop of the drive stretched away to a little wall screened by trees. Below the wall the hillside fell away in a precipitous crag to the plantation in the valley below. Near the front steps a pair of camellia trees, which I first remembered as small shrubs, were covered with waxy pink blooms, nature doing its best to imitate plastic. Outside my bedroom windows a long arm of evergreen shola, thick and mossy, ran eastward towards the escarpment to form a windbreak. Between its tip and the precipice was a level grassy corridor running southward. On the opposite side of the valley rose a huge grassy hill banded with outcrops of rock, Katari betta, the highest summit of the high eastern chain of the range and in fact the highest hill in the Biligiris. On either side of it other high hills blocked off the view to the east.

Having cast an affectionate eye over the hilltops to make sure that they were all safely there in their familiar order, I turned off diagonally, making for the corridor between the tip of the wind-break shola and the top of the cliff. On the way I paused a minute to search for a little landmark of the past, the inscribed headstone marking the grave of my grandfather's favourite horse, now almost lost in a tangle of long grass. Then along the path past the shola's end, on each side of which knobs and sheets of licheny granite pushed through the grass, interspersed with clumps of grey 'crown-of-thorns' with bright red flowers. Here the grassy corridor opened out as the flat top of a subsidiary ridge covered with grass and rocks, which ran south for a hundred yards or so before ending in a tangle of boulders and another little cliff.

From this point the view to the south had an ethereal beauty. It led the eye gently down the long forest-filled Minchiguli valley through which wound the road we had traversed the day before, now out of sight among the treetops far below. The valley was bordered on one side by the scalloped ridges of the eastern chain, grassy hills ribbed with rock and capped or caped with evergreen sholas. In the western foreground the central spine of hills on which the houses of Attikan and Honnametti were built rose to one final rotund grassy fell before dipping down to a tangle of lesser uplands among which lay the other three estates, spread out below like an aerial photograph. At the far end of the Minchiguli valley itself, one of my father's favourite adventure playgrounds, the great profile of Bedanaikana betta filled the horizon. A massif flanked with cliffs and skirted with evergreen forest, it was a long, long walk to reach its lonely environs. But if you wanted to be sure of seeing wild animals you walked there, as I had done so often with my father long ago.

On these latter-day visits to the hills the rocky vantage point at the end of this subsidiary ridge of the Attikan hill was my chosen refuge, and I sneaked off there whenever I could, to write up notes and diary, check the questionnaire forms, relax guiltily with a book, or just sit in the sun and think. The only fly in this idyllic ointment was literally a fly: a frail black creature with spindly legs which left a bright yellow smear when squashed. At this time of year it was ubiquitous outdoors on still sunny days at Attikan, crawling listlessly about on human skin and tickling unbearably till swatted, to leave its reproachful yellow stain.

When we were children there had been a little wooden hut at this point, a kind of arbour or gazebo containing two benches, presumably intended for those wishing to shelter from the sun while enjoying the view. We were always intrigued by little houses, and this one was invested with a fairy-tale glamour in our eyes, but it must always have been fairly ramshackle. My father told me once that he had asked my mother to marry him there. When she said yes he turned to embrace her and the bench collapsed beneath them. It was the kind of story Ralph loved to tell, since for him the momentous and the ludicrous were never far apart. So I was a little disappointed to find on my return to India that the hut had vanished without trace, although I have to admit that it wasn't much of a loss.

Beyond the windbreak shola and clearly visible from the lookout point, undulating slopes covered with lawn-like grass dotted with little shrubberies of wenlandia and yellow-flowering hypericum climbed to the saddle joining the Attikan hill to the bald fell which dropped away to the lower hills encompassing the other three estates a thousand feet below. This stretch of landscape had a singular charm of its own, particularly at this time of year when the sholas of broad-leaved rain forest looked like clumps of sphagnum moss — soft, lumpy and variegated, belying the term 'evergreen' with shades of red and salmon pink, the young leaves of the wild cinnamon trees.

Beginning to feel hungry I started up these slopes on the far side of the shola, entered the trees by a path leading back to the house, and began picking up bits of fallen branches as I went. By the time I reached the front door I had an armful of logs and kindling which I leaned against the wall to dry in the sun. When I first came back to Attikan, Baswa had deplored this habit, tut-tutting that it was not fit work for a doraisani. Having failed to dissuade me he began to appreciate that an extra pair of wood-gathering hands made for better fires and lighter work, and stopped arguing, but he never felt entirely comfortable about it and always eyed my personal harvest of fuel with an air of disapproval.

Fortunately his good nature triumphed over these little local difficulties, and today with his shining morning grin he produced a plateful of hot ragi porridge for breakfast, to be eaten with my tinned milk. I let him cook for me morning and evening, only substituting ragi, dal and rice for the durable chappattis with the texture of old welly boots he was otherwise wont to provide, because he was familiar with the vagaries of the ancient wood-burning kitchen stove and I was not. Besides, the kitchen was his territory. But I made my own tea in my bathroom on my primus-sized kerosene cooker, a triumph of intermediate technology if ever there was one, and boiled water there for doing my own washing up. This was because I had discovered that sterilisation of my drinking water alone failed to prevent my contracting at Attikan a mild but trying urinary complaint. The solution, it turned out, was to wash up in sterile water as well. It was clear that in Baswa's view my laboured explanations cast little light on this aberrant behaviour, but he had learned to put up with my eccentricities which, after all, saved him time and trouble.

Except on Sundays, the best time for interviewing the estate workers was in the evening, when everyone was at home. Sunday, still a holiday here as in the rest of India, was the hardest working day for the interviewers and me, but on weekdays the interviewers had little to do in the forenoon (if we couldn't find any household with a married couple of the right ages both at home) but check their forms before passing them on to me. We had almost completed the current group, the rural low castes of the taluka hinterland, and would soon be able to start on the Sholigas, who did not work regular hours and might, with luck be found in their podus during the day. The upshot of all this was that I told the interviewers I would take them for a picnic lunch today to Honnametti Kalu, the rock of the golden footprint. Having examined the morning's leech-bites, legacy of wood-gathering in the damp mulch of the shola, and to make sure they had stopped bleeding, I replaced my wet running shoes. Leeches inject an anti-coagulant before tucking in, and once they have been pulled off, or fallen off fat and replete, the tiny painless puncture continues for a while to hemorrhage impressively. The quickest way to stop the bleeding is to stick on a little wisp of cotton wool or paper tissue, as on a shaving cut. Leech bites are harmless in themselves but very itchy as they heal and therefore easily infected by scratching.

Into my light rucksack I put biscuits, water-bottle, bananas and oranges, notebook and ballpoint, polaroid and conventional cameras, and the presents I had promised my Sholiga friend San Mada, whom I hoped to meet shortly at Honnametti. On the way back to Attikan I would take the footpath which wound through the upper reaches of the coffee near the top of the ridge, but now I retraced last night's route from Yellehottay until the Honnametti turnoff was reached. Then steeply uphill, as the road contoured the flanks of the hillside, rising steadily through the green coffee bushes and the dappled shadows of the gravilia shade trees. The banks, revetments and culverts all along the way were feathered as usual with maidenhair fern and golden yellow with wild calceolarias. An occasional wood pigeon flapped among the branches above or a flight of green parakeets whirred off noisily. And once, although the monsoons were over, I heard to my joy a clear whistle, abstracted and musing and not quite a tune, reminiscent of a day-dreaming schoolboy: the sweet heart-piercing song of the Malabar whistling thrush, that beautiful blue bird of the wild wet rain forests. These sounds and sights and poignant scents all spoke to my condition, as the Quakers say, and the response evoked was, this is where I belong.

The Attikan coffee stopped abruptly along a narrow cleared boundary line which ran steeply up the hill above the road and as steeply down below it. On the other side of the boundary and below the road on which I walked, the first field of Honnametti estate began. This was the Doraisani Kadu, literally 'the lady's woodland', once my mother's share of the estate and still named for her. Here a subsidiary road turned off, soft and earthy, to zigzag down to Yellehottay through Honnametti coffee. It was the route Sheila and I had taken on our ponies when we were children, because the surface would not harm their unshod hooves and its level stretches allowed for satisfying canters. The Biligiris, in general steep and stony, don't offer much scope for pleasure riding, although horses, along with pack bullocks, were the only form of transport in my grandparents' days there.

We children rose at six and went out to ride before breakfast. Sheila's pony was a bay called Merrylegs (something of a misnomer) after an equine character in one of our horsey books. Mine was a silky dun called Papyrus, 'Pi' for short, who lived on to become our much younger sister Paddy's mount in turn. They both had the cow hocks of the local 'tat' ponies, but they were good-natured and well-behaved. There were other paths and tracks which followed contours or descended slopes in a series of hairpin bends which we sometimes used, but besides being easy on the feet, with long level stretches between the zigags, this route had a particular charm. Among the gravilias there were tall flowering forest trees, and massive boulders rose like icebergs from the sea of green coffee. Streams crossed the road from time to time, flowing through rocky bends, their banks planted with the palm-like fronds of cardamoms. There was also a little pond, bordered by wild ginger.

When we went riding we wore the round white solar topis then considered suitable for children, which made us look like mushrooms. These we wore outdoors when it was sunny until 5 p.m., at which time it was deemed safe to remove them without risk of sunstroke. The khaki sun-hats of our elders were much more becoming, and I looked forward to graduating to them. Unfortunately, within a few years of those happy days, topis went out and dark glasses came in.

Hopeful as puppies, Sheila and I inhabited a pristine world in which the wilds around us and the wilds of our imagination seemed to merge. Living on the edge of danger as we did, we nevertheless sought the stimulus of imaginary threats. The objective dangers we risked daily, attacks by bears, snake-bites, aggressive elephants and hair-raising roads when we were driven from or to the estate, jungle fires against which we had to take the precaution of burning firelines around, garden and estate, all seemed to, us routine. We had to invent dangers of the King Kong type, such as an enormous rogue elephant rampaging down over the top of the hill behind the house at twilight. The game was to get back to the house before it got you. This was exciting. Real dangers, when they did occur were frightening, a very different matter.

With no friends of our own age, no peer-group, we spent much of our time acting the parts of fictional characters. We also had an ongoing game in which we played ourselves, weaving around ourselves a whole new mythology. This we named the Girl Game. The imaginary characters were two sisters, greenhorns and townees (which in our world meant that their parents lived in the Nilgiris or Bangalore, to us centres of metropolitan ignorance of life in the raw). In the game we ourselves were older, cleverer and highly skilled in all the activites in which we normally engaged. Our shambling ponies were transmuted into thoroughbred steeds on which we sailed over the garden hedges and fences, and the girls were greatly impressed. It was a game of showing off, and because we had no peers with admiration to incite, we had to invent some. One would have thought that our real life was interesting enough for us to refrain from gilding the lily, but in our view it was humdrum enough to require embroidery.

An American sociologist once published a volume on the function of human conflict, maintaining that the unity of a given group is best ensured by conflict with another group. Sheila and I, constant bickerers, bore this out by closing ranks against posh urban rivals in the Girl Game. We got a lot of mileage out of it until we made the mistake of recruiting Heather's sister Polly, who was our governess for some years. She brought it to an end by her refusal to take it seriously. Our flights of fancy were always vulnerable to humour.

It is a measure of our isolation that in all those childhood years I can only remember three occasions when we had other children to play with at Honnametti. Once we were visited by a Canadian family, but the children were very small, much younger than us, and we had nothing in common with them. Once a French artist brought his daughter. She was older than us and we were impressed by her sophistication, but she wasn't really interested in being outdoors. And there was the time Mr. Sani, the District Forest Officer, came to stay with his son Omi. We got on well with Omi, who was a sweet boy. Fifty years later I had the pleasure of staying with him and his wife on their farm near Bangalore. He had grown up to be a lovely man. There were also the herd boys and garden boys who worked in the environs of house and garden, but they were a good deal older than we were. We admired them greatly and fraternised when we had the opportunity, but they had their routine and we had ours. The labour village down in the valley was too far away to provide us with companionship, and in any case we were much too shy of the shouting, uninhibited children there to venture unaccompanied all the way down to the estate, except just to Yellehottay....

At this point the road I was taking became the drive leading to Honnametti bungalow. Above it on the Honnametti side of the boundary line the orchard began. When we lived there an assortment of fruit flourished within the high chicken-wire fences intended to keep out pillaging porcupines and wild pigs. Peaches grew alongside hill-guavas and strawberry guavas, lemons and limes, pomegranates, tree-tomatoes and bananas, loose-skin oranges and tight-skin oranges. Pineapples grew in orderly rows in the vegetable garden enclosed within the orchard fence. In Heather's day she would take baskets of fruit down to the estate children. Today the orchard, rundown and unkempt, still provides some oranges and tree tomatoes for those who choose to help themselves. Certainly I did when passing by.

Further up the steep drive, lying between it and the Doraisani Kadu plantation, was a stretch of lawn under jacaranda trees which had once been a rose garden. Then a clump of hibiscus came in sight at the start of a path which led down to a row of staff and service houses and a stable. A hedge and some trees momentarily screened the field of vision, after which the drive suddenly levelled off on a shelf dug out of the hillside to cradle the house and its apron of lawns and garden, turned the corner of the house, and revealed a spectacular view.

Facing the house across the valley was a big forest-covered hill, Devara betta or the hill of God. Next to it rose the bald dome of Katari betta, with the rest of the chain running south. North of Devara betta the chain continued over two more summits and then dipped to a wide bowl-shaped gap with a fold of downland at the bottom of the bowl: Bellaji Gap. Framed in the gap a blue vista beckoned the eye; patches of distant cultivation on the band of level plateau country at the foot of the hills, and then a series of little hills and ridges clad in scrub jungle, the 'tiger country' of our youth. Beyond rose another range, smaller than the Biligiris, the wild Baragurs, and on the horizon a further line of blue serrations. To the north of the gap a semi-circle of grassy fells armoured with outcrops of rock nursed in their hollows fat cushions of mossy green rain forest. Just in front of them a smaller hill rose from the Bellaji downland. On its summit my grandfather lay buried in the heart of his beloved range. In front of the house the drive circled a long narrow oval of rose-bed. Beyond, a green ribbon of lawn and a low stone wall defined the outer edge of the shelf. On the far side of the wall the hill dropped away for a thousand feet, to the grey-green carpet of silver oaks shading the Honnametti coffee and covering the valley floor.

Honnametti means golden footprint. The hill tribe, the Sholigas, have a legend in which the lord Ranga, godling of the hills, once walked the range changing his shape at every step. At one point not far from where the house was built he left the footprint of a gigantic man on a flat rock. Close by a huge granite monolith stands balanced at the edge of a small cliff and gives a metallic clang if struck with a stone. There's gold in there, the Sholigas said, naming the rock Honnametti Kalu, the rock of the golden footprint. And who should know better? Wasn't the god Ranga the tribe's own brother-in-law, having married a Sholiga girl when the world was young?

The house faced east to the view. At its northern end was a broad lawn surrounded by flowering borders. Those which separated the lawn from the front garden used to be filled with larkspur and variegated phlox, while the eastern border had always flamed with scarlet canna lilies. I was glad to see that the latter had survived. At the far end of the big lawn, once the venue for unsporting if not violent games of croquet, was another rose-bed, and behind it towered a great wall of shola, shutting off the view to the north and forming a frame for the garden. Starting at the edge of the shola and running on behind the house and its outbuildings was a vertical bank, twenty feet high, the back of the shelf cut from the hillside. At its northern or shola end it was covered with a thickly tangled mass of honeysuckle and passion-fruit vine which, when we were young, bore delectable fruit if you could get to it in time. With the passion-fruit it was a case of first come, first served.

In my parents' day the contrast between the long rough journey through the jungle and the estates, shut in by trees, and its culmination in this airy platform brilliant with flowers against the dark setting of shola, was extraordinarily effective. It is striking even today, with the garden only a pale reflection of its former glories.

If the garden was beautiful, the house from the outside was not. For a start it had a corrugated iron roof, painted green. But in the old days it had looked welcoming and comfortable, a long, low ranch-like building made of sun-dried bricks, with a long front verandah. In deference to the climate in the two monsoons which draped the hills in mist and rain for several months of the year, the verandah was not an open gallery but was furnished with windows which in our day were always open — except of course in monsoon-time. Under these windows, against the front wall of the house and on either side of the stone steps which led up to the verandah, were two long rose-beds which Heather had carpeted with mignonette and pansies. The roses were still there.

As I came round the corner the interviewers, who had cadged a lift up from the estate by tractor, came to meet me. With them was a familiar figure, small, dark-skinned, with crinkly hair pulled back from his face and screwed into a knot at the back of his head: San Mada, my particular Sholiga friend, had been my father's favourite shikari and best tracker in the last years at Honnametti. Like most Sholiga men he never seemed to look any older. Although he had retired to his podu (except for certain periods when he worked for the estate, thinning shade for instance, or at crop-picking time), he always joined me on my out-of-working-hours forays over the hills. We exchanged beaming greetings, and I presented the sandals and umbrella he had asked me to bring. He received them very much as his due, with no more than a murmured "Santosa" and a polite lift of them to his forehead, before explaining that today he was overseeing a group of Sholigas temporarily employed on tree work not far from today's destination, and that he had come to enquire about further jungle ventures. I fully intended to mix business with pleasure while on the Biligiris, and to revisit with San Mada as many of the hills as possible within the limits of day trips. The interviewers produced four complete forms, having interviewed two couples the evening before.

"Already? When you'd only just arrived? There's enthusiasm for you."

"Well, the people were near by, so close to Sunder's house," Manjula said. "It was no trouble."

"It must have been you girls who insisted on it. I can't see the men being so keen."

Rajan giggled. "That is true. We wanted to play cards."

"Well, let's go in," I said. Contemplating the dreadful carapace of dusty wrought iron, I felt a wave of wistful yearning for the wide open casements of times past. But this was no time for such self-indulgence. Why did I have to make myself so miserable? Since I didn't know the answer to that I stumped resolutely up the steps maintaining a stiff upper lip, and turned the handle. The door remained closed.

"Damn," I muttered, knocking on the glass. " I forgot they keep it locked."

"You see?" San Mada gave a disparaging sniff and addressed the assembled company loudly just as Mr. Murthy, the clerk, flung open the door, full of bonhomie. "This is what it is like now. In the old days when the Dorai and Doraisani were here the house was full of treasures and the doors and windows never closed. Now, when there is nothing in the house, they lock it up." He turned and spat eloquently.

Since none of this was Mr. Murthy's fault and he was standing there hospitably to welcome us, I pretended not to hear and slunk hastily indoors with a valedictory "Barutane" to San Mada, who went off mouthing uncomplimentary things under his breath about the current state of the world.

Coffee had been provided, thick and sweet, and other secretarial staff members — an accountant, a 'writer' (clerk) turned up, including young Sunder with whom the interviewers were billeted. The interviewers knew them all by now and after the initial civilities had been exchanged I could lean back and, under cover of the odd nod and smile, let them all converse while I mentally re-furnished and populated the house as it had been when it was ours.

Five rooms with french windows opened onto the verandah. Like the verandah they all had wooden floors, polished in the old days to a perilous gloss, and each had a fireplace in which a log fire blazed every evening, and all through the day during the monsoons. These fires were the only way of heating and drying the place, which at an altitude of nearly six thousand feet was never too warm, often chilly, and exceedingly damp in mist and rain. The centre room, opposite the front door, was the hall, a narrow lobby between the drawing room and the dining room, the only passage between the front and back of the house and the only means of access to the dining room from the pantry and kitchen regions. Its french windows gave onto the central seating area of the verandah. From the hall there was a door into the dining room and, concealed by an archway, two more doors, one into the pantry and one into a single spare bedroom.

At Christmas a tall fir tree stood in the archway, flickering with candles, glittering with ornaments and imitation frost, intensely exciting to small people. The parcels were piled at its foot, stockings having been gleefully unpacked at daybreak after cautious manual investigation of their contours in the small hours.

At other times the hall was dominated by a huge pair of curved elephant tusks against the back wall, framed by the arch, record-breaking trophies of a rogue elephant shot by Ralph. In this room Ralph kept his collection of sporting guns and rifles, by such august makers as Westley Richards and Holland and Holland, in a tall cupboard, with ammunition and cleaning gear in a big bureau-chest against the wall. When I was older I enjoyed cleaning the guns. If you detached your mind from their lethal purpose and admired them for their workmanship they were beautiful things, superbly balanced, engraved and damascened. The radio was there, and if television had reached India while the family were at Honnametti, the box would have been there too. As it was, a great evening treat for us children was to watch films on the cine projector: Laurel and Hardy, Charlie Chaplin and Felix the Cat. There was also a documentary about a fight between a mongoose and a cobra. There were wildlife films taken in our jungles too, but these were less popular. It has to be admitted that Ralph was not at his best as a photographer or movie-maker.

Above the door to the verandah hung an enormous fully-mounted bison head. Tiger and panther skins and heads hung on the two long walls along with spears, bows and arrows, relics of Ralph's expedition to Burmese Nagaland. There was a black bearskin on the floor and Burmese brasses on the mantelshelf. Against the wall opposite stood an upright piano. I have an indelible memory of Heather listening to the news night after night during the war while standing stork-like on one leg with the other foot resting on the cover to the keyboard. Altogether the hall was a totally masculine room, principally devoted to Ralph's pursuits, where Heather had given up trying.

As my thoughts turned to the dining room I had a sudden vision of the past; of two little girls eating their breakfast cereal in a spacious room at the centre of their universe. One of these privileged children was my sister Sheila. The other was me. Sheila's straight blonde hair set off a pussy-cat face which in later years suddenly blossomed into beauty. My own brown hair, equally straight, framed a round solemn face with round solemn eyes reflecting the anxious approach to life of one whose headlong enthusiasms frequently led to bruised spirit and bloodied knees.

The walls of the room soared up to high rafters. It was so big that the dark rosewood furniture lent it a seemly air without diminishing it. French windows from the verandah let in light, and on one side a chimney-breast held a generous open fireplace in which burning logs crackled and spat. In each wall were shelved embrasures filled with books: exploration and ethnography; natural and man-made history; wildlife photography and Encyclopaedia Britannica. For round-eyes, obsessional reader, they were Aladdin's caves of treasure.

Above the solid sideboards and over the fire, the walls were hung with mounted trophies of the chase. Two huge tiger skins, the heads of panther, sloth bear, deer, antelope, and a wild boar. We children accepted their presence as we accepted the porcelain and the Georgian silver on the sideboards. They were simply known ingredients of our small cosmos. Concepts of conservation, the unity of the ecosystem, the rights of species other than man, which were to loom large in our futures, still awaited us. Meanwhile we loved our domestic animals, were fascinated by the wild ones, and could recite the legends attached to each example of the taxidermist's art. Here, for instance, was the head of the panther which had killed our mother's dog, and there was the tiger which kept climbing into the estate cowsheds. We also believed, awestruck, that the wild boar was the one which had killed our maternal grandfather, but in this we were mistaken.

With us at breakfast was our mother, Heather. She was slender, dark-haired, comely and, although a native Scot, as graceful as an Indian woman, particularly in the gestures of her hands. We, her daughters, could not imagine her at fault in any way at all. To us at that time, she was infallible.

The door from the hall to the dining room burst open, and this scene of sedate domesticity was immediately spiced with a whiff of anarchy as our father strode in. A tall thin man whose fair hair was already in disorderly retreat, he beamed at us myopically through gold-rimmed glasses. He carried a battered brown paper parcel in one hand which, having helped himself to porridge and sat down, he proceeded to open. As he chatted buoyantly about this and that a stream of white powder poured out of one corner of the package to settle on the surface of his oatmeal. Sheila and I eyed it speculatively. Our mother asked sharply, "What's that you've got there, Ralph?"

"Arsenic," he replied pensively picking up his spoon.

"Oh no, you don't," she cried, snatching away his bowl just in time.

He looked mildly disconcerted, we girls fell about with hilarity, and there was a loud explosion of mirth from the hall doorway, whence fled Damodaran the houseman, hand over mouth, to share the joke in the pantry with his assistant, Rama. Unlike Heather our father was all too fallible. It turned out that the arsenic was a weed-killer ordered through our agent.

We had a lot of fun in the dining room. On our birthdays we children were enthroned there in honour, crowned with flowers, our chairs decorated with an arch of the same flowers.

Sheila's birthday in August meant that her flower-bower and wreath were made from the wild white orchids that grew on trees in the south-west monsoon. My flowers in September were the madonna lilies which grew in profusion on the grassy hills at that time. When Paddy came along, her wreath and bower were fashioned from roses.

This room was also the scene of some of Miowke's more sensational orgies of destruction. Miowke was a male Hoolock gibbon, black with white eyebrows. He was brought back by Ralph from one of his Far East expeditions, and by the time I returned to Honnametti from school at the age of sixteen, he had grown from enchanting babyhood to become a professional pest. From his roomy outdoor cage he was carried every morning by one of the garden lads to a shola about a mile away where he was released to roam the trees in freedom, swinging from branch to branch. This he did until about mid-morning, when he got bored with brachiation and swung himself home. At the height of his career all doors and windows had to be shut at noon, to remain so until Miowke was recaptured and replaced in his cage. But he still managed to break in unseen from time to time and create havoc. Once he opened a desk and the drinks cupboard, drank a mixture of ink and gin, and poured the rest on the floor. Best of all he liked to seize a piece of Heather's treasured Imperial Russian china, climb into the dining room rafters, and drop it on the floor. He frustrated those who tried to get him down with long sticks or ladders by urinating on them. Fortunately he was devoted to my parents and very jealous. They had only to put their arms round each other for him to descend whimpering and try to insert himself between them.

At other times his entry was legitimate, carried in Ralph's arms, seated in his lap or on a chair, to eat sedately from his own plate. When he was young he was even taken into the drawing room from time to time to eat a piece of cake and drink tea out of his own cup. But what he enjoyed best, after breaking china, was to share Ralph's bath. They would lie there soaking side by side, Miowke abstractedly licking the soap off Ralph's chest.

On the other side of the hall was the drawing room: a posh description for a sitting room perhaps, but one which suited it. The verandah was our general living room, and when we went into the drawing room it really was to withdraw temporarily from the pressure of other people. It was hardly ever used in the day time. It came into its own, if there were guests, at afternoon tea, complete with silver kettle and tea service, drop scones, fruit cake and chocolate roll. Heather made the cakes on a kerosene cooker with a tin oven on top, which symbolised pretty well the way our life at Honnametti combined the primitive with the luxurious. The fire was lit in the late afternoon, and in the evening with the curtains drawn the adults in the family — which eventually included Sheila and me — relaxed there after the strenuous day. Sometimes, especially when Ralph was away, we didn't use the dining room in the evenings but ate a picnic supper in the comfort of the drawing room. I have a vivid memory of Heather, dressed up in a long evening housecoat for the benefit of guests, kneeling on the floor carving a joint. She always sat on the floor by the fire, even when she was over eighty, still slim and supple, barefoot, smoking her pipe.

This room was chiefly associated in my mind with the scent of flowers. A silver chalice was always filled with roses, and a wide vase on a stand in one corner held huge sprays of blossom from the garden or wild hill flowers: tall blue and white gentians, tall pink ground orchids, and the sweet-smelling madonna lilies. Although a practical person, Heather had a streak of artistic creativity which revealed itself in her garden and in this room in particular. It was her territory and strictly a no-trophy area.

Beyond the drawing room was a spare room and beyond the

dining room our parents' bedroom. These were the other two rooms with french windows onto the verandah. At the north end of the house was another spare room, entered through a little anteroom from a door at the end of the verandah. At the south end of the house the suite of the rooms, ante-room bedroom and bathroom, was repeated, and was always called the nursery. First it belonged to Sheila and me, and later to Paddy. All the bedrooms bore Heather's imprint and were free from taxidermic memento mori. Each bedroom had its own bathroom, and the bathrooms, like the other rooms, had fireplaces in which log fires burned in the monsoons and cold weather. Without them the damp would have encased everything in mould. Even with the fires, seldom-used possessions such as party shoes tended to sprout green whiskers in July and August, the months of the south-west monsoon.

Our parents' bedroom differed from the others in having two bathrooms, one each. Ralph's was attached to his dressing room, which like all the bathrooms, had a window opening onto the yard at the back of the house. This was the most lively part of the homestead, with lots of people coming and going, and from his window he carried on a great many high decibel conversations and transactions.

Heather's one self-indulgence was long, hot baths. A huge wood-fuelled boiler in a shed behind the house provided ample hot water. Her problem was to get away from the demands of people long enough to enjoy it. In fact even in her bathroom she was not incommunicado. Since it was a place where the family could pin her down and where she could not truthfully say "I'm busy," we tended to converge there. A frequent guest of the house once observed, "I used to wonder where the whole Morris family kept disappearing to, until I discovered that they were holding conferences in Heather's bathroom."

My memories of the nursery are epitomised by the image of Sheila and me kneeling on the windowsill, grasping the bars like monkeys in a cage. "Randolph C," we yelled in unison, "Come to tea." (The 'C' was for Camroux, Ralph's middle name.)

About two hundred yards away from this, the south end of the house was a small brick building which housed our father's office. Here he spent long mysterious hours dictating letters to the clerk and scribbling, among other things, endless memoranda. He also held a kind of impromptu court, interviewing villagers (usually employees) and/or tribesmen, who had turned up with grievances, petitions or information. There was no room inside for such transactions, so they stood outside and he stood in the doorway while everyone shouted at each other. Whoever had the grievance — sometimes it was Ralph himself — shouted loudest of all. In south India much communication is accomplished at the top of the voice, which was one reason why Sheila and I, instructed to remind Daddy that it was time for a tea-break, thought it only natural. to bellow at him from a distance.

The bars at our windows were to keep out marauding panthers which, bolder, smaller and more agile than tigers, might enter a house in search of a dog-dinner and settle for a child instead.

The nursery was fairly spartan, with bare polished boards surrounding a meagre central island of rug. There were two white wooden cots with cotton-flock mattresses and hard slats underneath. There was a small dressing table and a cupboard. Over the fireplace hung a crucifix (we were nominally Catholics, as our mother followed that faith after a rather perfunctory fashion), and two framed prints. These were Reynolds' 'Age of Innocence' and Landseer's 'Dignity and Impudence', relics, I suppose, of the Edwardian childhoods of our parents, but much admired by Sheila and me. Over our beds hung two more character-forming pictures. Mine portrayed fairies and Sheila's showed four angels around an infant bed. Since I felt that fairies were inferior to angels in the supernatural hierarchy, it is possible that my picture contributed to the sense of inadequacy which dogged my later life.

The ante-room of the nursery lay between it and the verandah. For much of our childhood it was occupied by Heather's young sister Polly, much loved and teased by us as aunt, governess and friend. Looking back on the period I am struck by the patience with which she entered into our games and endured the squabbles of our sibling rivalry. We rose at six a.m., partly due to our natural diurnal rhythm and partly because we went to bed shortly after six p.m. Polly's rhythm did not coincide, which gave us scope for a good deal of pleasurable pestering. Once we insisted on her going to bed with a rope round her waist, with which we hauled her out in the morning.

Like all other bedrooms in the house, the nursery had its own bathroom. Except for the cheerful bedtime blaze in its fireplace and a hearth rug woven with Noah's Ark figures, this was pretty spartan too, with its bare boards. But the big cast-iron bath on legs was the locus of long, imaginative discussions, sometimes erupting into furious argument, when we sat facing each other, chest-deep in warm water, ordering our world in a way that knitted fact and fantasy together almost indistinguishably in our lives. Our early literary tastes were also shaped here. Before we enjoyed the benefits of plumbing, four potties stood in one corner, two for us children, two on stands for adults. We saw them as a family, and called them John, Jean, James and Joan. Seated upon John and Jean, or maybe James and Joan, I well remember our study of the works of Beatrix Potter. Some of them, like The Tale of Mr. Tod, struck us as pretty sinister. The other thing I recall about the bathroom was the presence of a large yellow packet containing 'Bromo' toilet paper. The surface of the packet was covered from top to bottom with a lengthy eulogy, much of it in very small print, of this product. Sheila and I had memorised it, and were prone to recite it as one of our party pieces.

Occasionally Heather and Polly would go off duty together and insist on Ralph putting us to bed. This was very popular with us. Not only did he do everything all wrong, which was a bonus in itself, but he also conducted, as much for his own amusement as for ours, boxing and wrestling matches between us, with the nursery rug as the ring. There were times when it ended in tears, but with life's usual unfairness it was these infrequent and irresponsibly conducted evenings which stick in my mind as the joyful ones.

Over the fireplace in Polly's room hung a print of Millais' painting of Sir Galahad, at which I gazed adoringly from the time I first encountered the Arthurian legends. Ralph almost destroyed this romantic idyll by inventing for us scurrilous bedtime stories about the doings of Galahad and Lancelot along the lines of the immortal parody 'My stench is as the stench of ten because I cart manure'. But in spite of his disenchanting efforts and the games we played in our bath with two little wooden boats called Gallie and Lancie, he never quite succeeded.

Paddy was born when I was ten and Sheila eight. To console us we were given a baby doll and cradle each, and we played with them for a few months in an intensely emulative way, breast and bottle-feeding them, changing nappies and so forth. But contrary to Freudian theory, we had never been interested in dolls before in spite of our indisputable femininity. For much of every year we spent the daylight hours outdoors, playing with the dogs and other animals, building secret houses in the surrounding woodland, and passing the time of day with the household and garden staff. On days of heavy rain in the monsoons, when I was not reading with secretive passion or drawing pinman cartoon strips about the adventures of an archetypal trickster who bore the respectable south Indian name of Ninga, we played endless games on the verandah with lead farm animals. Since these models did not offer enough variety, we supplemented them with others we made out of plasticine or a pleasing material called Glitterwax.

These games involved a lot of preliminary hard bargaining and shrewd bartering of our livestock, which engrossed us as much as the inventive play which followed. In these, Sheila favoured cows, while I identified with dogs or wolves. At one time Sheila's ambition was to marry a cart-bull. Later she shifted her conjugal sights from cattle to herd-boys, with whom she regularly fell in love. Meanwhile my own allegiance shifted from Mowgli to Galahad.

The south end of the verandah, from which the door led into Polly's anteroom and our nursery, was our playroom. It housed our toy cupboard, bookcase and rocking horse. And, since the french windows of our parents' bedroom also opened on this part of the verandah, the tall white cupboard where Heather kept her medical supplies stood against one wall. A little further along, between our parents' windows and those of the dining room, stood a big kerosene-fired refrigerator. After that the ambience of the verandah ceased to be scruffy and utilitarian and became tidy and convivial, furnished as a communal sitting room.

If the family met at all between meals in the daytime (other than in Heather's bathroom), it was in the verandah. Enclosed mainly by glass, it provided access to all the rooms and, except for the nursery at one end and the north spare room at the other, light and air as well. The central part, between front door and hall, was the seating area, with sofa and armchairs. Here there was a carpet. For the rest, Persian rugs covered the polished boards at intervals and tripped up the unwary. Compared with the more functional southern end, the northern end of the verandah beyond this central area was dedicated to leisure. Here were the drinks cabinet, bookshelves, and an enormous telescope on a tripod so tall that a special pair of steps was needed to reach the eyepiece. The telescope was so powerful that, if you focused it on the hills across the valley in front of the house to watch animals come out of the forest to graze in the grassland, you could see every flick of a sambhar's ear or a bison's tail. It had been given to my parents by a millionaire associated with the American Museum of Natural History of New York, after they had hosted and guided an expedition to collect specimens and backgrounds for its Asian Hall.

There was a low table by the front door where the tappal, the post, used to be placed in the evening, to be distributed when the adults turned up for supper. The tappal was brought up every day from Kollepet by two specially employed men who took it in turns to carry the locked canvas bag by shortcut paths through the jungle, armed with a spear. This was trimmed with little bells to advertise their presence and thus avoid encounters with wild animals. Only the toughest and most self-reliant applied for the job, well-paid though it was, because of its inherent dangers. In fact none of them came to any harm in our day, though occasionally there was no post if the tappal man heard or saw an elephant on or near the path and decided to return to the bus-terminus village. Quite recently one of these men, now an old gentleman retired to a village near Lokkanhalli, had visited me at my landlord's shack. He was renowned locally for his telling mimicry of my father's stutter in moments of vexation.

After our morning ride and breakfast, Sheila and I used to settle down to lessons with Polly. I can remember little of these, but they must have been well-conceived and interesting because when we did eventually go to boarding school we had no difficulty with more formal classwork. But I also owed a lot to my love affair with the household books. Besides the treasures of the dining room bookshelves, our nursery bookcase contained nearly all the childhood classics and the twelve volumes of Arthur Mee's Children's Encyclopaedia, confidently sub-titled The Book of Knowledge, out of which I would read aloud to a reluctant Sheila during our enforced afternoon rest on a rug in the garden. I still find myself in possession of unexpected bits of information gleaned from this source. It also contained potted versions of adult classics which

— fortunately — led me to seek out and read the originals, and it was a good introduction to poetry, not all of which was received by us respectfully. For instance we found the works of an American lady called Ella Wheeler Wilcox a particularly pleasing model for parody, although I don't remember now what she wrote which we found so funny.

Sheila was always the comedy star of the plays and recitative entertainments we devised for the adults at frequent intervals, while I provided much of the material. But the kind of poetry I most enjoyed reading to myself then were ballads and narrative fantasies. There were two by Alfred Noyes, whose obscure verse I discovered in the drawing room bookcase and found strangely exciting. One was about the quest of two children for a magic ruby, in which occurred the alarming refrain, 'Then silkily whispered Creeping Sin, This is the jewel you wished to win.' Stirring stuff. The other was 'The Forest of Wild Thyme', which left me with a taste for topographical fables, from Erewhon to Tolkein.

The drawing room bookcase also housed the complete works of Kipling in the old soft leather and gilt bindings. These I devoured, especially the Jungle Books, which I tried vainly to reenact, reserving for myself the role of Mowgli, with Sheila unwillingly cast as Grey Brother. One result of this indiscriminate literary diet was that between the ages of eight and eighteen I fancied myself — abetted unreasonably by my parents — as both a poet and an artist, and still have verses and paintings put away which prove how wrong I was.

HONNAMETTI: the house

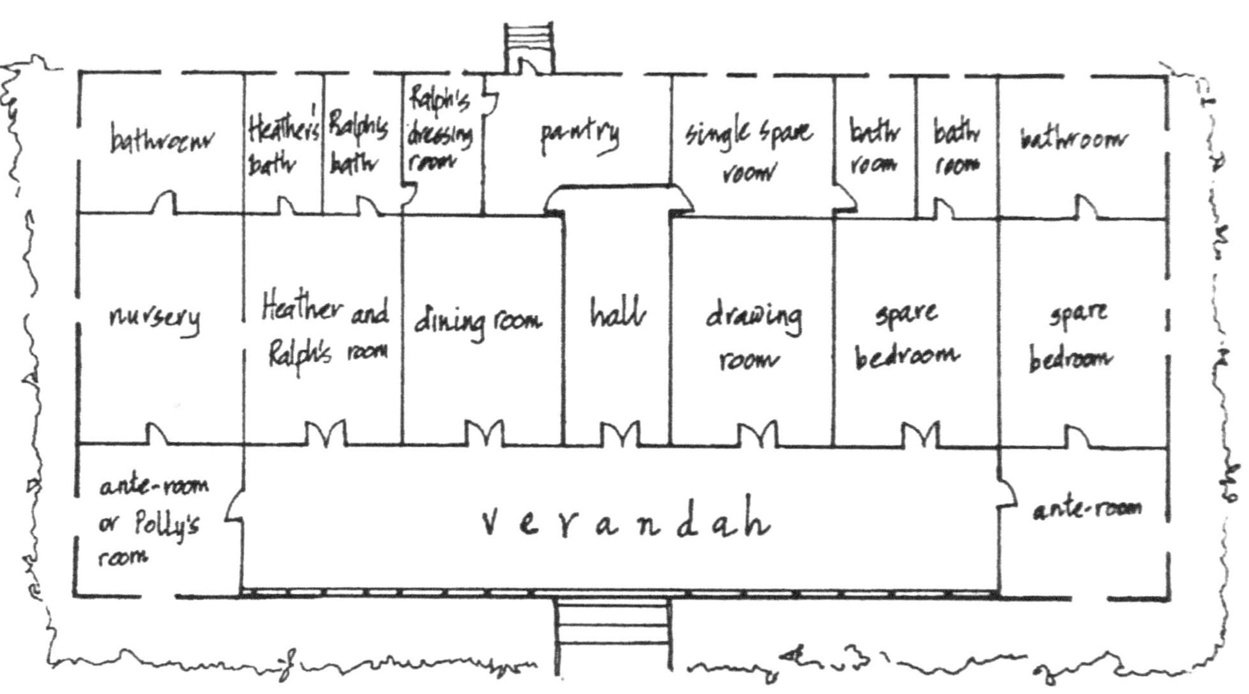

HONNAMETTI: the house & garden

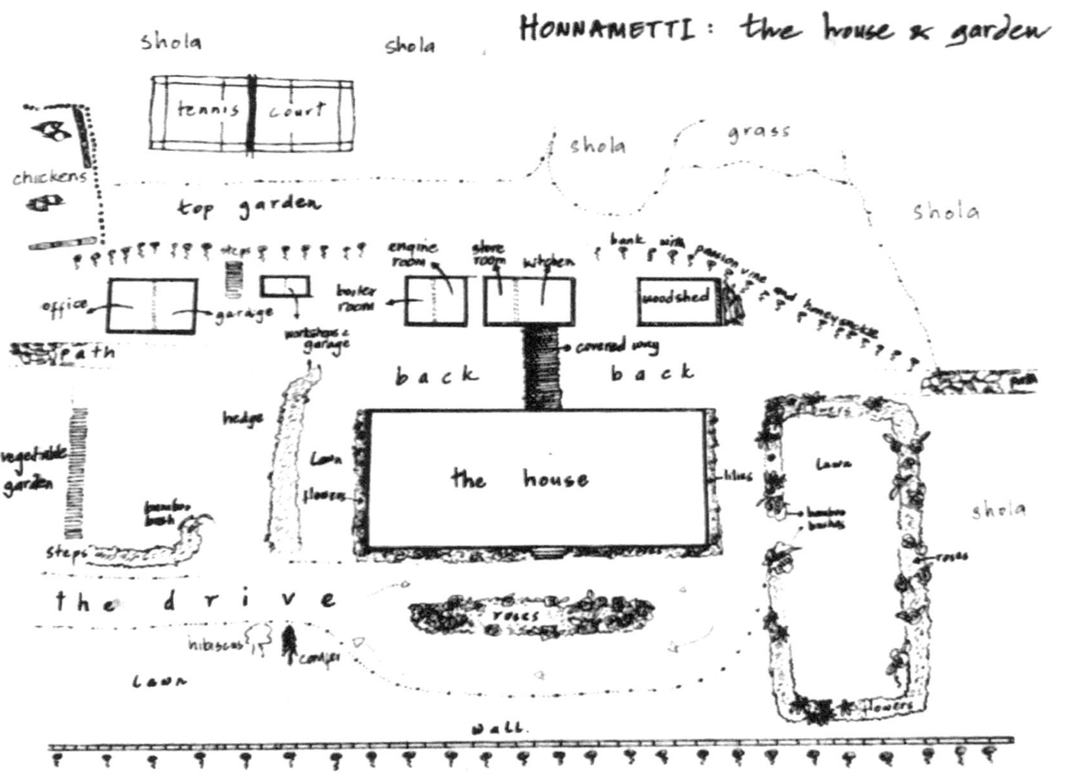

picnic at the rock

"You are being silent, Mrs. Monica," said Mr. Murthy. "You are thinking perhaps that we Indians talk too much."

"No more than anybody else, Mr. Murthy."

"You have been coming back for some number of years now. Tell us what you think of the Indian character."

"Impossible," I said, laughing. "Everybody's different."

"But you must have come to some general conclusions?"

This required thought. "Well, if you insist, there is one thing that strikes me. It's the way people waste time telling someone else to do something they are quite capable of doing themselves. It often saves a lot of time and trouble to do things yourself."

The staff members looked at each other. The interviewers giggled, having heard this before from me, sometimes as an admonishment. Mr. Murthy took a meditative suck of coffee and then slowly nodded agreement. "That is true. I have never thought of it before."

"But who am I to criticise?" I added, conscience-stricken by such acquiescence. "Europeans have some peculiar habits too."

"We don't mind you saying it," he replied solemnly, "because we know you are enthusiastic for India."

"And that is why you keep coming back," someone pointed out smugly and the talk went onto other things.

After a bit I consulted my watch. It was time we started, or at least the interviewers, with their preference for strolling, did. They were not great walkers, especially the girls in their saris and sandals, and though they always got fitter fast with all the walking they had to do in the hills, it was not fair to hurry them today.

When we rose to take our leave I said to them, " Look, you go ahead and I'll catch up with you. There's something I want to look at first."

They were quite happy to do this, especially as young Sunder said he would see them on their way, and they prepared to set off, taking with them their picnic food in that invaluable Indian artefact, a three-tiered 'tiffin carrier'.

We moved towards the front door, Mr. Murthy calling for the bungalow caretaker as he did so. But when the youth arrived he waved him away. "Paravila (never mind)," he said.

"Then why did you call him?" The accountant was curious.

"I called him to open the door. And then I remembered," admitted Mr. Murthy with a rueful smile, "that I was perfectly capable of opening the door myself."

Amid shouts of laughter we separated, the others going out through the front of the house while I hurried through the hall and turned into the pantry to reach the back door, bent on a quick retrospective tour of further haunts of my youth.

The pantry had definitely seen better days. Once it had been the spotless domain of one Rama Nair, a member of the famous (among anthropologists) matrilineal caste of Kerala. A proud man, he accepted Heather's training in meticulous hygiene but was not prepared to stand any nonsense from anyone else. "Yaru bloody fool? Ninu bloody fool (Who are you calling a fool? Bloody fool yourself)," he was once heard to bellow bilingually at another member of the staff who had ventured to take issue with him. He wouldn't have been seen dead in the present rundown state of his department.

Behind the house, and running its length, was a cemented yard at the rear of which, against the vertical wall which rose to the terraced top garden, was a row of outbuildings. This yard greatly attracted Sheila and me. Known to us all simply as The Back, on the lines of the Cambridge Backs, it was a sociable area full of goings on and intriguing happenings such as the feeding of the dogs, and the grinding of masala by the kitchen lad on a heavy square stone with a stone roller. It separated the bungalow itself from the row of outbuildings which contained kitchen, engine-room for electricity generator and water pump, and other workshops, and was intersected by a covered walkway from the pantry in the bungalow to the kitchen. Various memorable characters presided over the transactions at The Back.

The northernmost outbuilding was the woodshed where that genial soul Devera Gudda, husband of the enterprising Baswi, chopped cheerfully when he wasn't collecting bundles of fallen branches from the shola or entertaining us children with a little song and dance act or gossiping with passers-by. He was a Harijan, an 'untouchable', but he was also a Harijan priest, and so accorded a certain respect by higher castes. His other household responsibilities included the laying and lighting of the fires and polishing the wooden floors with half a green coconut to a lustrous finish. Sheila and I loved him dearly.

Next to the woodshed was the kitchen, joined to the pantry in the main bungalow by the umbilical cord of covered cloister or walkway. The kitchen cooking was done on a splendid black wood-burning cast-iron 'Bonnybridge' stove. Since washing up the saucepans was beneath the cook's dignity, it was done outside the kitchen by the same assistant who ground the spices. The cook and the houseman also came from Kerala, nephews succeeding uncles over the years in the matrilineal tradition. When we were children the cook was one Panguni, a simple soul who put up with us all for years and was affectionately nicknamed Ping Pong by Sheila and me. His cuisine was limited in scope and occasionally calamitous, but he stayed on until pensioned off in old age. The succession of housemen, his relatives, were handsome and dashing, unlike him. First there was Madhavan who, sad to say, took to drink. When he left his younger brother, or maybe his nephew, Damodaran, took over. Damodaran had an eye for the girls which proved his undoing and he died mysteriously (of Sholiga sorcery, it was rumoured on the estate). But he was probably poisoned for making a pass at a Sholiga girl. He was followed by his kinsman Gopal Krishna, whom Heather nursed through smallpox, and who stayed with our parents till they left. Adjoining the kitchen was the storeroom, at once the heart of the household and Heather's workshop. Here she sterilised the milk from our cows, separated the cream, which came fresh to the dining table, churned yesterday's cream into butter, and clarified butter into ghee, our cooking medium. Here too she made the cakes, jam and marmalade; planned the meals; checked and stored the grains and groceries ordered through our Kollepet agent, and our own fruit and vegetables; fed the calves and dogs; dispensed medical aid; and advised, consoled, treated and scolded a stream of people as diverse as those who crowded round Ralph's office door. The storeroom was clinically clean and rigorously ordered. When she spent most of her time down on the plantation during the war and I had occasionally to preside there in her stead, I was terrified of making some dire mistake and never lived down the time I let the marmalade burn while stirring it and reading a book at the same time.

Next to the storeroom was the generator engine room, rather dark, with rows of gleaming batteries. The estate mechanic looked after it as well as the cars and — later — the tractors, but if anything went really wrong Heather would be called in to fix it.

The last outbuilding behind the house was the boiler room, where the water was heated, clothes dried in the monsoons, and occasionally a sick dog was nursed.

Round The Back went a system of open cemented drains, that carried to a tank, bath and washing up water which was used for watering the garden. Sheila and I liked these drains, as my own children did in years to come. Another thing we liked was squatting outside the storeroom with the dog-boy, helping to groom and de-flea the dogs. This teenage lad, one Nai Mada (Dog Mada), was a particular buddy of ours. He had duties other than kennel man, such as assisting the malis (gardeners) with weeding and watering, but they were not very onerous, and he was easily persuaded to join in our games. He taught us to play jacks with pebbles and we taught him English. I think we were both a bit in love with him. The Back was separated by an escallonia hedge from an open space in front of two garages which doubled as machinery repair shops. In our young days it also held dog kennels, a wire pen for pet rabbits and guinea pigs, and a stone block with a hole in it for pounding cottonseed for cattle-feed. Behind it were the stone steps which mounted the vertical bank and led to the terraces of the upper garden and the chicken-run. Beyond the steps was another garage, with an inspection pit, and beyond this was Ralph's office. I can still see him sitting there in a cane and bentwood revolving chair at his cluttered rolltop desk, surrounded by maps, diagrams of the dentition and crania of wild dogs and other mammals, and correspondence with wildlife, countryside and natural history journals, under the portraits of his parents, ready to burst forth from time to time to harangue and be harangued. When he was overseas in the army in World War II, Heather ruthlessly cut out the paper work, writing brief business letters at night while kneeling on the floor by her bedroom fire. The rest of the day she spent down on the estate, which she reorganised energetically. It prospered exceedingly for the first time ever, but the learned societies greatly missed Ralph's commentaries on his jungle observations.

Sheila and I spent a lot of time hanging about in this area playing with animals. Though the dogs were kennelled during the night to protect them from panthers, they roamed freely in the daytime and were our playmates. Those which stayed around the house and garden lived to grow old. The wanderers all failed to come back in the end. Here too we would saddle the ponies, or harness Bully boy, Sheila's miniature black cart-bull, who drew a scaled-down cart. We had to be a little wary of Albert the gander as he wandered about terrorising one and all. He had once been the devoted mate of a douce grey goose, but she had died. After her death he was inconsolable and hated everybody. We imported another wife for him, a beautiful white goose, but he proved conclusively that geese are monogamous for life by trying to drown her in a water-butt. He remained fierce and friendless until he adopted a little old sweeper-woman called Chikki. She was semi-retired and returned his affection. They were a touching sight as they squatted in the shade for hours, his head resting on her shoulder. When Chikki died Albert became so vicious that our parents decided that the kindest thing was to end his life too. Sheila and I cried and cried, but that did not stop us eating him, still crying.

After the demise of 'Pi' another local 'tat' pony was bought for Paddy which Sheila and I, now grown up, undertook to break in. We lunged it dutifully on the tennis court while Paddy petted it and introduced it to grooming. Shortly after its arrival she said to Heather, "There's something in my hair." There was indeed. She had picked up lice from the pony and it was a tricky business getting rid of the parasites by washing her long hair with kerosene.

Not half so tricky, though, as getting rid of the pony's lice. Sheila and I decided to wash it with a disinfectant detergent. The operation of scrubbing an unbroken colt with a foaming liquid and rinsing it with a hose proved to be highly dramatic, but it achieved its objective.

This was not the first brush we had with parasites. Years before, when we were small, Sheila and I had picked up bird-lice from a parakeet brought to us by a Sholiga. We had been well fumigated, but were apparently stimulated by the possibilities of vermin to the extent of wishing to share our experience. Shortly after our stringent de-lousing a rather grand Indian Civil Service couple whom our mother had never met came to stay. They arrived unexpectedly early when Ralph was out. Heather, hurriedly changing in her bedroom, sent us out to entertain them until she was ready to emerge. Eager to oblige, we received them on the verandah with our version of social small talk and Heather, appalled, heard through her french window Sheila's piping voice remarking with quiet pride, "My head's full of lice. They often crawl down on my forehead and I catch them."

There were other animals from time to time. Young deer which wreaked havoc in the orchard when they grew up, a bison calf, sloth bear cubs captured too old, so that they attacked everyone but Heather who fed them, enchanting chestnut-coated Malabar squirrels, nesting as babies in old slippers and released, tame and trusting, in the adjoining sholas. Most of the latter disappeared mysteriously, probably through descending from the trees on to someone's shoulder once too often. Sholigas eat squirrels.

We twice fostered litters of tiger cubs. I can still see in my mind's eye Heather's old black spaniel, Sweep, walking along the front lawn on a sunny day, followed by Jack, a young Airedale, and following Jack in wavering single file, nose to tail, five tiger cubs. The mother of these had killed a man, and Ralph, sent for by distraught villagers, had crawled into the thorn clump where she lay and shot her as she charged him, only to find she had cubs with her. The second litter had been abandoned by their mother and gathered up by Ralph and Sheila, then pregnant with her fourth child.

Though they are delicate and difficult to bring up by hand when they are very young, tiger cubs make wonderful pets, intelligent, comic, friendly and affectionate. But unfortunately you can't have full grown tigers wandering loose about the place. While they would probably never intentionally harm the people who had nurtured them, this would not apply to others and a tiger is far too powerful to control on a lead. Besides, they require immense quantities of meat.

So those of our cubs which survived all went to zoos, sad to say, at the age of about six months, by which time their friendly play had already got a bit rough. A few more months and a friendly cuff from your still affectionate pet could break your neck. When the second lot of cubs were on their way to the Chicago zoo, Paddy was allowed to visit them during their stopover at Heathrow. At six months they were already half-grown. Delighted to see her they tried to climb up her like kittens the size of labradors, and practically tore the clothes off her in exuberant welcome. Homo sapiens is just too puny a playmate for felis tigris.

Today I walked quickly past The Back buildings, all in a sad state of decline, averting my eyes from the now moribund storeroom in particular with an acute sense of loss. Then round the corner of the escallonia hedge, to enter the triangular space backed by the garages and workshops. This too had been the scene of lively activity in the past, and was still busy this morning, with several people clustered round the tractor, attending to its toilet.

Leaving them to it after the necessary exchange of pleasantries, I ascended the flight of stone steps which led to the upper garden — the 'top garden' as we used to call it. It clung to the hillside in a series of terraces, some of which had supported the strawberry beds (now reverted to grass), with beyond them the long hen-run, no longer in use, which had once been wired in like a huge fruit cage or mosquito net to protect the fowls from kites, bandicoots and egg-hunting rat snakes. Sheila and I named each one and knew them all as individual characters.

The path up the hill zigzagged between what had been beds of amaryllis and agapanthus lilies, cosmos, African daisies, verbena and more cannas. The grassy banks of this hanging garden were studded with a bushy shrub, the name of which I forget, which greeted thunderstorms with an explosion of fluffy pink blossom like old-fashioned powder puffs. At the same time these banks and the steep slope below the retaining wall of the shelf on which the bungalow stood, produced masses of fragile pink 'thunder lilies' after a storm.

In the upper garden was a mulberry tree, and more jacarandas, canopies of blue bloom from March till May. Above these was the hard tennis court, seldom used for tennis as far as I can remember, since guests seemed more amused by the amateurish and unprincipled games of croquet we played on the big lawn below. Our parents did not have the time to play tennis, Sheila and I were absorbed with our relationships with animals or imaginary characters, and the court required too much upkeep. It now supported a crop of young coffee bushes.

A long spine of shola ran, in our young days and in these latter days, along the length of the ridge between Attikan and Honnametti. It continued along the top of the upper garden at Honnametti, and at its northern end sent down a tongue towards the house, ending at the top of the vertical bank behind the outbuildings and big lawn. I entered this stretch of shola and plodded uphill through the trees. The stretches of shola adjacent to the top garden had been kept clear of undergrowth in our day and provided a sylvan retreat in which Sheila and I safely played. Sometimes we were joined here by Nai Mada, with whom we communicated without difficulty in spite of the fact that our Kannada was rudimentary and his English vestigial. He was our good friend and though he left the bungalow staff to work full time on the estate when he was older, we kept in touch with him. He was the first person I asked about on my return, only to learn that dear Nai Mada had died. I look forward very much to meeting him again in the next world.

Coming out of the shola on to the grassy hog-backed summit of the hill on which the house stood, I began to walk down the other side, that is, to descend its western slope. Like the rest of the ridge of which it was a part, the gradient was gradual for about a hundred feet before it fell away very steeply. In places this sharp drop took the form of cliffs or rocky outcrops. The back of the hill behind the house tilted over in one such precipice after the initial gentle slope, and the path I took ran down to a level platform of rock at the edge of the cliff. This platform faced due west, and here I stopped to look and listen.

The Biligirirangan hills run roughly north and south for about sixty miles and consist of three parallel ridges divided by deep valleys. The eastern ridge is the longest, highest and most continuous, though it is broken by passes in places, particularly the wide one we called Bellaji Gap, through which our north-eastern road ran. Honnametti estate lay in the valley between the eastern and central ridges, and Honnametti bungalow perched on its shelf looking east towards the gap from a hill in the highest part of the central ridge. Attikan bungalow also faced east from a hill on the central ridge, about a mile south of Honnametti.

Between the outcrops of rocky cliff on the west side of this central ridge, well seen from the natural platform on which I stood, were tongues and fans of grassy hillside which were steep but not precipitous. They presented in our girlhood days a strenuous challenge to my black labrador dog Quailer, our chief companion and playmate. While we went flower picking among the masses of madonna lilies, gentians and ground orchids that starred these grassy slopes in their season (the Biligiris are very rich in orchids, the habitat of at least sixty-five different species), Quailer pursued one of his hobbies. He would select hefty boulders to dig up and nose over to roll hundreds of feet down, following them halfway down to the bottom of the ridge, a thousand feet below. Then, with a staunchness worthy of a more productive cause, he would carry them up to the top again.

Quailer was a dog of considerable eccentricity but endowed with patience and good humour. Cast as Bagheera, Owd Bob or White Fang, he would do his best to cooperate, and harnessed to a little wooden cart he would tow it until he was tired and then lie down immovably. But he enjoyed a private life as a collector. Small objects would disappear, to be sought vainly until suspicion fell on him and we would stalk him cautiously until we came upon him in some well-chosen hiding place, lying cosily surrounded by a jackdaw hoard of treasures. Whenever one of his toy cupboards, as we called them, was discovered he dismantled it in secret, carrying its constituents one by one stealthily to a new hiding place. His other hobby was stone-rolling, his regular pitch being the steep bank below the low stone wall that bounded the lawn in front of the house at the lip of the shelf on which the house was built. Here he undermined football-sized stones by digging them from below and nudged them with his nose until they started rolling. He would follow, barking joyously, until they reached the bottom, and then carry them up to roll them down again. This obsession gave him enormous neck muscles and broke all his teeth.

From my vantage point I gazed westward. The vertical drop

below the platform plunged for a hundred feet to long grass slopes which descended at an easier gradient to a sea of deciduous forest before rising again to a low line of jungle-clad hills, the much lower westerly ridge of the range. Beyond them lay the flat plateau country, sprinkled with kere or reservoirs which we called 'tanks'. On the western horizon, blue with distance, crouched the pantherine shape of Chamundi, the sacred hill of the city of Mysore. Nearer, the lights of Kollepet could be seen in the evening, while to the south-west the view was bounded by the far blue wall of the Nilgiri hills.

The Nilgiris. That distant bourne of shops and clubs, Planters' Week and Government House parties, mimosa and the ubiquitous eucalyptus trees. All the appurtenances of what was later to become known (in Britain) as 'the Raj', although as far as I know this term, which simply means 'rule' was seldom used, in south India anyway, until popularised by the BBC. In our childhood the Nilgiris meant Granny Kinloch's house outside the little town of Kotagiri, the smell of eucalyptus woodsmoke, eating appams and mangosteens, and the marathon journey by car to get there and back. Although the distance from Honnametti to Kotagiri was not much more than a hundred miles, the drive there (indeed anywhere from our hills) was an undertaking of some magnitude. Supposing the fifteen miles of our south-western road, the Punjur ghat, to be passable, and that no rogue elephant had chosen to patrol it, there was still the hazard of crossing the Punjur river at its foot. Should the river be fordable, there were many miles of forest road to be traversed where elephants were still the chief hazard before reaching the hamlet of Dimbam and the spectacular descent to the blazing plains of Tamil Nadu, then the State of Madras. Miles of dusty road, innocent then of tarmac, led us, via the town of Satyamangalam, which had about as much charm as Kollepet, to the railhead of Mettupalayam with its graceful plantations of areca palm, at the foot of the Coonoor and Kotagiri ghats. We left for the Nilgiris at four a.m., and arrived late at night. Since it was our parents' business to change tyres and refill boiling radiators, we children seldom failed to enjoy the adventure.

To this observation platform, where I now sat down dangling my legs over the edge, we often used to come to watch the sunset turn to vermilion the innumerable kere which irrigated the stretch of plateau that ran westward towards Mysore. On such evenings we might well look down the slopes below to see a rummaging bear or watch a herd of elephant, sambhar or bison come out of the jungle to graze. The jungle was known to us as the Jagir, as it had once formed part of the fief of a petty lordling or Jagirdar. If you sat on the rock platform by day, as I did now, you became aware that the Jagir throbbed and hummed with a familiar sound, the chirping of a myriad green barbets, common bird of the hills and coffee plantation pest. If you waited long enough you might also catch the boom of a startled grey langur, the beautiful long-tailed monkey of the south Indian hills, and you would certainly hear the plaintive cry of the rust-and-white brahminy kite, watch the kestrels hover and stoop, and perhaps see a black eagle in soaring flight.

But no more time now to sit and admire the view or meditate on temps perdu. Promising myself a longer visit soon, I got up and hurried back the way I'd come. I could have gone on northward along the top of the ridge and descended further on to catch up with the interviewers, but the going would have been rough and slow. This way it took me no time to retrace my steps down to the house and round to the front garden. At this point I paused, looking at the little hollows in the drive near the edge of the front lawn. They had always been there, filling up as deep puddles in the monsoons, and there Sheila and I used to play in the pouring rain when we were small, buttoned into stiff canvas raincoats with elasticated knickers to match, shod in shiny welly-boots, making mud pies. What we liked to do was to sit in the puddles, thus putting to the test the waterproof qualities of our gear. We also wandered about making concoctions from such substances as the tongues of arum lilies which we hoped, like alchemists, would turn out to have useful properties, or to gouge from the steep bank behind the house handfuls of pink and yellow clay, easily moulded. For this reason, and the fact that we were discouraged from doing it, the bank attracted us as wasps to jam.

Crossing the big side lawn I entered the shola that hemmed in the garden to the north, to follow the wide path which ran through it, contouring the hillside. This was another stretch of home woodland in which we were allowed to play. The chief attraction of the one above the house, the hilltop shola, was that we had invented an imaginary country there, of which a big tree, bent almost horizontal by some arboreal accident, was named the City. In the shola I was now passing through, we built fairy houses of twigs and the thick pads of moss which grew on boulders and tree-trunks, or made secret hidey-places for ourselves in the thick undergrowth of strobilanthus, which we revealed under seal of silence as classified information only to Devera Gudda and old Knoot Ranga, the gardener. Where was Nai Mada then? If he was still with us then he would have shared the secret.

In the monsoons we were firmly discouraged from playing in the sholas, as the leaf-mould underfoot swarmed then with leeches. Not that leeches held any terrors for us. On the contrary, when Sheila and I were once competing as to the number of leech bites we received in a monsoon, I have a guilty memory of cheating by dropping a leech into the welly-boot I was wearing on a walk. No, the problem with leech bites is their messy aftermath because the flow of blood is so hard to staunch. I remember one evening, when we were much older, we had returned, drenched and dirty after a day in the soaking monsoon jungle with our father, and were chased off to share a bath at once. We climbed in together, soaking luxuriously in the big white bath- tub full of steaming water, by a blazing log fire, and watching with dispassionate interest the water slowly turning a delicate shade of pink, dyed by our seeping blood.

My first real taste of adventure in our own wild world came when I was eight and first went camping with Ralph as a birthday treat. The camp was in a shola-filled hollow in the hills of the high eastern ridge not far from Katari betta, and one sharp impression of it remains with me. It is of sitting by the camp fire at night, watching in a state of exaltation the sparks float up through the tree tops, seeming to join the glittering stars in the black sky. Then, looking down, I saw a leech looping up the inside of a cylindrical tin that had contained shortbread biscuits. Somehow the leech in the biscuit tin seemed to me both comic and cosmic, epitomising the glorious departure from the normal in which I was involved.

Walking across the big lawn and along the path into the shadowy shola beyond, I remembered another familiar background noise, the sleepy buzz of the cicadas in the shola during the hot weather, so continuous that it was only noticeable when it suddenly stopped, to start again in a little while in miraculous synchronisation.

At the end of the shola the path contoured round what had once been open grass hillside but was now becoming overgrown with wenlandia shrubs and hillside strobilanthus. Ralph always used to insist that moderate grazing by cattle, which are not extractive feeders like sheep and goats, was an aid to reforestation, and this hillside, grazed for years by Honnametti cows, certainly seemed to prove it. The hill strobilanthus would soon die away under the forest growth, which in some ways was a pity, because when it flowered, once in twelve years, the hills were deliciously mantled with purple blossom smelling of honey, rather like heather, but softer and more delicate in colour. For the rest of the time the shrub, like heather, was horrible to walk through, so perhaps its disappearance was really no loss.

Passing a huge granite monolith split by lightning which rose from the long grass below the path and which in the past had been my delight to climb, I came to another shola. Through it a stream ran down from the saddle between the bungalow hill and the next hill to the north of it. On the edge of it, about a mile from our garden, my parents had built a little wooden summer house, where we were taken to play when we were small children. Only the foundations now remained, plus a single buddleia and a tall tree which had once been a small ornamental conifer. The stream had been dammed three times, to form three reservoirs, one above the other, before it ran on down to the estate. Its banks were thickly planted with the long green fronds of cardamoms, another useful cash crop of the hills. The middle reservoir, encased in concrete, supplied bath water to the house through a pipe running along the path.

Past the dam I came out of the strip of shola along the stream to follow the path round the flank of another great grassy hill. Here a second monolith rose from the grass of the hillside below the path, this one resembling a primitive carving of Virgin and Child. The path went on to cross the middle dam of three more reservoirs on another cardamom-fringed stream descending to the estate in the valley, and plunged into a huge shola which Ralph had completely planted up with cardamoms. Now the shola was sadly thinned out and the cardamoms replaced by coffee. At this point I caught up with the interviewers, and we went on together for two miles or so until we came to the end of the woodland.

San Mada was there, supervising some other Sholigas who were clinging light-heartedly to the tops of high trees with their toes and one hand while with the other they wielded short axes to thin out the branches. "How far are you going?" he asked.

"Only as far as the kalu (rock)," I said, and he seemed relieved.

We walked out into the open on to a flat grassy hilltop with the bones of the earth showing through as rounded boulders. Before us rose the third granite monolith of the morning's walk, Honnametti Kalu, perched in an apparently precarious position on a slanting slab of rock at the top of a little crag. It was a lovely place for a picnic: sunshine, grass, flat slabs of warm dry rock to sit on. But first, I suggested, let's examine our feet for leeches.

We all found one or two, tenaciously attached. The others couldn't bring themselves to touch the black rubbery things, so I pulled them off everyone's feet and produced tufts of cotton wool to staunch the flow of blood.

Leeches dealt with, the interviewers and I duly tapped the standing stone to hear its metallic ring, and searched for the footprint in the rock, which we found hidden in new undergrowth and decided that it was not very convincing. While they spread out the picnic and admired the great panorama to the west, pointing out to each other the Biligirirangan temple perched on its foothill and the site of Kollepet, distinguished by the gleam of Dod and Chik Kere, I wandered off to take in the eastward view. Looking down, I could see where the silver-grey treetops of the estate ceased at its northern end and the great rainforest of the Gundal valley began. The Gundal stream rose at the watershed of Yellehottay, ran northward down the valley in which lay Honnametti estate, defining the estate's eastern boundary, and continued on its course through the gradually widening forest-filled valley, until it left the hills at their northern extremity to join, eventually, the great Kaveri river. On the way, some miles below the end of the estate, it passed through the Dodsampagi reserved forest, so called after a huge sampagi (champak, frangipani or temple) tree, sacred to the Sholigas, which grew near the river. In this forest, at the edge of a marshy water-hole, my parents had built a platform in a tall white cedar from which we would go, at a time of full moon in clear weather, to spend the night watching animals come to the pool to drink. On one such night my parents had watched a herd of elephants come down to drink, much plagued by a naughty baby which would not be kept in order, but frolicked about, falling into the great holes left by the feet of the adults, splashing round the tuskers and generally causing its mother a good deal of concern. And once I sat up there with a friend and saw a tigress and two cubs look up at the platform as if puzzled and then go off quietly about their business. It was always exciting to watch the animals unseen, but apart from this pleasure visits to the observation machan were mostly uneventful. Not always, though. Once an elephant objected to the long homemade ladder by which the tree was climbed and pulled it down, which presented my parents with a problem when they wanted to descend in the morning. And another time, when they had come down and walked back to their car, which they had left on the track near the Dodsampagi tree, they found that a jungle fire had passed that way, leaving the car a burned-out skeleton. Since this was India the car was hauled back to the estate by bulls, cleaned up, refilled with petrol, and the skeleton driven to Coimbatore to have a new body built around it, after which it enjoyed many more years of useful life.

From where I stood I looked straight across to Bellaji Gap. From there my eyes travelled northward to the great dome of Namagundi betta, equivalent in height and difficulty of access to Bedanaikana betta to the south of the range. The hill was crowned by a patch of shola, Namagundikan, and seamed by a shoIa-filled watercourse, Hoolpatchyhulla. It is a wild and inaccessible part of the hills, favoured by both bison and elephants.

Ralph used to say that Namagundi betta seemed to be used by bison as a kind of sanatorium, since so many solitary bulls he had seen there were either injured or diseased. Two were blind in one eye, two were lame, others had suffered a variety of injuries, and three had been mauled by tigers. Tigers try their luck with bison from time to time, usually hoping to get a calf straying at the fringe of a herd, but sometimes attack full-grown animals, although not with much success as a rule.

Ralph had once been watching the antics of a tiger stalking a bison herd and being chased off again and again with snorts of rage and fear on the part of the herd and an unhurried lack of concern on the part of the tiger. As he and the friend with him set off home, they met one of the bulls on their path and just had time to leap behind trees as he lowered his head and charged. The impetus of his rush carried the bull over the edge of a steep slope, down which he rolled, flattening the undergrowth, to make a crash landing at the bottom.

Whereupon he got to his feet and made off, apparently none the worse for his fall.

This happened near Hoolpatchyhulla and a few years later while camping there, Ralph and a Sholiga called San Eera heard the snorts of an angry bison coming from a nearby patch of shola. In the morning they came suddenly on a large bull, which promptly lowered his head and charged. San Eera whisked himself behind a tree with a startled yell while Ralph, finding himself short of nearby trees, flung himself flat on the ground. The bull bounded over him, striking his head with its foot, and then galloped off. Examination of the shola where the snorts were heard the night before showed that a tiger had been around, infuriating the bull.

Not long before that a Sholiga had been killed by a bison bull. When his body was recovered by a search party they found not far away the half-eaten corpse of a bison cow which had been killed by a tiger.

Ralph once wrote that bison have many of the pleasant characteristics of the elephant with few of its vices. The two species share the same haunts: bamboo forests and tall grass, moving to the short grass of the hilltops and the evergreen sholas in the hot weather. As a rule they ignore each other, though Ralph actually saw a male elephant kill a bison bull when they came face to face on a game path. But both animals had been frightened by his presence.

Elephants are social animals, showing true concern for one another. They do their best to help those of the herd that are ill or injured, and mourn their dead. Our parents once saw elephants gather in great distress round a cow of the herd which had died calving of a breech delivery. They tried to raise her, the whole herd keeping up a continuous clamour, and stayed around, visiting her body from time to time for days after she died. Cow elephants sometimes devotedly foster another cow's calf even when the mother is still alive and suckling it, and lone bulls — even rogues — often adopt a young elephant as companion and treat it with loving care.

So, herds tend to act in unison and this can be alarming if you get in their way. Ralph's parents and sister once inadvertently camped on a game-path near Hoolpatchyhulla used by elephants to get to the water. A herd surrounded the camp and spent the whole night threatening to break in. They were only kept out by continuous shouts, banging of tins, and a circle of fires. My aunt was so frightened that she climbed a small tree, which bent gently under her weight and deposited her into the stream.

Since my father and I had once found ourselves between a herd and the water it was making for, we had every sympathy with Aunt Muriel. In our case there were no trees to climb, and I hate to think what would have happened if the herd had not changed its corporate mind about that particular approach to its evening bath. For some reason that part of the Biligirirangan hills not only attracted sick and solitary bison but also solitary bull elephants. Several of the latter subsequently abandoned a hitherto blameless course to become homicidal rogues for no known reason (in one case after twenty years as an inoffensive recluse), and Ralph eventually had to put an end to their careers of destruction.

On Namagundi betta two Sholiga friends of Ralph's had been killed by a rogue elephant as they crossed the ridge carrying ragi to sell at the Udhatti shanti (market) at the eastern foot of the hills. Though their relatives searched for them when they did not come home, their bodies were not found for some years, not in fact until Ralph and a Sholiga companion found patches of ragi growing at the edge of the shola and, hunting around in the hope of solving this mystery, came upon their crushed and broken skeletons. The same elephant later ambushed Ralph and another Sholiga, having first hunted them through the undergrowth and long grass and then stationed itself further up the path at an open glade which they would have to cross. By this time it had been prescribed as a rogue, and Ralph shot it as it charged them.

This was by no means the only encounter my parents, especially Ralph, had with rogues on Namagundi. Some of them were hair-raising, and it made a change to think of a more peaceful occasion near Hoolpatchyhalla when we had watched a tigress playing with her cubs in a sheltered hollow, rolling about with them and generally having fun. Although tigers don't like walking in the heat of the sun after a meal they are not averse to sunning themselves, and I remember watching a tiger on Namagundi strolling along in broad daylight, at peace with the world. According to the Sholigas there are still tigers there, probably because it is difficult for deer poachers to reach, and also because indiscriminate cattle-grazing from the spreading villages at the foot of the hills has nowhere near reached Namagundi, and therefore the bison herds there may not have been decimated by rinderpest, the cattle disease which has killed so many of the herds in more accessible areas of the hills.

Thinking of bison (or more correctly of gaur, the official name of these wild cattle), I returned to Honnametti Kalu and looked down the western slope of the hill below the little escarpment. From here we had several times watched a herd grazing peacefully. In fact from the top of the adjoining hill we had watched them grazing in friendly proximity to our own cows, the herdsman so used to their presence that he barely noticed them. According to Ralph it was not an uncommon sight in the past to see bison and elephants grazing near each other in amity, and occasionally a solitary bison bull will attach itself to the outskirts of an elephant herd, perhaps for security.

Bison are on the whole non-belligerent animals, except for bulls made restive by tigers or by some nagging injury which makes them fierce. Quite close to where we sat was a little shola, beyond which the grassy ridge continued, gradually losing height. No more than a mile along the ridge from Honnametti Kalu Ralph and I, with my daughter Susan, aged then about nine or ten, and two young men, had approached a herd. Our American friends, sons of a trustee of the Natural History Museum in New York, wanted to photograph bison and collect a big bull. We had got close, some of the herd eyeing us phlegmatically, others still grazing, when without warning a huge old bull put down his head and charged. Ralph and Cottie were armed and stood their ground. Danny and I were ready to run when I noticed a small commotion going on beside me: Susan jumping up and down with excitement and squeaking, "This is the greatest experience of my life." She says now that she was terrified. She certainly did not act terrified, which is more than can be said for Danny and me. But before the bull reached us, two high velocity rifles roared in quick succession and the great beast dropped dead. The poor creature turned out to have been recently mauled by a tiger, and had lost an eye.

The picnic over, we were sitting on the rocks enjoying the view when I noticed two late-blooming Nilgiri lilies surviving in the long grass below. "Oh look," I said, "those are the lilies I told you about. I'll get them for you." I jumped up and was just going to plunge down through the long grass on one side of the crag when for no particular reason Heather's warning of some years ago came into my mind: be careful of Russell's vipers in long grass near sholas. Turning back I picked up a stick someone had brought and started down again. The grass was thick as well as long and it was a tedious business parting the tufts with the stick to see where I was putting my feet. "Oh, this is a bore," I thought. "I can't be bothered." But in the process of thinking this the stick had automatically thrust aside yet another tuft, and there, just where I was about to put my foot, was a great fat Russell's viper, the most venomous snake in India after the krait and the king cobra.

I stared at it, fighting a strong inclination to retreat. But I wasn't going to let the interviewers see me in ignominious flight. Besides I did want to pick a Nilgiri lily again. Reminding myself that Russell's vipers are a sluggish lot that don't move unless they have to, and that snakes (except for the king cobra) don't attack unprovoked, I made a detour, taking good care to test every step in case the viper had any relatives in the vicinity Having picked the lilies I could bear this cautious progress no longer, and returned by a rock-climb up the crag to a chorus of "Oh, Auntie, do be careful." "I am being careful," I snapped, reaching for a better handhold. "I prefer it here to down there." Somehow the lilies survived being held between my teeth like a boarding pirate's cutlass, and were duly admired by the girls, who tucked them in their hair. The only time I have ever seen a snake strike at anyone was when I was climbing Namagundi with Ralph. He must have trodden on the tail of a Russell's viper, as it suddenly reared up and struck him with a whack on the calf. Fortunately, he always wore long canvas boots reaching to just below the knee, and the snake's fangs failed to penetrate. He was quite unmoved by this experience but lacking his moral fibre, I never forgot it.

As we rose to go San Mada turned up. I told him about the Viper and he nodded. "Yes," he said in a matter-of-fact voice. "You would have died or you would have had a thin leg for life." I knew what he meant, having seen Sholigas who, having been bitten by a snake, had tied a tourniquet and left it on too long, resulting in a withered leg. Personally I'd have appreciated a little more concern on my Sholiga friend's part, but reminded myself that the risk of snakebite to a Sholiga is much the same as the risk of crossing a busy road to us.

After all, nobody raises their eyebrows much if you say, "I was narrowly missed by a van today." The interviewers set off to retrace their route to the house: whence they hoped to cadge another tractor ride to the 'lines', the labour village. I had to go back to Attikan, having arranged some interviews of my own there. But first I decided to climb the hill behind the big shola. I have forgotten its name, but it is an attractive mountain, steep enough from the south to constitute a hands-and-feet scramble, and studded with rocks. Approaching its summit from the north I plodded up a narrow strip of rock and grass, part of the fireline enclosing the estates which was burnt yearly to keep out the hot weather jungle fires, which ran between the edge of the shola and the sharp drop on the western side. It was rough and heavy going, and I noticed with surprise, signs of the relatively recent presence of at least one elephant. Funny, I thought, they don't usually come so high in wet weather, and the north-east monsoon has just ended. But no doubt it had its reasons, same as me.

When I was six Ralph gave me this hill for my birthday. I already had an urge to possess hills with interesting shapes which amounted to a kind of personal geomancy, and for a long time I really believed it belonged to me, when in unromantic fact it was the property of the Forest Department. It still had claims on my affection. This hill threw a long spur westward into the valley of the Jagir, and as I stood on the summit looking down I remembered the time my father had taken my children there, aged about seven and five. From the top they had seen a tiger descending the spur. His first thought was that the children would like a closer view of it. There were no second thoughts, about his being unarmed for instance, and lumbered with two tots. He simply plunged downhill, the children sliding and scrambling in his wake. Down at the bottom it was very hot, the grass was long, and the tiger was out of sight. Susan, tough as they come, was disappointed. Simon, always affected by heat, turned white and collapsed. His grandfather had to carry him back for over a thousand feet, while towing Susan by the hand. Nobody offered him any sympathy when they got home.

He didn't have much luck with Simon. Another time he took him, aged about three, for a walk in the shola adjoining the house during the monsoon, forgetting that Simon had a horror of leeches. Trying to prevent the leeches attaching themselves to his boots Simon started to run, tripped, and fell on his face among soggy leaves alive with the rubbery creatures looping purposefully towards him. His screams were so terrible even after he had been picked up that he was hurriedly carried home, still shrieking. Curiously enough, instead of saddling him for life with some grim phobia, this experience appeared to act on my son like aversion therapy in reverse. A week later he came to me beaming. "Guess what I've got in my pocket."

"What have you got?" Illicit matches? Grandfather's sweeties?

He brought out a handful of squirming black objects. "Leeches."

"I don't really think you ought to keep leeches in your pocket," I said dubiously.

"Why not?"

"Well...um...lsn't it rather cruel?"

"No, it's not," he explained with a beatific smile. "They're my friends now." If you can't beat 'em, join 'em.

I sighed. All this was long ago, though it seemed like only yesterday. Simon was grappling with his own children's nightmares these days, and it was time I returned to my duties at Attikan. I left the hilltop, scrambled down between young coffee and cardamoms in the big shola and rejoined the main path, which would take me back to work.

the view from god's hill

On a beautiful sunlit cold-weather morning I was wakened by the call of the jungle fowl to the realisation that a strenuous day lay ahead. First I had to walk over to Honnametti to personally interview two couples there. Many of the questions on my survey forms dealt with intimate issues, and some of the couples who agreed (probably out of curiosity) to be interviewed, nevertheless preferred to confide in me rather than in the young interviewers.

And after that a long day's walking lay ahead. So, up betimes, a hurried packing of the rucksack with fruit and biscuits, parched rice and spiced cashew nuts, filled water bottle, cameras, and the inevitable ballpoint pen, forms and notebook. A hasty 'namaste' to Baswa when he appeared sleepily from the back regions, and then off along the road to Honnametti, rejoicing in the poignant scents of early morning in the hills.

Three hours later, interviews over and coffee and chapattis duly consumed with one of the couples in their staff house below the bungalow, I set off back along the upper path which ran through the top fields of first Honnametti and then Attikan coffee, skirting the shola that ran along the ridge between the hills on which the houses stood. I had avoided this route in the early morning because of bears, but returned by it because it was shorter, wilder, and a source as yet untapped on this visit for recollection of past times.

I walked quickly past Ralph's old office, where the accountant was already busy, and on along the path, with the orchard below me on one side and the cowshed, my mother's pride and Sheila's joy, above me on the other. The cowshed was still in use, housing a few nice animals. In our day the cows were familiar characters with strong, individual personalities, and I remembered those of my childhood with special clarity: Nancy, with an elegant sweep of horn signifying her half-Ayrshire ancestry; big black Daisy; bad-tempered Molly who would sometimes chase us if we met her on the hill; Monica, half-Jersey and sweet of temperament. There were others in supporting roles, but these were the leading ladies.

Beyond it was a small coffee field, in our day known as Paddy's clearing, having been planted when she was born and its proceeds banked for her. Here, among the coffee bushes, were the remains of a building which had housed cart-bulls when we lived at Honnametti. It had once been entered and some of the bulls slaughtered by a remarkable animal which earned itself the title of 'the phantom tiger', as it managed to get away without being seen or heard until the day it was finally dispatched by my father. In the course of a year it killed forty-four cows, buffaloes and cart-bulls, but hardly ever ate them. It had a strange preference for getting into well-protected sheds and only once killed a cow grazing on the hill. When it was finally shot it was covered with scratches from forcing itself through barbed wire into the shed. Once there, it was never satisfied with killing one animal, a most un-tigerlike trait except in the case of a tigress teaching her cubs to hunt. But this animal was a male and worked alone. Like my father, it may have just enjoyed living dangerously, and certainly it enjoyed a prosperous year of breaking, entering and killing beyond the requirements of hunger. Until it made the mistake of returning to its kill a second night, we had begun to regard it as a larger edition of Eliot's Macavity, the Mystery Cat:

'For he's a fiend in feline shape, a monster of depravity...

He's broken every human law, he breaks the law of gravity....'

Crossing the boundary between Honnametti and Attikan estates, the narrow path wound high up through the coffee bushes, just below the strip of shola on the ridge. At the dip between the two hills, a short track led off westward into the shola trees and through them to the open hillside beyond. Here I turned off, to look once more down into the Jagir and to revisit, just for a few minutes, Farewell Rock.

In the old days, before the Punjur road had been built, my grandparents and their friends used to come to and fro from the hills on horseback, their baggage carried by pack bulls, along this track. From the dip or pass between the hills it dropped westward into the Jagir in a series of hairpin bends and continued through the deciduous forest and the foothills to the plateau below, eventually joining the road to Kollepet and Mysore. There it began to descend an outcrop of rock shaped rather like a squatting toad thrust out to overlook the downward path. Here my grandparents came to take leave of departing friends. My own memories of the rock were concerned with childhood walks to it and were associated with a fear of bears. Because of the ever-present danger of meeting a bear and all the warnings ("run away from a bear uphill and from an elephant downhill") ' and cautionary tales about them which conditioned our childhood, they haunted my nightmares until long after I grew up. Then I was actually attacked by a bear and narrowly escaped being killed by it, not in India but in the Cilo Dag mountains of Turkish Kurdistan. This happened about twenty years ago and strangely enough, since then the bear nightmares have ceased.

The environs of Farewell Rock certainly constituted a desirable residential area for bears, with the fig forest nearby and rocky caves up and down the western slopes of the ridge. Ralph had entered one such cave regardless of bears and found in it some ancient artefacts. There was a rusty sword, a curved wooden ceremonial sickle, and some corroded ritual vessels. The Sholiga with him declined to enter the cave, which he said was undoubtedly guarded by an evil spirit, and advised Ralph strongly not to remove the relics. But my father was no more afraid of spooks than of more corporeal threats, and rescued them from their hiding place. "Rather you than me," said the Sholiga, prudently keeping his distance. It would be artistically satisfying to be able to report on a succession of subsequent calamities betokening a curse, but nothing happened. There was another occasion, though, when Ralph had performed one of his unnecessary feats of valour by crawling after a bear into its cave, when he nearly lost his life. Having reached the end of the cave he turned back to find the bear between him and the narrow entrance. But by some miracle the animal decided to give way and retreated down another tunnel with a lack of aggression most unusual in a sloth bear taken by surprise.

From Farewell Rock to Attikan by the upper path was only about a ten-minute walk. Part of it was through a lovely shola, so reminiscent of my childhood with its patch of ladies-slipper plants still growing in the same spot that I felt as if I had been transported back in a time machine, and quite expected to see again the coral snake I had once encountered on the path, with its glossy black back and glowing coral underside. The effect of this déja vu experience was a sudden decision to climb up the fireline beyond the shola to reach the summit of the hill above Attikan bungalow and cast an eye westward once more down its broad westerly ridge.

Once on the top of the broad, grassy, rock-studded dome I looked into the wilds of the Jagir, heard the whistle of a pariah kite, and was suddenly reminded of the time when Sheila and I had once courted trouble down there. In the forties we had a very old Ford jalopy among the estate vehicles, and one day she and I decided on an unauthorised attempt to drive it to the Biligirirangan temple in the western foothills by a forest road, then disused, which started from Kartikerri, our uncle Leonard's estate. We kept the plan to ourselves for fear of veto.

The road had not been repaired for years and we chugged and scraped our way through the young growth upon it, the high clearance of the ancient car preserving its undercarriage from hidden boulders. The wooden bridges across the nullas were full of holes and we bounced madly over them, hoping to get over before they gave way. At last we came to a watercourse where the bridge had already given way, which meant executing a difficult turn before retracing our route. By this time it was late afternoon, the jungle was beginning to fill with long shadows and enigmatic sounds, and we began to feel uncomfortably conspicuous, in the noisy old car as it swished through the grass.

Sheila, who was driving, began to force the pace and this was too much for the Ford. It stalled, fortunately at the crest of a long slope.

When this happened we always had to get out and push, and I was just opening the door when there was a surging commotion in the tall grass beside the track and the earth-shaking uproar of a trumpeting elephant. Sheila punched the starter and slammed the car into gear... and for once that old jalopy fired immediately. We went clattering down the track in a terrible hurry, practically becoming airborne at the bridges, and finally reached home well after nightfall, considerably chastened. Our mother was not pleased with us. Our jaunt, she informed us, had led us into the ambit of a particularly vicious rogue, which had not only taken to seeking out and chasing Sholigas food-gathering in its vicinity, but had recently attacked a forestry cart and torn the driver and his bulls limb from limb. We looked at each other. Suppose the car hadn't started? It didn't bear thinking about.

Within a few years of this episode we were both married and starting a family, but I can't truthfully say we settled down. I'm not sure that I even know what settling down means. In my experience people tend to grow more and more like themselves as they grow older, although some traumatic event may bring to the surface dormant personality traits. I can still see Heather, barefoot and wearing jeans, standing on a chest of drawers to change a light bulb at the age of eighty. And Ralph never 'settled down' or grew up at all.

He had quite a bad time in the war (World War II, that is), but it failed to sober him. One day he and Heather were informed by their Kollepet agents that some large packing cases had turned up at the railhead and could the estate lorry please be sent for them as they were very heavy. When these huge wooden crates arrived at Honnametti they were found to be euphemistically labelled 'officer's kit'. What they contained was loot from the Western Desert campaign. But loot of a peculiarly eccentric sort. Among other things, there were quantities of Italian uniforms, which Ralph presented to the maistries (recruiters and overseers of workers from their own villages) on the estate. And very nice, if somewhat unusual, they looked, swaggering about in military gear, complete with epaulettes and brass buttons.

Another box held Italian signalling flags. "Why on earth did you collect these?" asked Heather, gazing bemused at the piles of green and red pennants. "Clothes for the children," was the smug reply of one who knew he had used forethought. "You're mad," she said, but in the end she did hire a tailor from Kollepet to make up dozens of little shirts and pants from the good strong cotton flags, which were in fact very well received by the estate children. If there was method in his madness where the foregoing items of 'officer's kit' were concerned, there was none in certain other boxes, which turned out to contain not only unlovely souvenirs in the shape of old shell cases, but a number of live hand grenades.

"Ralph, get rid of these things at once," his wife exclaimed, horrified.

"All right," he agreed gleefully. "I will."

And he did. He made a bonfire in the top garden behind his office and spent a happy morning throwing in the grenades one by one, dodging behind a corner of the office wall as each one exploded with a shattering crack. The noise was dreadful and the rest of the household cowered indoors or in the most distant reaches of the garden until the grenades were all disposed of. Everyone also was glad when it was over, but Ralph had a lovely time while they lasted.

In anthropological literature much has been written about the way the men of 'primitive' societies tend to see the female as representing nature, the mysterious and dangerous other that has to be controlled, while the male represents culture. It has been suggested by feminist anthropology that this way of looking at things has become the authorised version because in the past anthropologists were mostly men, who spoke to the men of the societies they studied and therefore failed to take into account — or even discover — the ideas of the women. Certainly when I came to analyse my questionnaire data I was intrigued to find that the most frequent arguments against divorce given by my female respondents was that men have no control over their own uncouth proclivities and need the firm hand of a good woman. These arguments cropped up even in those caste groups where divorce is institutionalised. As one sardonic Upliga woman put it: "What's the point of getting divorced and marrying again? The next one will be just as bad." That our mother's part was that of culture and nurture while our father's was that of nature was an idea that would have been entirely acceptable to the women of Kollepet taluk.

I had to go down to Attikan bungalow to deposit the morning's questionnaire forms before walking on down to the estate. Having done so, I trotted through the fig shola on my way to Yellehottay thinking about the couple who had invited me to breakfast after the interview. He was a quiet Brahman, the only person among all the staff and labourers on the estates who was genuinely interested in the wild and who loved walking for its own sake. His colleagues tolerated his interests as amiable eccentricities, but I had learned to respect him. She had been a lecturer in chemistry at a women's college in Mysore before her marriage, had resigned herself to the loss of her career because her husband loved his job and did not want to leave the hills, and was devoting herself to tutoring their two little boys. They had both married late in life by Indian standards, she because of her training and work and he because his father had died when he was young and left him with several sisters to marry off. It is considered bad form among high caste south Indians for brothers to marry before their elder sisters have been provided with husbands, and the cost of his sister's wedding had meant that he had reached early middle age before he himself could afford to marry. I had enjoyed the interviews with them because they had discussed the questions dispassionately and I found some of their opinions both interesting and enlightening.

But now the problem of high caste petty bourgeoisie had to be pigeonholed. I had reached Yellehottay and my next objective was a visit to a very different, though even more admirable, category of person: my old friend Sholiga Jeddia. Jeddia had been one of my father's best and most trusted shikaris when they were both in their prime. One day when I was about nine years old, Ralph took me on a trip down to the ghat road he had built that ran from the estate through Bellaji gap and down the eastern side of the hills towards the 'tiger country', that stretch of scrub jungle which rolled away eastward from the foot of the Biligirirangan range. This private thoroughfare joined a Forest Department road at a hamlet called Udhatti, and thence it was possible to drive northward to Bangalore via the main town of the adjoining taluk and the mighty Sivasamudram falls of the Kaveri river. With us were Jeddia and two other Sholigas.

I forget why we left the car on the road, to plunge down the hill on foot through very tall grass. Perhaps I had expressed a covetous wish to collect by climbing a rocky knoll called by the Sholigas Kurridi Guday (bear hillock) because among the rocks were deep caves much frequented by bears. More likely I had done no such thing and my father had decided on a whim of his own to take me there, judging this a suitable adventure for a child of tender years. Or, of course, he may have seen a bear moving about the knoll and was unable to resist the temptation to pursue it. Whatever the reason, there we were, pushing our way through the long grass when we practically fell over two bears. Fortunately they chose to rush downhill, expressing their displeasure in a series of grunting roars. They might just as easily have rushed at us instead, the behaviour of sloth bears being unpredictable, except that they do prefer going downhill in a crisis. My father, carrying his rifle, set off after them in enthusiastic pursuit, followed closely by his faithful henchmen, who probably felt safer under the circumstances in the vicinity of a firearm. All of a sudden I found myself alone, unable to see over or through the six foot high grass surrounding me.

I was lost. There were bears about. I could even smell them.

In a distinctly half-hearted manner and near to tears, I began to push through the claustrophobic tussocks in the general direction in which the others had disappeared, although I could not hear their voices. Suddenly there was a heart-stopping rustle ahead, and the long blades parted to reveal the smiling face and curly head of Jeddia, kathi, or curve knife in hand.

"Aiyō, kusu, ba," he said.

Which means, roughly translated, "Dear me, child, come along." Whereat he stuck his kathi into his waistcloth, heaved me up effortlessly, set me astride his hip, and pushed on down the hill, a one-man rescue party, to find the others. They were standing at the mouth of a crevasse-like cave into which the bears had vanished. "Oh, there you are," my father said in mild reproof. "You really must learn to keep up." Forty-five years later, on my first visit to the hills when I returned to do research in the taluk, I walked down to visit the manager of Kartikerri estate, and near the estate office encountered a figure from the past. We both stopped and stared.

"I know that face," I said.

"And so you should," was the dignified reply, "considering I carried you when you were a child." We embraced.

Of course I'd often see him between the time of the bear incident and my parents' retirement from Honnametti. He had been a familiar friend, with his rather simian face offset by a high, intellectual-looking forehead, typically Sholiga in appearance. Like most Sholigas he had changed very little over the years, but he had developed a powerful presence. As a tammadi, a Sholiga priest, he had presided for years over the little Sholiga temple in the shola above Yellehottay, to which my parents had donated a massive stone Baswa, Shiva's bull. After our family had all gone, the new proprietors of Attikan and Honnametti decided to convert the shrine to a devastana of establishment Hinduism and put in a Brahman priest. The ousted incumbent took himself off to a Sholiga podu near

Kartikerri, where he became tammadi of the shrine there. And one night, he and some of his friends went to the Attikan temple and achieved the remarkable feat of removing the heavy stone bull, which he regarded as inalienable Sholiga property given to them in trust, to its new home. He had now retired, full of honour, to a typical Sholiga wattle-and-daub hut near his old Attikan haunts, whence he emerged from time to time to conduct ritual ceremonies or do a little coffee picking, and this was where I went to visit him, taking as a gift the sandals he had requested.

From Yellehottay I walked a little way back along the road we had driven up on the evening of our arrival which ran between the Attikan coffee and the evergreen shola above which enfolded the foot of Katari betta. Turning off along a narrow ferny path I climbed steeply up through the trees for a while to emerge panting into a grassy clearing, a gently sloping curve of downland in the gap between two big hills, Katari betta, which faced Attikan across the deep valley in which lay the estates, and Devera betta, which faced Honnametti. At the top of the slope on my left was the Attikan temple, with a few cattle sheds and dwellings clustered round it. Some distance from it and immediately before me was Jeddia's hut, a neat piece of basket-work thatched with grass and surrounded by a well-swept patch of cow-dunged earth.

He was lying on the ground in front of the hut, sleeping in the sun. I thought of slipping away so as not to disturb him, but as soon as I appeared one of his daughters who had been sitting nearby ran over to shake him awake, and he rose unhurriedly, hands joined in greeting.

"I hope you are well, father," I said when the preliminaries were over and the sandals presented and approved.

"I am old," he replied gravely. "There is nothing left for me now but to wait. I am waiting for your father to call me to join him, and then I will gladly go."

My eyes filled. Tears were never far away when I returned to the Biligiris. This old man, learning that I was anxious to obtain samples of the bark of a jungle tree, the kambi mara , used by Sholiga women as a contraceptive, had recently walked miles in search of it, returning footsore with a bagful. The gift of sandals seemed a feeble return for such staunch loyalty to an ancient alliance. While I now deplore in principle all sport involving the killing of animals, I knew that it was partly the fellowship of danger shared which had united Jeddia and my father in a friendship that lasted beyond death. I could only bow my head in recognition of an expression of constancy and faith before which my own pessimistic mourning was revealed as unenlightened.

After a while we began to speak of other things. On my last visit to the hills I had met an elderly Sholiga who had asked me about my work. When he learned that I was studying the links between caste, marital customs and fertility he told me, laughing, that his son had married four wives in succession and that each one had left him after a short time. Thus he had no children. What did I think of that? I thought it was interesting. Did he know why, I asked, the wives had left? He shook his head and went off grinning, much amused apparently by his son's misfortune.

Now it so happened that this man was Jeddia's father-in-law, though he was no older than his aliya. As Jeddia had once explained to me, he himself had remained celibate during his youth and priestly service. But when he began to grow old and think of retirement he married a young woman, the daughter of his friend. Sholigas say that all old men and women should marry, or at least set up house together, since people need care and company in their old age. In fact, Jeddia's wife produced a family of four so promptly that she had informed me that she now proposed to take 'bark-juice', (brewed from the kambi mara), which she was convinced would henceforth render her infertile. While Jeddia himself was probably past siring any more offsprings, his wife was almost certain to marry again after his death and she felt she had done quite enough childbearing.

Since the young man whose wives kept leaving was thus Jeddia's brother-in-law, I asked as delicately as I could whether anyone knew the reason for these marital fiascos, suspecting impotence, homosexuality or some interesting perversion, though l couldn't imagine why the father should find the whole thing so funny. Jeddia started to laugh in his turn.

"They couldn't stand his mother." (Jeddia's ma-in-law, to be precise.) "And he wouldn't leave her house."

But things were looking up, he told me. The most recent wife had said she would come back to her ex-husband if he would agree to their starting afresh neo-locally (as anthropological jargon has it). This time he had acquiesced and had at last flown the parental nest. The reunited couple were getting on quite well together and the wife was pregnant.

I listened, fascinated. Unlike the high castes, Sholigas don't go in for patrilineal joint families. In fact it is rather the other way, as one form of Sholiga marriage requires the prospective bridegroom to live with and work for the parents of his bride-to-be for some years. No wonder the Sholiga girls, never easily coerced, had objected to living in the household of their husband's mother, who was clearly a possessive and strong-minded lady.

It would have been nice to have spent the rest of the morning sitting on the grass outside Jeddia's hut, listening to his stories. But, as I explained, I had an appointment with a mutual friend, a long way to go before nightfall, and time was getting on. We said au revoir, or rather, I said "Barutane" and he said "Hogi ba" (go and come; the patois equivalent of the more formal "Hog bit banni") and I left him to continue his siesta.

From Yellehottay I had to follow the winding estate road until I reached the turn-off to Bellaji, which crossed the Gundal stream by a bridge just above the top of the Honnametti waterfall. In our day there was a beautiful road from Yellehoua through the shola above and to the east of the estate which was a short-cut to Bellaji. But as it had fallen into disuse and gone back to jungle I had to run the gauntlet of the children at the 'lines', from whose persistent cries of "Photo, photo" I only escaped after considerable expenditure of polaroid film.

Leaving the estate behind at the bridge over the Gundal I walked up the road a mile or so till I came to the huts of the Sholigas who had opted to work on the estate, where San Mada was temporarily staying. The settlement was not far from the Bellaji cattle sheds, at the foot of the little hill where my grandfather was buried. At the top of the hill, in a walled enclosure with a few flower beds kept tidy by the estate, to the credit of the staff, were four monuments: one over my grandfather's grave; another over the grave of a lady who had died at Attikan on a visit to the Biligiris long ago; one a memorial to my grandmother who had died in Mysore; and one more, the latest which I had raised to my father. I had had a stone engraved in memory of my mother, and walked up to the cemetery to see where her memorial could be placed. San Mada came with me, and together we placed a few flowers on the monuments.

"Where do you want to go today?" San Mada enquired as we walked down the hill again.

"Anēri betta, Beltalli betta, Devera betta."

He looked relieved. He had found our last expedition nerve-racking, and so to be honest, had I. Walking unarmed in the jungle was a very different matter from the old days when we went armed for self-protection, mainly against bears and boars. He and I had traversed the semi-circle of hills to the north of Bellaji, a fine continuous ridge with only the dips between the hills filled with shola. The quickest way to the start of the ridge was through a large patch of shola in the hollow of the cirque. But we had no sooner entered its margins when San Mada grabbed my arm and stopped to listen. "What is it?" I whispered. He turned away, beckoning me out of the undergrowth and walked away for about a hundred yards. "Kurridi. Erudu kurridi." He explained there were two bears in the shola, robbing a hive of honey. This accounted for the noises I had heard when he stopped, unidentifiable to me but fortunately not for him. No way were either of us going to enter the shola.

After some argument he agreed to go the longer way round the shola to reach the ridge, and after that unpromising beginning we did have a wonderful day. But not noticeably tranquil because every time we prepared to plunge into a shola filling a dip on the ridge, San Mada began to pray loudly, a prophylactic tactic which may have made him feel more secure but thoroughly disconcerted me. He was probably right to pray. It was a bear-infested area.

From the ridge we had a grand view over to Namagundikan and the nearer precipitous heights of a pointed hill called Sigiwadi, on the summit of which were the remains of a little ancient fort.

My husband, Bob, and I had once walked from Bellaji through the valley between this ridge and Sigiwadi. "Surely we don't need to take a rifle with us," he had said with a touch of scorn when I automatically made for the gun cabinet in the hall before setting out.

Already in love and in no mind to argue, I deferred to his objection and as we got home safely he turned out to be right. But whether or not we needed to be armed, we certainly wished we had been before the walk was over. While we were making our way along a grassy slope with a long strip of shola below us, we became aware of a rhythmic sound coming from the woodland.

"Sounds like somebody sawing wood," Bob remarked with an innocent lack of disquiet.

"It's not a person. It's a panther," I said, walking a little faster.

It was a panther. They make this noise like sawing. While they also growl and roar, this is their own particular sound, like a cat's miaow. We walked on faster and faster but failed to leave the 'sawing' behind. Down in the shola the panther was keeping pace with us, and it stayed with us until we climbed up the hill above to return along the ridge, somewhat subdued.

Curiously enough, my father had the same experience of being accompanied by a 'sawing' panther some years before on Namagundi betta. What the panthers had in mind is a matter for speculation, but there was something uncanny about the experience, like heavy breathing down the telephone.

Today San Mada and I turned our backs on these northern fells and climbed south-eastward, up a long grassy spur armoured with rocky outcrops which took us to the summit of the hill that framed the south side of Bellaji gap. Thence we walked on to the next hill to the south by an old game path which the Sholiga found. Ralph used to encourage the Sholigas to keep the game paths open but this one had been overgrown for years and San Mada had to use his kathi constantly, hacking a way through for us. From this hill we dropped down into a deep valley filled with heavy rain forest, which my parents had named the Silent Valley. It was indeed silent, very still and somehow secret, and the height of the trees gave it the soaring quality of a cathedral. It was full of elephant tracks and droppings, and we proceeded with due caution.

Up again, then, out of the forest and steeply up grassy slopes with views to the east of the great cliff of Marguli betta, a favourite camping ground of my father's. We were now traversing the eastern slope of Devera betta, the forested west face of which confronted

Honnametti bungalow across the valley in which lay the estate. I was curious to see what San Mada would do next, because the summit of Devera betta, the Hill of God, was a particularly sacred Sholiga place, and nobody in our day ever went there for fear of retaliation by sorcery. The other castes greatly feared the tribe's bent for sorcery and this very fear made it a potent weapon. Even my father had only been up there once, sneaking up to take a look when he knew there were no Sholigas about.

Sure enough, San Mada led me round the eastern slopes well below the summit. At last we came to a path which would have led us down again into the shola-filled valley between Devera betta and Katari betta. Here I stopped, suddenly filled with an overpowering desire to visit the summit of Devera betta.

"San Mada," I said hesitantly, "I wish very much to go up there. Will you show me?"

He considered for a moment and then favoured me with his rare smile. "Yes, we will go. But take your shoes off."

Divested of sandals and gym shoes we turned up the hill and climbed, not without a muffled yelp or two on my part, to the flattish top of the sacred hill.

There was not much to see there apart from the view, just grass and rocks and a small shrine like a cairn, but the place felt old. And holy. I sat myself down unobtrusively on a flat slab of rock at a respectful twenty feet or so from the shrine and said a little prayer of my own while San Mada approached it and addressed the deity with a long loud scolding harangue in the archaic Kannada of the Sholigaveru which I was unable to follow. When he had finished we sat together on the rocks and amicably shared the biscuits, fruits and parched rice and nuts which I had brought in my rucksack. After this we turned around to contemplate the wide and rolling prospect of the east. Before us the grassy eastern slopes of Devera betta fell away to a saddle beyond which a long ridge ran up to the rounded summit and plump sholas of Marguli above its beehive-hung cliffs. To our right rose Katari betta, its northern sholas dropping steeply down to the deep valley which divided its eastern slopes from Marguli's precipitous south face. Above them a pair of black eagles soared and dipped, nesting perhaps in a niche of the summit crag, or on the more sombre cliff of Dupabarri a few miles to the south of where we sat. To our left was the green fastness of the Silent Valley and rising above it the tops of the hills we had climbed earlier that day.

And beyond the foot of the hills a flattish expanse of scrub country soon lost itself in a rolling panorama of small hills clad in deciduous forest, leading the eye to the blue ridges of the Baragur range, an uninhabited wilderness in our day, dominated by Ponnachi boli, its big baldheaded northern massif. This had been the Tiger Country, a stretch of jungle enclosing small pockets of cultivation where the villagers endured beleaguered lives, with elephants making inroads into their hard-earned crops and tigers making inroads into their scrawny cattle. (In 1934, over a period of only four months, one hundred and twenty-four cattle from just six of these hamlets were killed by tigers or panthers.) But today the cultivation covered most of the level land and filled the little valleys between the forested folds of the hills.

Over there to the north-east was the Minna valley, to which Ralph had built a cart-track at the villagers' request and made it motorable, thus benefiting himself as well as them with easier access to this happy hunting ground. In our day the Minna villagers had tigers like other people have mice. They were persecuted by them and sent regular deputations to the estate imploring him to go there and dispatch or scare off yet another feline cattle-rustler. I never remember going there without encountering in one way or another a big cat, sleek and glossy on an ample diet of venison and beef. Watching, one warm and sunny day, a tiger stroll regally through the Scrub, unaware of our presence and in no hurry, it struck me that Blake's lines 'Tiger, tiger, burning bright' are strikingly apposite. Tigers in the wild do almost glow with a lambent orange sheen, but in the daylight rather than the night.

There was the time when a cri de coeur from the Minna villagers coincided with the visit of a young army friend bent upon jungle adventure. My father, hoping to satisfy Tony and solve the villagers' problem at the same time, decreed a visit to the valley. Sheila and I, aged about thirteen and fifteen, went along too.

On the first day after our arrival Tony and I were parked in a low tree on the side of a nulla about halfway up the little glen which it drained. The tiger had killed a cow at the foot of the nulla and was said to be lying up there to sleep off its meal during the hot hours of the day. Accompanied by a body of village men as beaters, pounding drums, blowing temple trumpets and clattering bamboo rattles, Ralph and Sheila walked up the nulla, the disgruntled tiger retreating before them.

It passed us, walking slowly through long grass on the other side of the little watercourse, looking as big and burnished as a chestnut horse. Tony, fired, but reckoned without the weight of Ralph's high-velocity rifle. He missed the tiger completely with the right barrel, the kick nearly knocked him off the tree, and I just grabbed him in time as he started to topple backwards. The left barrel never got fired as the tiger had departed, much to my relief. The villagers were not very pleased.

That night another cow was killed, this time by a pair of tigers, mother and nearly full-grown son, which had been decimating the valley cattle for some months. It was Sheila's turn to sit with Tony in a strategically placed tree chosen by Ralph, and mine to stay with our parent. Ralph decided that he and I should sit on the ground on a patch of bare hillside some way up the side valley drained by the nulla, to act as a stop in case the tigers broke back. But pretty soon it was evident that all was not well with the beat. The tigress was suspicious and hostile, as she might well be, and kept stopping to roar defiantly at the noise of drums and shouts moving up the nulla from the kill where the pair had been lying in the shade. Then we heard her make a series of short charges down the nulla. As the beat approached our position, the roars of the tigress and the yells, thumps and rattles of the men mingled in a fearsome din. At the sound of yet another furious charge Ralph, who had been getting increasingly restless, picked up his rifle and stood up. "I must go down to them before someone gets mauled."

l rose obediently and prepared to follow him.

"No, no, not you," he said. "Somebody ought to stay here."

l sat again with reluctance. He turned away down the hill and then stopped, struck by a thought, and bent to pick up some stones. "Here," he said kindly. "If the tigress comes your way, throw these at her. And use the ciné camera. You might get a shot of her." Honour satisfied, he waved cheerfully and set off, to disappear among the trees of the nulla.

If he believed there was nothing unusual about leaving an unarmed teenage lass sitting on the ground in the vicinity of an angry tigress, I felt — upon further consideration — that I could not agree. Naturally it was his duty to protect the villagers, but I would have preferred to have gone with him. The subversive thought crossed my mind that he had been rather irresponsible. If the tigress comes up here and I throw stones at her I'll only attract her attention, I told myself reasonably. So I won't. I clasped my arms round the ciné camera on my knees and awaited events, quietly quaking.

I didn't have to wait long. Just as the outliers of the line of beaters reached me, the tigress gave a shattering roar and charged downstream again amid shrieks and the sound of two rifle shots in quick succession. All the men I could see shinned up the few saplings nearby. As the available trees, such as they were, had thus been pre-empted I stuck perforce to my post on the ground, though not from choice.

Suddenly there was a series of crashes and a tiger, its black and orange coat flaming in the sun, galloped down the hillside on the opposite bank of the nulla. Mother and son, it turned out, had both broken back. Unharmed, I'm glad to say, as Ralph had merely fired over the tigress's head in the hope of turning her. The story had a happy ending even for the villagers, as the tiger pair, justifiably incensed by the goings-on of the day, decided to patronise some quieter village elsewhere and took themselves off.

On another tiger country trip, Sheila and I were with Ralph when he decided to go and look at a solitary tusker in a patch of forest to see if it was indeed the proscribed rogue he thought it might be. "Stay here and wait for me," he adjured us. We sat at the foot of a bamboo clump and waited. And waited. And after a while we could hear the feeding elephant draw nearer to us. No sign of our Daddy. When we could actually hear the heavy foot-falls of the approaching elephant, the tracker loaded the shotgun he was carrying. I knew well enough that to fire a shotgun at an elephant could be literally fatal, but I daren't speak for fear of attracting the tusker's attention. Just then Ralph suddenly appeared from a totally unexpected quarter and whispered, "Come on. Quick." We came on quick with no further urging, and once out of the elephants earshot he informed us with satisfaction that yes, it was the rogue.

In his younger days he found it hard to countenance weakness in others. When we set off with him on our exploration of the Baragurs I was fourteen and Sheila was only twelve. He walked us hard, anything from eight to twenty miles a day over rough country. One evening when we were making for yet another far-flung camp site, Ralph, striding ahead on his long legs, had to keep stopping at intervals to wait for us impatiently (incidentally getting a rest while he did so) before marching on again as soon as we turned up panting. On this occasion Sheila was really tired, and as she trotted up to where he stood waiting she implored him, tears pouring down her dusty cheeks, "Please Daddy, couldn't we stop here and rest a bit?"

He looked at her as if she'd asked to be conveyed in a litter by Nubian slaves. "We could," he replied judicially. "But it's getting dark, as you see, and there's a man-eater about in these parts." He was not making it up. He had been told about the man-eater in the last village we'd passed through, but hadn't considered it worth mentioning till now. Needless to say we went on, having lost any urgent desire to hang about.

Still mulling over past adventures, San Mada and I pointed out landmarks to each other. He told me about his last year with my father, when Ralph had been collecting specimens for the London Natural History Museum. He was over sixty then, and San Mada still a young man, but it had been a good partnership. Halcyon days, as the Sholiga told it in his soft unempathic voice, before old age, a shrinking forest, and latter-day threats to the tribe's identity had come to plague him.

At last we turned to go, retraced our steps to where we'd left our footgear, and wandered slowly downhill into the valley, along the path past Jeddia's hut (but he was out) and on down to Yellehottay, where we arranged to meet again in a few days time. Then we clasped each other's hands between our own for a moment of affectionate farewell, and went our ways, he back to Bellaji and I back up the road towards Attikan bungalow and the evening's homework on the interviewers' forms awaiting me there.

best laid plans...

Tuesday began badly. This would have caused no surprise to the average resident of Kollepet taluk, for whom Tuesday is traditionally an inauspicious day: the day on which people try to avoid such pursuits as getting a haircut, starting a journey, initiating a business deal, or conceiving a child. It didn't surprise me either when I thought about it. Waking up with a nasty headache after a restless night of discouraging dreams was probably the result of sleeping with the bedroom windows shut. There was of course a reason for this unhygienic practice, which I had adopted for the first time on my current visit to Attikan.

The last time I was here, Bob had been with me for a brief reunion with his beloved India, not to mention truant wife. We had slept peacefully with the transom windows above the casement open, as I had always done hitherto, but on the last night before our departure we had made the mistake of putting our food boxes, ready and packed for the morrow's exodus, on the floor of the hall outside the bedroom door. That night, with the house in darkness, long after the generator had been switched off, we were woken by a scrabbling noise outside the window, followed by a thump as something jumped into the room. By the time we had fumbled for our torches and switched them on, the intruder had pattered across the bedroom and was scratching energetically at the door into the hall. Converging beams of torchlight revealed a jungle rat, and we jumped out of bed to chase it out. But that rat didn't want to go out. It wanted to get into the hall. A ridiculous game of hide and seek ensued, and eventually we managed to herd the rat into the adjoining bathroom and to slam the door, shutting it in. We got back into bed triumphantly. Come the morning we would release the rat. Now we could get some sleep.

We had reckoned without the rat's tenacity of purpose. It immediately began a frenzied scratching at the bathroom door accompanied by piercing squeaks.

"Shut up," we yelled.

"Lemme out of here," it yelled back in rat language. "Lemme out, or you'll be sorry."

We were sorry. After enduring about an hour of clamorous protest we could stand it no longer and let it out in desperation. Whereupon it went straight back to the door into the hall and began trying to gnaw its way through to the food boxes, punctuating its efforts with shrill complaints about our lack of co-operation. It went on trying all night. Every time we got up, alternately giggling and swearing, to chase it away, it literally ran rings round us, along the mantelshelf, over the dressing table, under the beds and back to its post to take up its fortissimo labours. By dawn we were exhausted. So too, it seemed, was our visitor. As the first light outlined the windows, the assault on the door suddenly ceased and a small shadow scurried across the floor, up to the transom, flopped down on the outer sill, and vanished. Exit rat.

On my first night back I had heard a scrabbling noise outside just before I fell asleep with an inward snigger at the frustration of the extramural rodent. Since then I had been left in peace, but at this morning's price. It occurred to me belatedly to ask the estate manager to get Baswa to tack some chicken wire over the transom, thus thwarting mini trespassers while permitting the window to stay open. Feeling a bit livelier after several cups of tea and a cold wash, I dressed, ate my ragi porridge, collected a bunch of pink camellias, and set off for Yellehottay via the Manager's office.

At the Honnametti turn-off, which we used to call the Sharp Corner, I met Mr. Lakhani coming up in the jeep and learned that the picnic to which he had invited the interviewers and me for next week was to take place today instead. Could we come before going down to Mullayparthi? Yes, we could, I said. But in that case could he arrange transport for the interviewers to Mullayparthi this evening, as otherwise the double walks might be too much for them? He agreed and explained the reason for the change of plan. When the tappal came last night he had learned that the Kollepet family planning campaigners were to hold a 'camp' at Kartikerri estate on the Wednesday of next week to which the Managers of the estates were asked to send as many people as possible. He handed me an official-looking envelope which contained a personal invitation for me to attend the presentation. Since it was very much in the line of duty to do so, I acquiesced with only a slight sinking of the heart.

We arranged that the picnic party would meet at Yellehottay at noon, in spite of the connotations of Tuesday. The interviewers, it seemed, had already been informed, and nobody was to bring contributions. Mrs. Lakhani and her mother-in-law were making a portable Maharashtrian meal for one and all. So we parted, and I went down to Yellehottay to undertake a little ceremony of my own. I wanted to put the camellias on Subba's memorial.

At one corner of the crossroads, where the old shola road to Bellaji, now abandoned, used to take off, my parents had put up a stone pillar with an engraved tablet in memory of Subba, the head maistry or overseer of Honnametti for sixty years or so. He had been our grandfather's right-hand man and had even been to Europe with him, though he wisely showed no desire ever to repeat the experience. He had held in his arms, as babies, my father, my sisters and me, and my children in turn and managed to avoid dropping any of us.

Subba was a man of honour, strong-minded, reliable and experienced. When my parents were away together it was he rather than the English-speaking 'writer' who was in charge. We all loved him, though the affection Sheila and I had for him was tempered with awe and we were always abnormally meek and unobtrusive in his presence.

A devout Hindu, member of the Naikar caste, a self-respecting cultivator community of Karnataka, he never bothered with the appurtenances of Westernisation beyond wearing the tweed jackets my parents gave him for Christmas from time to time. My memories of him are always in his working gear, with a few days' grey stubble on his otherwise distinguished-looking face, sandalled or barefoot, knobbly knees below khaki shorts or furled dhoti, jacket over collarless shirt, khaki knitted cap on his head, and a long stick like a scout's pole, symbol of a maistry's status, in his hand. He did not often smile but when he did, it was singularly sweet and however scruffy he looked, he carried with him an aura of quiet authority.

Altogether Subba was a man of charisma. He was a wise man too. Once, when he had told my father that he was going to his village where his wife was about to give birth to a child and Ralph had proferred the conventional good-luck wishes for a boy, Subba replied with grave reproof, "You, of all people, should know that whatever its sex the child will be wanted and loved."

Subba died suddenly when my parents were both away. My father told me later how he returned alone and full of grief to the vacuum left at Honnametti by the loss of his old friend. He went to bed that night not only sad but guilty about his absence at the time when Subba most needed him. And then suddenly he saw Subba standing by his bed.

He sat up and said, "But Subba, you're dead."

"Yes", Subba answered quietly. But there was something he had to say. He had died owing my parents five hundred rupees. The money was in a box under his bed in his village house and he wanted my father to have it. Would he please go and look for it? Before my father could speak he was alone again. His friend had gone. Ralph told me he found himself sitting there in his bed, tears running down his cheeks, crying, "Subba, please come back."

In the morning he told himself it had all been a vivid dream. It was true that Subba had died before he was able to repay the loan, but Ralph had no intention of going to the village to demand it back from the bereaved family. And there the matter rested for a few days. Until a letter arrived for my father from a man in Tamil Nadu whose name was familiar because Subba had often spoken of him as a cousin and a great friend.

"Although we never met," the letter began, "I am writing to you because last night my cousin Subba appeared to me in a dream. He was troubled because he died owing you money. The money is in the box under his bed in the village and he wants you to go there and take it."

From the date on the letter it was clear that both dreams had come on the same night. Convinced as he was by this that he had indeed received a communication from the far side of death's frontier, he still couldn't face going to the village himself. So he sent a trusted deputy. But too late. Subba's second wife, a hard-bitten character with a disreputable son by a former marriage, had found the box and gone off with it. Yes, said the neighbours, Subba had kept cash and valuables in a box under his bed, and no, they did not know where the pair had gone. They went unexpectedly in the night and nothing more had been heard of them. And nothing more was ever heard of them. That was the end of the story. It could all have been a remarkable coincidence of course, but my father never thought so.

Now, obeying the morning's impulse to lay them on the memorial that day, I carried my sheaf of waxy pink flowers and dark shiny leaves to Yellehottay. To my surprise when I got there, I found Mada maistry, the present head maistry of Honnametti and Subba's son by his first marriage, with his wife carrying out the customary 'thi thi' ceremony performed by Hindus on the anniversary of a father's death. I hadn't realised that this was the day. The surprise was mutual. Feeling a little uncomfortable, I laid my offerings on the stone, stayed with them for a while and then crept away. For some reason I had never developed any rapport with Mada maistry, still less with his rather formidable wife, and our relationship had never progressed beyond polite pleasantries although Mada was very like Subba in appearance. He was quite a personality in his own way, but nothing like Subba in character.

Neither was his son, an extroverted entrepreneur who owned a bus which he drove regularly when it was in a roadworthy — or nominally roadworthy — condition to Kollepet and back. The bus replaced the old tappal runners and was a great boon to the estate workers. I often had recourse to it during my years of research and never failed to regret it. Fears of such minor highway hazards as elephants faded into insignificance as the ramshackle vehicle hurtled round the bends of the ghat, outer wheels skimming the edge of the abyss, or overtook another vehicle on a blind corner of the Coimbatore-Kollepet road. Perhaps the driver, a man of steel in his career (appropriate word), learned from his other passengers that I was a woman of straw who prayed with closed eyes and whitened knuckles all the way from Yellehottay to Lokkanhalli or vice versa, and had informed his parents of the fact. In this respect, as in many others, I fell far short of being my father's daughter. As passenger, Ralph was nerveless. As driver, by the same token he was almost as unnerving as Mada's son.

The picnic went well, even hilariously. Followed by stoic estate employees charged by the Manager with the task of carrying the grub, the Lakhanis, the interviewers and I walked from Yellehottay to the grassy saddle overlooked by the Attikan temple. Thence we followed the many-stranded cattle track which carved a way up between tree roots and boulders through the shola on the west side of

Katari betta, to cut diagonally across the grassy flank of the hill above the cliffs till it faded out on the summit ridge. From there it was a fairly easy walk up the moderate slope to the summit cairn.

Although the highest point of the range, the top of Katari betta like Honnametti Kalu and the top of the hill behind Honnametti bungalow, had become domesticated territory. Approached by a not particularly strenuous walk from the estate, it was frequented from time to time in the 1970s and 1980s by cattle and their herders, occasionally by members of the estate staff bent on al fresco entertainment, and commonly by me aspiring to a little solitary exercise in the course of my working days at Attikan. For the interviewers, of course, and for beautiful Mrs. Lakhani in her filmy sari, the ascent, and even more so the descent, was a real adventure. And it was fun. The food was delicious. The company was good. We laughed a lot and pointed out to each other Honnametti bungalow, pinned like a brooch to the breast of the opposite hill, the green policies of Attikan and, looking eastward, the site of the estate ragi fields. Mr. Lakhani, an amusing raconteur, told the others of the epic day when he and I had walked to the ragi fields and back. It was in the first year of my return to the hills, when the eastern ghat road, approached through Bellaji Gap, was still disused, breached in several places by landslides. At that time, it was a Sabbath day's journey by motor vehicle to reach the ragi fields: down the Punjur ghat, southward to Hassanur and then back northward along the eastern foot of the hills. On this occasion the jeep was out of order or something. Or maybe the Punjur river was in flood. So we arranged to walk, Mr. Lakhani and his strapping assistant, me and my young assistant and some recruited Sholigas. All would have been well if Mr. Lakhani had not chosen to divulge to me just as we were setting off, that Mada maistry's comment on this expedition had been, "She'll never make it." Whereupon, possibly blinded by fury, I tripped, fell heavily, and hit my knee agonisingly on a stone. Everyone picked me up and urged me to go home and nurse the injury. But what I was already nursing was an enraged determination to prove the maistry wrong. Gritting my teeth with a fortitude born of this unworthy purpose, I brushed off their well-meant advice and soldiered on, insisting that I was quite all right.

We walked down the long, steep valley between Katari betta, Devera betta and Marguli, three thousand feet to the foot of the hills, then northwards to the fields and then on Udhatti at the foot of the breached ghat road. Here Mr. Lakhani, who was recovering from a sprained leg and beginning to feel it, suggested that he and I should take the daily bus, then due, to Hassanur, and another bus the next day to Punjur, where we would be met by some form of estate transport.

"You go," I countered with manic obstinacy. "I'm going to finish the walk."

This really left poor Mr. Lakhani with no option but to walk back too. It came to twenty-two miles with six thousand feet of descent and ascent. The assistants' complaints of tiredness were received by their limping employers with a certain lack of sympathy and it was a morose and taciturn party which arrived back at Honnametti that night. The next day my knee was swollen to monstrous proportions. It took a year to recover completely.

Whether or not Mada maistry ate his words with due repentance I never discovered, but at the Katari betta picnic, Mr. Lakhani had the others rolling on the grass with his tale of our misadventures. The picnic over, and Mrs. Lakhani, Manjula and Ramani assisted down the hill, we went our separate ways. The interviewers planned a siesta before the evening's visit to Mullayparthi, and I intended to skive off on a little ploy of my own. To climb the Honnametti waterfall.

I had done it years ago with Bob, my husband. It was only climbable in the dry weather. During the monsoons the flooded Gundal stream boiled over the hundred feet or so to fall in a roaring spate of white water which could be heard all over the estate. It was an impressive sight then, if you didn't mind the leechy approach. But by now the flow would be confined to the middle of the drop and the rock on either side should 'go', as climbers say.

About half a mile down the main estate road from the lines, a subsidiary track turned off to the Honnametti pulp-house. This consisted of a tall building built on two levels. At the top was a large flat area where, in the crop-picking season, the baskets of ripe red coffee berries were brought to be weighed and measured and then poured down a chute which connected with the pulping machinery on the lower level. Water from the nearby-stream was conducted through the machines, which discharged a mixture of pulpy skins and skinned beans into a series of concrete tanks where the beans were separated from the floating pulp, washed and re-washed. The cleaned beans were then spread out to dry in the sun on the long drying 'tables' set up on both levels until they reached the stage of silvery-yellow dehydration when they were deposited in vast heaps in a high storage shed prior to being transported for further processing in the coffee-curing works in Coimbatore. The pulp was carried to various sheds strategically placed about the estate, where it settled down, stinking of silage, to form an excellent organic manure. This was an exciting time for Sheila and me when we were small because we were allowed to play in the heaps of dried coffee beans. We would climb to the top and jump down to land in the silky yielding embrace of the shifting beans. Or we would roll down. Or bury each other. It was like a cross between a hayloft and seaside sand dunes, and to us one of the greatest treats of the year. The time I remember best was the year the Maharaja of Mysore came to stay with us, and was taken to see the pulp house in action. Shown into the storage shed where we were shrieking and cavorting in a great bean heap, he smiled indulgently and when we were extricated to be introduced, patted our tousled heads while we smirked coyly at him. This was in our eyes the real thing, a proper kingly visit, totally unlike that of the poor shabby British Collector of Coimbatore. The Maharaja arrived at Honnametti with a retinue of aides and servants. Grand tents were pitched on the lawn to provide His Highness's own kitchen and extra accommodation for his staff. The drawing room was converted into his puja room (private chapel), so the verandah became the centre of social activities. It was all tremendously exciting and we revelled in the royalty bit to the depths of our snobbish little souls.

In fact, that Maharaja was a truly good man. A devout Hindu, he headed a triumvirate of which the other pillars were his upright Muslim chief minister, Sir Mirza Ismail, and his equally high-principled British adviser, Sir Charles Todhunter. Together they transformed Mysore into both a modern and a model State where people of various creeds and colours co-existed tolerantly. That is, until the Christian community, with remarkable arrogance and lack of foresight, chose to build a cathedral in the Muslim quarter. When the spire of the cathedral overtopped the minarets of the mosque the Muslims, equally bigoted, erupted into violence and set fire to it. But such a riot was rare. Mysore was a peaceful State then, prosperous, well-run and beautiful. Its cities were garden cities, and everyone loved the honest and unpretentious prince Krishnaraja Wadiyar.

These reminiscences lasted me while I descended from one level to another of the pulp-house complex, slithered down a steep earthy slope thickly planted with cardamoms, and battled through the undergrowth and fallen branches of the strip of shola on the estate side of the stream. Across the water the hillside rose steeply, heavily forested with sub-tropical vegetation and tall trees. Walking upstream was difficult, impeded by fallen trees, spiny rattan canes and strobilanthus, but eventually I reached the foot of the fall and looked up. As I'd expected, the volume of water had been reduced by dry weather so that it plunged down the middle of the scarp, leaving a tempting series of dry rock walls, slabs and ledges above me. With a surge of pleasurable anticipation I began the ascent. All went well and enjoyably until I reached a narrow ledge about half-way up. The wall immediately before me was smoothly water-polished, but to its right it was more broken, affording holds for hand and foot. A deep horizontal crack afforded the first foothold, and into this I thrust my right foot, shod in canvas gym shoe. The result was startling. With a loud hiss and an explosion of movement a large, gaudy snake shot out of the crack on to the ledge, while I nearly fell off backward in surprise. The snake and I looked at each other. Neither of us liked what we saw. Furthermore, there was no room on the ledge for both of us to carry on with our affairs without discommoding each other.

I didn't know whether or not the snake was poisonous. Many, if not most, water-snakes are. I had seen a couple of smaller ones of the same sort near streams in the past few years, and as I could not remember ever seeing this kind in the old days, I had described it to a herpetologist friend. But as he was unable to identify it from my report of stripey green body and viper-shaped head with orange patches, the issue was still in doubt. Meanwhile here we were, both indignant, the snake justifiably so since my invasive foot had intruded where it was minding its own business, and both debating our next move. Now that the crack was presumably vacant, I thought about replacing my foot and going on with the climb. There were two things against this move. First it meant practically nudging the already worried snake before stepping over it. Secondly, the wise climber likes to be sure of being able to reverse a move or series of moves should further upward progress prove impracticable. Reversing the next few moves would entail returning via the snake's crack and ledge.

"You've spoilt my fun, you silly thing," I said unfairly. "I'd better try to go down. If I can." With infinite care I lowered myself backward off the ledge, feeling for the little finger and toe holds by which I had ascended while keeping a careful eye on the shiny coils of the handsome victor of our battle of wills. A few breathless minutes later I was back on a lower ledge and, acknowledging ignominious defeat, set about reversing the rest of the climb. After which I took myself off back to work, indulging en route in self-commiseration over the undue amount of snake trouble encountered during the past few days.

It was time to take the road that followed the Gundal stream all the way down to Mullayparthi at the northern tip of the estate and get on with my job. By the time I arrived the interviewers, conveyed by jeep from the 'lines', were ready to start. We found a few couples who were warily willing to submit to our long boring questionnaires, and we in our turn listened with grateful patience to our respondents' views on the issues raised by our inquiries. Many of them, especially the women, found in these sessions an unprecedented opportunity for airing grievances and opinions to a sympathetic audience, which meant that it was never possible to estimate with any accuracy the duration of each interview.

But at last it was over for the day. I said goodnight to my young friends and accepted an offer from the jeep driver of a lift to Attikan from the labour village later that evening. Then I walked on quietly and alone down the Gundal valley along the track through the tall creeper-hung rain forest, almost dizzied by the volume of the birdsong. A troop of grey langurs with silky tassled tails whooped through the branches, and a beautiful auburn-coated Malabar squirrel with contrasting creamy underside paused in its airy progress to regard with a bright eye the pedestrian stranger-below.

The jungle around me, still and secret, though by no means silent, filled me with a sense of the numinous as I looked up mm the green canopy of those towering trees. This was the forest primeval, where time gave way to eternity, and I was part of it. I wanted to hold and possess the moment forever, but as the light began to fade and the birdsong to die away, the aspect of the forest slowly changed. My heart began to beat a little faster and I found myself glancing back over my shoulder. Time to disengage from communion with nature and to walk back towards civilisation in the form of the jeep, a bath and the fireside at Attikan.

rogues' gallery

A few days of resolute endeavour had completed over half the sessions required by the survey for the Sholiga group. Most of these were achieved either at the Honnametti 'lines', where Sholiga couples who had moved to Bellaji for temporary work on the estate came to buy subsidised grain from the shanti there; at Bellaji itself, where there was a shifting population of Sholigas from outlying podus; or at Mullayparthi in the Gundal valley close to the northern end of the estate. The latter site necessitated a longish walk for me and cadged lifts for the interviewers. Although my friendship with some of the older tribespeople was often productive enough of new qualitative data, it was the quantitative variety collected from the questionnaires, raw material from which a wealth of statistics could be hewn, for which my paymasters thirsted.

Now, except for a few more couples at Mullayparthi and a small group at a fairly isolated podu called Nellikatherahatti near the foot of Namagundi betta, which was San Mada's home ground, we had nearly finished with the Sholigas accessible from Honnametti. Our attention would shortly have to be directed to the big podu near Kartikerri, one of the three lower estates. This would mean a move on the part of the interviewers, as the podu was at least seven miles from Honnametti and my expectations of them did not include a daily walk of fourteen miles, the return part of it uphill all the way. I had received the Kartikerri Manager's permission to rent them accommodation in the house of a bachelor clerk on that estate, whence it was not far to the podu. For myself I hoped that the walk there and back, down and up the old tappal path from Attikan, would effect a state of gratifying fitness.

It seemed a good idea, therefore, to combine another Monday off on the hills in San Mada's company with the Kartikerri Manager's open invitation to lunch with him at his house to discuss details of the move. I decided to walk with San Mada southward along the eastern ridge of the range from Katari betta to Dupabarri, and then to drop down to the main estate road in the deep valley between the two main ridges, whence the Sholiga could return at leisure to Bellaji while I went on to Kartikerri.

From the top of Katari betta, the highest summit of the range, our westward view was bounded by the ramparts of the central ridge just across the valley wherein lay the estates of Honnametti and Attikan, each falling away from the watershed of Yellehottay, while to the east, long slopes led the eye down to the rolling landscape of the plateau country. But to the north and to the south a tumble of big hills, green sholas, golden grass and dark rocky outcrops stretched away into the distance. Those to the north were dominated by the heights of Namagundi betta, rising over the lower cirque of those hills where San Mada had prayed so fervently for deliverance from bears, to dwarf the rocky crown and tremendous cliff of Sigiwadi. We paused by the summit cairn, gazing once more at the long green groove of Hoolpatchyhulla descending from the mossy fastness of Namagundikan, and at the marginally lesser heights that clustered round Namagundi and thrust out spurs and ridges that screened glens and hollows which had been the scene of so many dramas long ago when we were young.

I pointed to the saddle of Kappali Kanave, where Ralph with Sheila (on a visit from America and heavily pregnant), once watched two other mothers protecting their young: a tigress with cubs and an elephant with her calf, circling warily round each other, trying to avoid a confrontation on a game path before they continued on their legitimate ways. San Mada nodded. "There are still tigers up there," he said, "and a great many elephants. It is even more dangerous to go there now than it was in the past. We don't go there any more." That part of the Biligirirangan hills used to attract not only sick and solitary bison but also solitary bull elephants and indeed, according to San Mada, this was still the case.

At one time my parents had a permanent camp, consisting of a few wattle and grass huts, by the clear waters of the Hoolpatchyhulla. One day they left the camp to walk the hills accompanied by two Sholigas and Heather's dog, a cocky Irish terrier called Peter. They were out longer than they had intended, and it began to get dark as they made their way back. They stopped at a nulla — a watercourse — to light a lantern. Ralph had a .375 Mauser with him, while one of his shikaris carried his .450 high-velocity rifle. Absent-minded as usual, he put the Mauser down and picked up the heavier rifle when they moved on again, leaving the .375 behind.

As they approached the camp, tired and leech-ridden, expecting to see through the trees the welcoming glow of camp-fire lit by the Sholigas remaining at the site, they were surprised to see nothing but darkness. They and the Sholigas with them called the others by name, "Bomma, Ranga, Nivu elliddare?"

Whereupon there was a cry, apparently from the top of a tree in the vicinity of the camp: "Don't come, don't come."

"Go back," cried another tree-borne voice. "The elephant is in the camp. He came very angry and we had to run. He is pulling down the huts and trampling on them."

Sundry sounds of demolition in the darkness ahead confirmed this information. My parents' party stopped to assimilate it, and were discussing in whispers their next move when the decision was taken from them. Peter the dog suddenly became aware of the unauthorised havoc on his territory. Without warning he streaked off into the gloom to bay the rogue. This added a new and undesirable element to the confusion. They could see very little in the starlight but they could hear Peter barking and the rogue screaming with rage — that awesome squeal of an angry elephant. Now Peter had once before driven an elephant out of a camp, an innocuous looker-on whose precipitate departure had given him a false sense of his own ascendancy. But this time a rapid reassessment of the situation prompted him to come scurrying back for protection to my parents. With the rogue in purposeful and noisy pursuit. Heather snatched a box of matches from her pocket, and they feverishly tried to set fire to the damp grass around them, while Peter crouched trembling against their legs with a "don't-just-stand-there-do-something" whimper.

A few seconds later the great bulk of the elephant emerged out of the dark, ploughing through the long grass towards them. Ralph lifted his rifle and began to fire shot after shot over his head, and at the last moment it suddenly changed its mind, veered off and went thundering away into the night.

While the party ruefully surveyed the wreckage of the camp Ralph asked, "Who's got the .375?"

"You left it in that nulla," Heather said, remembering.

The next day they went to fetch the rifle, but the elephant had got there first and smashed it to bits. It had then gone on, met a poor wretched stray cow and crushed her to death.

As soon as this rogue was duly proscribed after further acts of unprovoked mayhem, Ralph went after it accompanied by a friend, stalked it, and shot it. But a few years later its place was taken by a second rogue which began to terrorise this part of the hills. It trampled to death a Sholiga working in his podu, a woodcutter collecting fuel, and then two Sholiga brothers gathering lichen in the jungle. From the camp at Hoolpatchyhulla my father sought it out and disposed of it.

The third rogue, based at Dodsampagi in the valley at the foot of Namagundi betta, first waylaid a Sholiga father and son and tore them apart, following this horrific assault by a course of systematic destruction, raiding podus and charging the Sholigas who tried to drive it away.

At this time our friend Salim Ali, the ornithologist, was staying at Honnametti. One day he and Ralph set out at dawn to tramp the slopes of Namagundi, photographing bison and trying to get a specimen of the streaked grasshopper warbler, a tiny elusive bird living among grass stems. As they descended the hill in the evening on their way home, they met the rogue. They had reached a grassy amphitheatre crossed by strips of shola and were about to enter the first when a Sholiga burst panting out of it and made for them, gasping "Āne āne." He had been crossing from Bellaji to his podu in the Gundal valley when he encountered the rogue, which immediately gave chase. Moreover, he said, the night before it had entered their banana grove and wiped it out, including the watchman's hut, which it trampled underfoot, the watchman having leapt for safety as it advanced.

Since the rogue now appeared to be bestriding their path home and the light was beginning to fade, Ralph loaded his rifle, Salim held his camera at the ready, and they proceeded with caution, hoping to make a detour round it unobserved and get a picture of it while they did so. The Sholiga, not unnaturally declining to accompany them, borrowed a torch and hastened off to make a much wider detour back to his podu. Within half a mile they suddenly saw the elephant ahead, looking like a great grey rock in the middle of the amphitheatre where the single-file path intersected it. My father's practised eye caught a flick of its ear, and he whispered, "There he is."

The terrain on either side consisted of tall grass concealing boulders and little gullies. Not the best country in which to escape a determined pursuer in poor light. Ralph decided to try to bluff the elephant into moving off the path. Accordingly he fired in the air while they shouted in unison. Elephants are short-sighted but have an excellent sense of smell. This one had not yet seen them, but as soon as it heard the noise it lifted its trunk and began to 'take the wind'. Suddenly wheeling, it moved behind a small hummock, and they were just about to make a dash for safety while it was out of sight when it reappeared and began to close up on them.

In a few minutes it would be too dark for my father's rifle to afford much protection. He was slowly raising it when the oncoming rogue, still confused by the wind, again veered off, weaving back and forth in its efforts to locate them. This was their opportunity, and they hurried along the track as quietly as possible. Looking back after covering a hundred yards or so they could just see the elephant quartering the ground at the spot where they had been standing a few minutes earlier.

This was not Ralph's last encounter with the Dodsampagi rogue. He was to have one more. A few weeks after it had hunted him and Salim that evening as they returned from the hill, he was walking with a shotgun in the Gundal valley along a game path through heavy evergreen forest, accompanied by a Sholiga carrying his rifle. Their minds were on jungle fowl and wood pigeon as 'food for the pot', and the rifle was only there in case of emergency, the way we always took a rifle along if we went far into the jungle. The wisdom of this habit was demonstrated that morning. As they were walking peacefully along they were startled by a strident trumpet, and out of the bushes ahead charged the rogue, meaning business. With great presence of mind the Sholiga thrust the rifle into Ralph's hands before running for his life. My father just had time to fire first one barrel and then the other at the head of the oncoming monster as it reached him, and the Dodsampagi rogue fell dead, almost at his feet.

From the top of Katari betta we walked southward down the ridge and into a shola which filled the gap between that high summit and the next hill on the eastern ridge. As we came out of the greenery into the open a scuffling and rustling in the undergrowth brought us to a halt, wondering what might appear. What did appear was a small foxy disembodied face which eyed us rather reproachfully and then vanished again in the manner of the Cheshire Cat. I thought for a moment that it was a young wild dog, but San Mada, laughing, said it was his own dog, which must have followed him from Bellaji. I asked him if there were still wild dog packs in the hills, and he replied yes, there were some, but like all the other animals except for bears, elephants, pigs and porcupines, their numbers had dwindled.

In our day the ecological niche, shared in north India by the Indian wolf and the dhole or red dog, was in the Biligirirangan hills entirely filled by these red dogs, almost as large and sturdy as Alsatians. They were a force to be reckoned with. Although they mainly hunted deer and never bothered people on the hills (except in the dreadful days of the rabies epidemic), most other animals tried to avoid a wild dog pack. A Sholiga told my parents how he and some friends had once come upon a pack surrounding a tiger eating its (the tiger's) sambhar kill. The tiger, growing uneasy as the circle of dogs closed in, jumped up on a boulder, whereupon the dogs fell upon its dinner. This was too much for the tiger, which launched itself at the dogs. But as it sprang they rushed in and disembowelled it. Having killed the tiger they set about eating it, abandoning the dead sambhar. They went away when their hunger was satisfied and when they were safely out of sight, the Sholiga witnesses helped themselves to the carcass of the deer.

When we did occasionally come across them in our day, the dogs ignored us and we were never afraid of them; but it was distressing to hear the cries of hunted sambhar and barking deer. This was one jungle sound I was happy to do without. Today the remaining dogs must live principally on the wild pigs, since deer are relatively scarce and in the process of being hunted to extinction (in spite of, or even because of the area being declared a wildlife sanctuary) by that far more dangerous predator, man.

From this little shola we emerged on to the steep face of the next hill, up which we plodded in the growing heat of the morning sun. At the top of the hill was a big shola, quiet and secretive, with soaring trees but also with a thick undergrowth of strobilanthus through which we had to push our way with considerable effort. I was glad to come out of its claustrophobic depths on to a rocky hog's back which led us in time to another but more friendly patch of rain forest and out of that upon a flat saddle or col upon which stood the ruins of my great-uncle's shooting lodge, which had been destroyed by a forest fire. This was Dupabarri bungalow, built by my grandfather's brother Charles (my father's Uncle Chas) who had owned Gorrayhutti, the first of the three lower estates, had died there, and had been buried on the col of Dupabarri. After my parents left Honnametti, Ralph had bought Dupabarri and had lived there when he had returned to the hills to collect for the London Natural History Museum.

North of the grassy level on which we now wandered around, looking at the ruins of the little house, finding the spring from which its occupants had drawn water among the trees behind it, searching for my uncle's grave, rose the sombre escarpment of the Dupabarri cliff, nesting place of black eagles. To carry on southward along the ridge it would be necessary to circumvent the cliff, but there was no time for this today. Instead we walked slowly eastward for a few hundred yards until we happened upon the headstone and small neglected grave we sought. Here we stopped to pay our respects to the old man who lay there in the place he had loved.

Then we moved forward again until we came to the edge of the saddle, and here we sat down on the grass to enjoy the prospect before us. Long steep grassy slopes fell away from us towards the eastern foot of the hills, merging as they descended into scrub jungle. As the land levelled out three thousand feet below us, an apron of cultivation was revealed. No more than twenty years ago this had consisted of little patches like islands in a sea of thorny scrub and bamboo, where the inhabitants of a string of tiny hamlets along the foot of the hills led a precarious existence, harried by the animals which found their fields and flocks a rich source of nourishment. Directly beneath us was the hamlet of Bailur, still no more than a few meagre fields and a crumbling forest bungalow. It was here that Ralph had been chased round and round the thorn bushes and bamboo clumps by an elephant when Sholiga Punjur Eera had decamped with his rifle.

North of Bailur the cultivation patches at the foot of the hills, which today tended to merge with one another, included those owned by Honnametti estate. During World War II my parents had acquired this land near two settlements called Yerragabalu and Uginimulay so as to grow the millet ragi, the local staple cereal, for the estate workers at a time of food shortages. Herds of elephants converged appreciatively on this heaven-sent new source of fodder. Protective earthworks in the form of banks and ditches were deliberately and patiently trampled down, and the shouts of watchmen treated with contempt or confrontation. These fields had long ago been abandoned by the local people for this very reason, and the future of my parents' food programme hung in the balance. The introduction of electric fences had some effect but even so, a large male would often rush the fence, tearing up the posts and short-circuiting the current.

As Ralph was in the habit of pointing out to villagers harassed by elephants, crop-protection guns were really counterproductive because the injured and angry elephants only became more dangerous. The difficulty was to suggest an alternative, since raiding herds had scant respect for the cries and drum-beating of watchmen in the fields, and a family's entire subsistence for a year could disappear in a night when their field was entered by a herd.

This was when Ralph invented his harmless rocket-gun, which proved most effective. It consisted of a piece of metal tubing through which a firework rocket could be fired horizontally at the encroaching herd to frighten it off. He tried it in our ragi fields with great success, enjoying himself immensely. The herd fled out of the field with mystified and indignant squeals, their morale considerably shaken. Ralph became a keen proselytiser of this simple solution and was pleased to see it fairly generally adopted. On that first occasion, however, the elephants had the last word. They found Ralph's picnic basket, left outside the field, and trampled it flat in retaliation.

Beyond this first level stretch we looked across the blue hummocks of small hills crowned and buttressed with rock to the bluer line of the Baragur range. In May and September east (and west) of the Biligiris you can watch the thunderstorms marching like armies across the plateau country, transforming the dry nullas into instant rivers in roaring spate.

The tiger country, though hot and dry compared to the

Biligirirangan range, had its own arid beauty. From the foot of the hills it flowed eastward as rolling park-like terrain composed of glades of short, parched grass between clumps of bamboo, lantana thorn with its drifts of pink, orange and white flowers, and the bristling terralobia indica shrub with its wicked thorns. Between the scrubby growth there were stretches of open 'maidan' covered with a knee-high leguminous plant which the Sholigas called koggi gidda. Sandalwood grew in this jungle too, though it may be poached out now due to its inflated value and refusal to grow to order as a cash crop. Bigger trees thrived along the banks of nullas, among them a smooth-barked variety known locally as nir mutti which had a special attraction for tigers. In our day the marks of tigers' claws could be seen on them up to the height of about twenty feet.

All that country was once as populated as it is now and though in our day it had gone back to jungle, it was — still is — full of antiquities, including carved memorial slabs and prehistoric stone circles containing swastika-shaped stone-lined graves. The Sholigas who live there differ from the Biligirirangan tribe, calling themselves Yerl kula (seven clan) people as opposed to the Eid kula (five clan) kad averu, forest people of the high hills. They believe their countryside was once inhabited by a race of tiny people whose ploughs were drawn by hares. The koggi gidda were their tamarind trees, which they climbed with twelve-rung ladders, and the stone graves their houses. When my father asked how such small people managed to move such big stones, the reply dismissed the problem. "Oh, that just shows what clever little people they were."

Several of the rogue elephants which my father dispatched, taking blood-curdling risks in the process, had beset villagers around the foot of the Baragurs. The stories of these exploits deserve a book to themselves, but I shall confine myself to one in particular that came vividly to mind as San Mada and I breakfasted on fruit and parched lentils at Dupabarri and contemplated the distant range.

I remembered this rogue because I met him. He had been terrorising a place called Makanapalayam for some time, and had developed the habit of waiting in ambush beside the main path to the village with the sole purpose of waylaying and killing people. After several horrific deaths the headman sent an urgent message to my father at a time when my parents had two friends staying who had some experience of shikar. It was decided that they would all go to

Makanapalayam, taking Sheila and me along as well.

As soon as we arrived at the decaying forest bungalow, infested, as so many were, with termites and scorpions, we were told that the elephant was grazing in a hollow in bamboo jungle not far from the village. To make sure it was the right elephant my father decided to go and take a look at it that evening, followed by our shikaris and a justifiably nervous villager. When we reached a ledge of rock overlooking the hollow we saw the elephant feeding in the bamboo forest below. It was the rogue all right. We turned to go, and as we did so my father felt the wind shift and saw the questing lift of the elephant's trunk.

Feeling uneasy with so many hostages to fortune around he signalled to us to leave quietly. Which we did to the best of our ability but not very successfully, as the dry bamboo leaves crackled at every step. Our caution delayed us, and the remaining daylight began to fade fast. At one point we stopped to get the big flashlight out of its case only to find that the bulb had gone. Another delay ensued while the Sholigas tied bunches of bamboo stems together and lit them to form makeshift torches.

Through the gathering dusk, lit by the flickering gleams of torchlight, we hurried on without speaking, out of the bamboo now, moving through an area of thorn scrub and open glades. As we entered one such glade my father, still on the que vive, heard a twig snap behind us.

"That's the rogue," he said with certainty.

Shikaris and villager melted away into the darkness. The three armed men turned around to face the direction from which we had come. Mummy, Sheila and I looked round for a friendly tree and, finding none but low thorny acacias, moved into the shadow of the nearest.

As we did so a huge shape came silently out of the bushes.

And charged.

The three rifles roared together, flashes of flame from their muzzles piercing the darkness, and the elephant fell dead within a few feet of us.

It had been stalking us so noiselessly through the dry forest that it would have caught and slaughtered some or all of us if it had not been for my father's sixth sense and quick ear. I don't remember feeling frightened. It had all happened too quickly for thought.

Had San Mada heard these stories? Yes, he replied, before he became my father's chief shikari he had heard them all from older men. But things were better then, he added pointedly, because at least the Dorai was armed. Grasping his drift I pointed out that at least we were about to return through the estates instead of retracing our steps over the hills and through the sholas, and suggested that we should try to descend by the old approach road to Dupabarri bungalow, now more or less overgrown. He seconded this with some relief, and we walked down to the coffee-filled valley by less adventurous ways. But we did find fresh tiger droppings on the Dupabarri track.

Lunch with Mr. Coates, the kindly Anglo-Indian Manager of Kartikerri estate, was very pleasant. The charming principal bungalow at Kartikerri was now empty and forlorn. It had belonged to my father's uncle Leonard, warm-hearted and funny like his nephew Ralph but unlike him a canny businessman, with interests that kept him an absentee owner for much of Sheila's and my youth. Mr. Coates lived alone (except for school holidays when his wife and children joined him from Mysore), in a pretty little house nearby, built in the same style as the old bungalow with a roof of curly red Mangalore tiles and a well-kept garden in front. He complained that sambhar and barking-deer (muntjac) constantly raided his borders and though I sympathised with the problem, it was nice to know that there were still enough sambhar in the vicinity of the estate to be a nuisance.

We talked so long over lunch that it was getting late by the time we parted. Our conversation, moreover, had included an exchange of bear stories, as Kartikerri, like Attikan, was a great place for bears. I told him how my uncle and his wife, driving home one evening, had encountered two bears which rushed down a bank above the road and set about their car, leaving it badly scratched and battered by the time they had managed to drive on and outstrip their pursuers. He told me that the clerk in whose house the interviewers were to lodge, had recently met one on the road one evening, which had immediately given chase with every intention of rending him with tooth and claw. Fortunately he was young and fleet and chose to run uphill, and thus disappointed the bad-tempered beast. He was lucky. Many an unfortunate Sholiga has been horribly mauled, even had his whole face clawed away, through an unexpected meeting with a sloth bear.

In view of the lateness of the hour when I started back, all this ursine chat had an unsettling effect on me and provided a powerful motivation to get safely back to less exciting territory. I fairly scampered up the steep and stony footpath back to Yellehottay and arrived so breathless that I had to sit down for a while on the steps of the Attikan schoolhouse to compose myself before calling on Mr. Lakhani to report the outcome of the conference with his Kartikerri colleague.

Thence I set off again, following the principal Honnametti estate road as it curved gently down the valley to the site of the labour village. There I first passed the house of the head maistry (overseer), son of dear Subba, head maistry in our young days, then two streets of workers' houses below the road and a terrace of dwellings inhabited by a different caste above the road. More maistry's houses, the shanti or shop, where foodstuffs subsidised by the estate were available, and up on the hill beyond a house belonging to a 'writer' or estate clerk. The smoke of cooking fires filtered upward through the shade trees, children ran about everywhere, hens pecked and scratched around the vegetable plots and occasional banana tree, and women fetching water from the pipe connected to the cardamom-fringed stream, stopped to greet me: "Namaste, Amma." "Namaste," shouted people relaxing after the working day and "Namaste" chorused the children, crowding round in the well-founded belief that I was a reliable source of sweeties. "Namaste, namaste," I replied, edging my way through the clustering juveniles.

Sunder's house was next to the school which, I had noticed with surprise on my last visit, was sparsely attended. This was because of the difficulty of engaging a suitable teacher. Husbandless career women are rare in India and male primary teachers were reluctant to work in such an out-of-the-way place. It seemed a pity in view of the passionate desire for education so evident in south India. Little tots run after foreigners in town and village begging not for money but for "pennu, pennu, pencillu, pencillu". Education, far from being compulsory, is hard to come by among the poor, and therefore immensely valued in spite of white-collar unemployment.

Armed with forms and clipboards the interviewers began their task while I supervised first one pair and then the other. The interviews went off quite well, though Jagan and Rajan had to be reminded to query contradictory statements. There were only a few more to be done with the Harijans and Upuligas working on the estates, and within the next day or two we would only have Sholigas left to interview.

The last interview of the evening took place in the Upuliga 'lines' and was undertaken by Rajan and Ramani. I had been supervising Manjula and Jagan and wandered over to the other two, to find Sunder shamelessly eavesdropping, sniggering all the while. "Come and listen to this," he whispered gleefully. Ramani had reached the section of the questionnaire which dealt with attitudes and was innocently recording some remarkably puritanical replies from the wife. Oh yes, a woman's first duty was to her husband. She must live only for him and be subject to him in all things and so on. "Dear me," I murmured. "She doesn't sound much like an Upuliga, does she?" He exploded with mirth. "To hear her talk you'd think she was a Brahman." She was notorious, it seemed, for being the most promiscuous woman on the estate, and her husband had no influence on her whatsoever.

So we couldn't use that couple's forms. Well, at least it wasn't raining and there were no mosquitoes. According to Sunder, the couple next door were honest souls and moreover they were agreeable to being interviewed, mainly out of curiosity. We started again. It took another hour, by which time darkness had long descended. Gathering the forms to put in my rucksack and bidding goodnight to my young friends and the usual semi-circle of onlookers, I switched on my torch and set off back to Attikan hoping I looked more debonair than I felt.

Bears were in the forefront of my mind, and after that boars. Trying to avert my thoughts from the time two bears came out of the coffee to attack our car one night, and the time I rode my horse June up to Yellehottay on my way home one evening, to see an enormous wild boar come out of the bushes, I trudged apprehensively on uphill in the darkness. "He who would valiant be..." I sang, out of tune. "That's me. Why can't I be intrepid like my papa?"

Why indeed? Not fair to be denied the parental genes one would have chosen and landed with unsatisfactory ones like absent-mindedness. Rallied a little by indignation I increased my pace. But the darkness was Stygian as I entered the fig shola, my torch casting a miserable sliver of light, and I suffered a relapse, especially when I remembered how often I might have to repeat this crepuscular ramble. It then occurred to me that I wouldn't see an animal, hostile or amiable, unless I fell over it, and for all I knew the road was lined with crouching beasts. The unlikelihood of this cheered me up and I began another song: "Show me the way to go home. I'm tired and I wanna go to bed." Almost devil-may-care now (especially as I had left the shola behind), I strode on, belting out off-key a potpourri of hymns and old pop, till I saw the lights of the house and stopped singing for fear of alarming Baswa. Never was his betel-stained grin and the genial glow of the fire more welcome.

But the unseemly haste, on top of a filling pillau, of my return from Kartikerri, plus the long walk earlier on the hills and the usual strain of interviewing, led to unwonted fatigue and a distaste for concentrated questionnaire-checking. "Why am I doing this?" I asked myself, throwing down in exasperation yet another form in which one spouse flatly contradicted the evidence of the other. "I've gone off fertility. There's no future in it."

With these all too prophetic words I shoved the homework aside to brew myself a soothing cup of the panacea 'Boost' and returned to put my feet up by the fire and settle down to a luxurious re-read of Mansfield Park. Which meant that the remaining forms would have to be added to my work-load the following evening.

By the end of the next chapter conscience and common sense were nagging away too persistently to be ignored. I would not have time in the next few days to trot off to my favourite lookout place with the heavy pile of forms and sit in the sun alternately working, brushing away the wispy black flies and gazing southward at that superb view down the Minchiguli valley, where the green and bronze of the nearby hills became subtly modified into the greys and blues of those in the distance. It was silly and lazy not to finish my day's quota of checking and I'd only regret it if I failed to do so. Groaning an acceptance of the logic of these strictures, I laid my book aside and picked up another form, to find to my surprise that the disenchantment of an hour before had passed, and that the individual testaments I now had the privilege of reading seemed to me once more appealing, funny or poignant and always thought-provoking.

When the job was done I went off to bed by candlelight, Baswa having long since turned off the generator at what he considered to be the decent hour for retirement. But I really was tired by now, too tired at first for sleep. I thought of my father's adventures, and it occurred to me that although liberal opinion in the modern world is rightly opposed to big game shooting, the villagers' vision of Ralph as the knight in armour delivering them from dragons had its own truth. It is, after all, just as terrible a fate to be crushed or torn apart by an elephant or mangled by a tiger as it is to be bombed or beaten up by human enemies. He performed for them a service which there was nobody else around to undertake; and though it is true that he shot a good many animals, he also protected a great many more. The sad diminution of the once teeming wildlife of our hills and the surrounding jungles did not come about gradually after we left. It happened with appalling rapidity with a wave of indiscriminate shooting, poaching, poisoning of felines, and the influx of rinderpest-bearing cattle, as soon as he was no longer there to walk through the forest and keep watch. I thought, too, of our mother and reflected ruefully on her trials, with her husband disappearing into the jungle for days on end while she coped with the problems of household and estate, children and employees. It must have been particularly hard for her in wartime, with her husband incommunicado in the army, trying to cope with the theoretical assistance of two nubile daughters preoccupied with boy-friends and dare-devil ventures to the exclusion of sense, and with a third all set to leave the nursery and take off after them. But she always held her own. I smiled in salute, turned over and fell asleep.

shrines

As I walked down the road from Attikan to Yellehottay on a sunny morning I met Mr. Lakhani driving up in the Honnametti jeep. We stopped to exchange pleasantries.

"You are coming to the ceremony?" he enquired.

"Ceremony?"

"You did not know? But I sent a message by Ranga...."

"I didn't see Ranga last night or this morning," I replied truthfully, having taken good care to hide from him on both occasions. "However, I'll be glad to come. Jeddia did mention something of the sort, but I hadn't realised it was to be so soon."

Upon further enquiries it transpired that the new shrine to be established on the recently repaired Udhatti ghat was to replace one that had been there before the road fell into disuse. In a way the induction was to be of the deva or spirit itself, because the old one was deemed to be no longer present. When Sholiga Jeddia had mentioned this project, saying that he was to conduct the rites in his role of tammadi, I had assumed that it was to be a purely tribal affair, possibly conducted from Nellikatherahatti podu. But no, it seemed that it was to be an ecumenical gathering to which everyone on Honnametti was to be invited, and represented a kind of re-inauguration of the ghat road.

Like the Karti Baswa shrine on the Punjur road, this one was to serve both prophylactic and memorial services. Early in the 1950s a Christian mechanic and carpenter employed by my parents, a charming and talented person named Lawrence Pais unfortunately prone to occasional alcoholic bouts, had driven a tractor bound for the ragi fields over the precipitous edge of the road and killed himself at the spot where the deva's shrine was to be installed.

As to the Ranga mentioned above, he was the Attikan tappal (postman), who brought the mail up from Yellehottay and shared bungalow surveillance with Baswa at night. A simple soul, he was possessed of one eccentricity which irritated me beyond endurance. He would walk uninvited into whatever room I happened to be occupying, stand in silence and stare. And stare. It was not any kind of nasty stare. It was a trance-like gaze of total fascination. Asked what he wanted, he would reply, "Nothing," with a disarming smile and go on standing there, drinking me in.

When Bob was with me over Christmas he drank us both in. If Ranga had been a crowd he'd have gathered. When we put up our Christmas cards we had a respite because he scrutinised them instead. He loved those cards, dusting them tenderly each morning, and he was so upset when we took them down that we gave them to him.

Mind you, Ranga lived with his father, ailing mother and several younger siblings in a two-room house in the Attikan 'lines', so he was entitled to his innocent study of alien life-forms. After all, I was in the business of people-watching myself. But he did make me feel very self-conscious, so I guiltily tried to dodge the lad when I was feeling frail.

Sunday was another lovely cold-weather day: blue skies, green jungle, golden grassland, wild hypericum shrubs in yellow flower, the haunting cry of Brahminy kites circling overhead. An evocative day. Walking along the road through the tall trees of the Bellaji shola after crossing the bridge over the Gundal stream above Honnametti waterfall, I heard a crashing noise in the undergrowth below the road, indicative of the passage of heavy animals. Peering over the edge in some excitement I caught a glimpse of the backs of a shiny black bull and several grey-brown cows. A herd of bison, a rare sight nowadays, and all the more pleasing for that.

When the herd was out of sight I went on, following the winding track until it emerged from the trees on to the open Bellaji downland. Walking past the long cattle sheds I reflected that they had been there as long as I could remember, and consequently it had been a great place for those tigers which reckoned they had discovered a soft option: unsuspecting cows, buffaloes and cart-bulls instead of wary deer. The 'phantom' tiger had patronised the Bellaji sheds before moving on to Honnametti, and there was one my parents called 'the head-biter', because it always chewed off its victim's head before starting to feed. This was another for which Ralph had waited sitting on the ground with his rifle across his knees.

Before following the road through Bellaji Gap I decided to climb again the little cemetery hill where Grandfather was buried. On the way up I picked hypericum flowers to lay on the graves, the monument to my grandmother, and the new monument to my father. It was quiet and peaceful up there, and I wished that I could be buried there too, on top of the hill, surrounded by bigger hills, all wrapped in their wild and secretive dignity, still undesecrated by human greed and folly. I thought too of my other grandfather, Angus Kinloch, who had also died as the result of an attack by a wild animal. He had been killed by a wild boar when I was still a baby. My sisters and I and my children too, had loved his wife Nan and I wished I had known him.

Walking down the cemetery hill, leaving the cattle sheds behind, on through Bellaji Gap, and along the section of the ghat road above the slopes that fell away, clad in long grass and prickly wild dates, towards Kurridi Gudday and on down to the foot of the range, I wondered how many tigers remained in the Biligiris. When we left they were still numerous and bold, but their numbers had been drastically reduced within the past twenty-odd years by the introduction of a weedkiller called 'Folidol' which — the local people quickly learned— was lethal to both humans and felines. Murder by 'Folidol' became for a while a popular method of eliminating human encumbrances and enemies, and they poisoned the corpses of tiger and panther kills until they nearly exterminated the big cats.

But San Mada and I had found those fresh droppings coming down from Dupabarri, and he had told me that there were still some tigers in the more remote parts of the hills such as Namagundi. There were also quite a few panthers about. Though the numbers of the deer had diminished sadly anywhere near human habitation because of unrestrained shooting by poachers, the panthers were subsisting quite successfully on porcupines, according to the Sholigas. They must have become cleverer these days at killing them without getting a faceful of barbed quills. Looking down at the tumbled rocks of Kurridi Gudday I thought of that day when Jeddia, like some knight-errant from my favourite literature at that time, had lifted me out of danger in his strong young arms. It seemed fitting that I should be on my way to form a part of the congregation as he, in his honoured old age, presided over rituals to afford safety to those who travelled, on foot or on wheels, in those parts.

The ceremony was amply attended. Jeeps and tractors had set off from the estate carrying workers and staff, including the interviewers (now staying at Honnametti again), plus huge kadais for cooking food, as the function was to end with a feast. It had been arranged that the Nellikatherahatti Sholigas should supply wood and kindling and stoke the cooking fires. The deva was enshrined by Jeddia and acolytes with prolonged prayers, oblations and anointing in a natural niche in a tall outcrop of rock on the inner side of the road, more or less opposite the outer edge over which poor Lawrence had driven to his death. After the rites were concluded we all sat down on the road in two long rows and were served on banana leaves with the good food which the high-caste cooks had been preparing for the past few hours.

The outcrop was enticingly wrinkled and the ceremony long drawn-out. During a lull in the proceedings when everyone's interest was beginning to flag, I could not refrain from trying a few rock-climbing routes up the face. A number of young bloods among staff and labourers (as usual there were no women present apart from Manjula, Ramani and me) at once began to join in the game, and in one way or another a good time was had by all in the sensible Indian fashion which makes no distinction between holy day and holiday. With the deva installed and the feast over everyone began to straggle home at last. The interviewers and I piled into the waiting jeep with Mr. Lakhani and we set off to bounce and judder homeward through the brief Indian dusk.

Watching the last flush of sunset drain from the summits and the stars begin to appear as the dark shapes of the hills enfolded us, I reflected on all the times I had traversed this rough road in my life: hopeful journeys down to adventures; tired homecomings like the present one. A young man, the driver's mate, clung to the outside of the jeep, clutching the top of the door to avoid being jolted off. He was grinning with enjoyment, and I thought of the times when Sheila and I, on trips to and from the plateau country, had likewise enjoyed sitting on the wings of our shooting brake, legs astride the headlamps.

Sometimes, when we went en famille 'shooting for the pot' we were allowed to have the .20 bore and 4.10 shotguns outside the car with us, hoping to put up partridge, quail, jungle fowl or peafowl. We were not strikingly successful (I once came third in a clay-pigeon contest solely because none of the also-rans hit anything at all), but we loved being there on the outside with the wind in our hair and the shadows lengthening as one or other of our parents drove homeward.

Once, returning from the Minna Valley with my father we had approached in this way a sleek golden panther sunning itself on the track. It let us come right up to it, only jumping away at the last minute with an almost playful 'woof'. And another time, Sheila and I astride the headlamps, we came upon two panthers, a female and half-grown cub, rolling and playing in the dust. Ralph was driving and drew up as the panthers sat there and looked at us, almost close enough for Sheila and me to prod them with our toes.

"Don't move," Heather whispered unnecessarily.

Neither of us had any intention of moving. We weren't that silly. Eventually the sinuous spotted pair got bored with the frontal view of the car, strolled over to the side of the road and sat down again, alternately contemplating Ralph through the open window and Sheila, sitting on the wing a few feet from them. Daddy, impelled by the spirit of mischief which lurked, the eternal boy, in his adult soul, began to whistle softly to see what the panthers would do. The mother panther stiffened and began to growl.

"Drive on, Ralph," our mother hissed imperatively.

There was that in her manner — to say nothing of the mother panther's manner — which brooked no delay. He engaged gear quietly and drove on for about a hundred yards. We all looked back to see the panthers still sitting there, looking back at us with feline surmise.

At this point Heather insisted that we got inside the car. She'd had enough excitement for one day, she said, and she wasn't as keen on having her daughters tangle with defensively maternal panthers as Daddy seemed to be. Furthermore she intended to take over the driving, with the intention of getting us all home in one piece. Forty-five years later one of these daughters, still more or less in one piece, was driven home safely up the same road. The road itself had hardly changed at all.

A few days later I found myself in the same jeep, reversing the previous journey. This time Mr. Lakhani and Mr. Coates had invited me to travel with them to the Honnametti ragi fields. I had accepted on condition that they would agree to my walking back from Udhatti at the foot of the hills to Nellikatherahatti, San Mada's podu , and thence back to Attikan.

Today we trundled down the narrow road, repaired so recently after being abandoned for some twenty years since my parents' departure. As we passed through the strips of luxuriant shola bordering the watercourses tumbling down their stony channels, I amused my polite audience by pointing out favourite picnic places of the past. When we were small these were often special treats, celebrating birthdays, for instance. We would stop the car at a spot where a tree-shaded burn crossed the track and scramble up or down a bit before opening the old cane picnic basket and spreading out the goodies: curry puffs or curry and rice, mangoes in their season, or oranges, tree-tomatoes, bananas or peaches. Cold water in the big thermos. Beer for our parents and Polly. Sheila and I would explore the stream, bare-legged in khaki shorts and gym shoes, getting scratched, wet and muddy, absorbing the sights, sounds and scents of the wild. Privileged children.

Because the interviewers and I were to return so soon to the dusty, noisy and variously polluted environs of Lokkanhalli and Kollepet town, this trip had a poignant flavour of departure, and I paid intense attention to every detail of the landscape, investing every bend in the road with its quota of associations with the past. Here, for instance, I told the managers, was the corner where my mother and I had almost bumped into a herd of elephants. Driving home at dusk after a sojourn in Bangalore we had found the road in such a parlous state after recent thunderstorms that I had to get out of the car and walk ahead, filling up the deepest ruts with stones. I had just got in again as we reached a comparatively smoother stretch when we rounded the corner to find the view blocked by the massive backsides of the elephants, who were strolling in a leisurely manner up the road. Heather braked, turned off the lights, rolled down the window, and let the car run gently backward as she leaned out, trying to keep clear of the edge of the road in the semi-darkness, while we both held our breath and refrained from whispered comment until we were safely back out of sight. It was not until crashing noises below about fifteen minutes later indicated (we hoped) the herd's exit from the road that we dared creep forward again.

Today the drive was hair-raising enough to keep us fairly quiet while we negotiated its offering of obstacles, but once we reached the bottom of the ghat we were able to relax under an old sampagi tree, the sweet fragrance of its creamy flowers mingling with the smell of dust and of the strongly scented lantana thorn. Insects buzzed a background to our talk and laughter as we shared our food. Mr. Lakhani was in the strong position of one whose high caste precluded him from accepting cooked food from those whose culture did not debar low-caste cooks, thus giving him a head start in the reciprocity stakes. But he accepted fruit from Mr. Coates and me, while we non-Hindus tucked into everyone's contributions. I came off the best, food-wise, having only biscuits and marmite, fruit and nuts to offer, while Mr. Coates's cook had made him delicious pakoras, which I gratefully scoffed, along with Mr. Lakhani's wife's biryani.

Then we parted, the managers driving on to inspect the fields while I started back on foot up the road. A young Sholiga who lived at Udhatti caught up with me. He said he was on his way to visit his father at Nellikatherahatti, so we went on together. He turned out to be remarkably acculturated, apparently knowing little or no Sholiga lore, and few place names of the hills. In fact it turned out that I knew a good deal more about the hills than he did. The discovery surprised us both and this evidence of the vanishing of an irreplaceable cultural tradition saddened me. My young companion looked even more surprised when I scolded him for his ignorance, and I had to remind myself hastily that from his point of view my testiness was unreasonable, not to say mysterious.

Eventually we turned off the ghat to brush through the long grass of the deciduous jungle, following in single file a narrow footpath which climbed sharply uphill for what seemed a long way until it emerged suddenly into a relatively more open area which turned out to be the edge of the podu land.

Nellikatherahatti, the place of the nellikai trees, had been an abandoned podu in my young days, and overrun by jungle. But a few years before my first return in 1974, a group of Sholigas decided to go back to this site in a wild part of the hills not far from Namagundi betta. Before the reopening of the Udhatti ghat it was pretty remote, and when I was first invited by San Mada to visit it I was interested to learn that a Sholiga called San Eera was one of their number. San Eera had been one of my father's most valued shikaris but latterly he had become a man of substance (for a Sholiga), owning cattle and fields at Udhatti. He and his family, San Mada and his family, and a few others had made a considered decision to go back to the old ways, obviously motivated by a deep feeling of loss of identity and an almost inarticulate sense of being cheated of their heritage. Not that they put it like that to me. When I asked San Eera what had led them to this decision, he replied with simple gravity, "It was in our hearts."

Today I accompanied my young friend in search of his father, who lived, to my joy, in a splendid tree house which I had at first taken for a mere watchman's shelter. Our introduction was somewhat prolonged on account of the son's insistence that I should photograph his father and himself and the father's insistence that this should only be done when he was dressed for the occasion. So he climbed into his eyrie to change, the result being a nice polaroid picture for each of them and a considerable hiatus in my programme.

When all was disposed to the satisfaction of my new Sholiga friends I went to look for the old ones. The podu was now a large one, supporting about fifty people, members of several families.

It consisted of a large clearing stippled with trees, some of them tall, such as that which housed the Sholiga father, and some of them smaller, with feathery leaves and the round green fruit looking like walnut-sized gooseberries which the Sholigas call nellikai (nelli fruit).

The standard of cultivation was par for the course with Sholigas, which means poor. There seemed to be more weeds than ragi in the plots under the trees. Clearly it was easier to harvest food directly from the forest than to bother with hoeing. Indeed, patches of smoothly swept packed earth on which all kinds of jungle produce was spread to dry bore witness to the fact. So did sundry holes in the approach and perimeter paths from which yams had recently been dug.

I once walked with my father and some Sholigas eastward from Namagundikan, down a long rocky ridge which led from the high hills towards Udhatti, passing from the rainforest zone, through the long grass and deciduous zone to the scrub jungle of the plateau. And as we went the Sholigas told us what was and what was not good to eat, plucking us bits of this and that to sample. Bright yellow raspberries; honey on a twig; purple nirulu fruit which look like damsons but taste nicer, more like grapes; leaves; fungi and tubers. Before we could stop them they would break off a laden branch and proffer it. Sholigas, having been accustomed to the sole use of thousands of acres of jungle, are still alarmingly wasteful of currently scarce resources.

As I approached San Mada's huts I came across an ingenious contraption: a kerosene tin slung diagonally between a tree and a bush on a thin creeper. When the creeper was touched the tin swayed and loose stones inside it rattled. It was a scare-pig, with which the podu residents hoped to frighten foraging wild pig out of the grain plots without risking their own lives. The night-watchman in the tree swung the rope at intervals and hoped the noise would deter prospective porcine invaders.

San Mada came to meet me and to introduce his wife Madi and other relatives of all ages. We sat on the ground and talked for a bit after exchanging gifts: woollen vests, Marks and Spencer biscuits, cough mixture, as requested, and band-aids from me to them. Sholigas are prone to bronchitis in the monsoon and short of irresponsibly dishing out antibiotics this was the best I could do. Homegrown bananas from them to me. I asked after San Eera.

"San Eera is dead," they said. It was a shock, though he had been a very old man when I last saw him. But Sholigas have an ageless look, and my parents long ago nicknamed San Eera 'Peter Pan' when they spoke of him among themselves. The acute sense of loss I felt was as much a feeling of indignation that mortality had after all been one of his attributes as of mourning over the severance of yet another link with that pristine past. I asked San Mada whether he believed in the mainstream Hindu doctrine of reincarnation.

"No," he replied philosophically. "We just bury and forget."

But Jeddia believed he was going to join my father, and he was a tammadi. Sholigas, like everyone else, vary in their metaphysical convictions.

We sat for a few minutes in the silence due to San Eera's life and death, and then San Mada rose and walked towards a hut adjacent to his own, built like his of interlaced twigs reinforced with mud and thatched with grass. I followed him to the door and looked in. When Bob had been with me that time we had walked together to Nellikatherahatti to call on San Mada. After greeting us and introducing his family he had said he wanted to show us something, and led us to this hut.

The whole interior was a shrine to my parents. On a kind of central altar built of earth were their framed and garlanded photographs. Around these were smaller photographs and various little artefacts from our house which Ralph had given him before he went away for good. There didn't seem to be anything else in the hut at all.

Bob and I had been deeply touched and I had started to cry. True to form, my eyes filled with tears again today and overflowed while I groped for my grubby handkerchief. San Mada admonished me with kindly "Tch tch" noises to help me recover myself, and in the end I managed between sniffs a few disconnected phrases. "Bahala olledu, Appa. Bahala santosa." (It is very good, father. Very pleasing). It seemed to be what he expected, as he nodded in satisfaction and showed me round the rest of his domain. There was a hut containing a vast brass kadai, a pot about two feet in diameter and four feet high which had once graced a Honnametti lyre-plumbing bathroom and subsequently heated water for special posh camping reachable by bullock cart, like our occasional Christmas camps with guests. My parents had given him this as well and it was now used for storing grain. Other things like bedding were stored here too. Sholigas tend to use their huts for storage and to do all their living in the spaces outside unless it is actually pouring with rain. If anyone dies in a Sholiga hut they burn it down. Which is one reason why forest officials recently found to their surprise that Sholigas could not be prevailed upon to use the custom-built brick houses they were provided with (in an attempt at permanent settlement) for anything but storage. The Sholigas reply to official protests was, "How can you burn down a brick house?" A reasonable question in the circumstances.

I met various members of San Mada's and San Eera's families again. Some of the younger ones had now grown up, married and had their separate huts. I found the relationships somewhat confusing as Sholigas tend to re-marry rather frequently. Unlike orthodox Hindus, their weddings don't cost much, so they can afford to. They have more than one form of marriage too, the most common being what Srinivas calls 'ratified elopement', when the girl and boy go off together into the jungle to consummate the union, come back to a token scolding and then celebrate at a feast given by the boy's father. Another form is for the boy to work for a number of years in the girl's parents' household to prove himself a good husband. If acceptable, he stays on as son-in-law.

About an hour of chat and sightseeing round the rest of the podu ensued: the podu deity's shrine; the stream providing clean water all the year; the stored produce; with of course a tacit avoidance of such delicate subjects as ancient shotguns buried under hut floors and illegal cannabis plots. My father once pointed out one of these with raised eyebrows to a podu resident. "I can't imagine how that got there," said the owner blandly. Which Ralph and all the onlookers received with colluding mirth and exclamations of "eh", the Kannada expression of incredulity.

At last it was time to set off on the long walk home. San Mada insisted on accompanying me part of the way, so after a chorus of "Hogi banni" (go and come, the rustic form of goodbye in Kannada), and cries on my part of "Barrutane" (I will come back), we left along another single-file footpath which would lead us in time to the ghat road.

I looked back once more at the clearing in the forest with the huge shoulder of Namagundi rising above it and planned to come and stay for a long time at Nellikatherahatti. San Mada was quite enthusiastic when I mentioned the idea. "If you come to stay here we will build you a house like mine."

"That would please me very much," I said, loyally quelling a hankering for a tree house.

"But you will have to be careful when you go walking. The jungle is very dangerous now. Too many bears and elephants."

Difficult to be careful enough, though, as many a food-gathering Sholiga has found. All the same, I thought, it would be lovely to go back and stay with these people with whom I felt so much at home, maybe for a year, to see out the round of ritual and production. Perhaps they would let me attend the Rotihabba, the big annual harvest celebration about which they are so secretive that little is known. And perhaps I will yet.

When I was about fourteen and still under the impression that I was a poet, I wrote a good deal of verse about the Biligirirangan hills. One poem, addressed to Honnametti Kalu, predicted that I would keep on returning there all my life. And curiously enough, I have not yet knowingly left Honnametti for good. When I went away in the early fifties it never occurred to me that this was the end of an era because I had no idea that my parents would sell up and leave. Honnametti was the geographic centre of my life: the one fixed reference point. And each time I went back there in the subsequent years of my research projects, I left assuming that I would be back shortly. There has never yet been any question of saying goodbye forever. But I'm not at all sure now that I want to go back any more. In my dreams of Honnametti I wander through a dusty shell looking for my mother, and there is enough truth to the dream to tinge every visit with sadness. Besides, the trees as well as the animals are being destroyed. The sholas are dwindling. On the other hand I am nearer my father there than anywhere else. He still walks his beloved hills with the shades of his friends, waiting, it may be, for old Jeddia to join him at last, and to see the jungle reinstated in the tiger country, as it was reinstated years ago. So perhaps I'll go home once more, to come to terms with past and present in a Sholiga hut in Nellikatherahatti, or looking down the Minchiguli valley from the belvedere at Attikan. Moreover, I need to give a decent burials to that part of my soul which, at odds with my Quaker conscience, cries to be reborn as a defiant little devi with a large stockpile of sakti — supernatural female power — to put a curse on the head of anybody who fells a tree, harms an animal, or patronises a Sholiga in the White Hills of Rangan.

postscript

While I was on the hills I was invited to attend a meeting organised by the Chamarajnagar Family Planning Unit. A team of doctors turned up in a jeep; a platform had been improvised; all the staff plus the maistries (overseers) on Honnametti, Attikan and Kartikerri Estates were present; the work-force were given a day off; and loudspeakers summoned one and all to listen to words of wisdom.

The speeches were excellent. The advice on contraception, hygiene, and the care and feeding of children in the well-spaced ideal family was unexceptionable. But trouble arose with the advent of question time. Nobody in the audience seemed to have any questions, or indeed, comments, at all and the prolonged silence became uncomfortable. Eventually I rose with some diffidence to my feet.

"I do have a question," I said. "We have been listening to invaluable instruction on the vital subjects of birth control and child-rearing. But, as we all know, it is the women who conceive and bear, feed and bring up the children. Yet, apart from the lady doctor on the platform and myself there are no women present here today. My question is, where are the women?"

The answer, after another embarrassing silence, was a hasty assurance from those on the platform that of course they did sometimes hold such meetings for women. I didn't press the issue. It was not the doctors' fault that the women had not been invited to, or expected to, attend an occasion of so much relevance to their sex; and I was after all the guest of the estate managers, a mere researcher with no executive standing. But my question highlighted the situation in India (and elsewhere in the so-called Third World) which underlies, in fact precipitates, their problems of over-population: the traditional presumption of female marginality.

This being recognised, it must be added that in India this traditional perception, still much in evidence today, is cross-cut and complicated by three important cultural dichotomies: the cleavage between attitudes in the South and in the North; the cleavage which echoes it between the high castes and the low castes; and the new chasm opening between the dictates of caste and class.

The first contrast seems to reflect ancient and fundamental differences in outlook in Hindu India. The North places a particularly low value on the female, which may be partly related to high marriage and dowry expenses for daughters, to the exclusion of women from inheritance of property, and to the low work participation of women (who have to be restricted and protected to preserve male 'honour'). Basically, north India appears to be part of a 'high masculinity' belt which stretches from the Mediterranean through the Middle East and Pakistan to the Assam border. In north India the ideal of hypergamy (wife marrying upward socially) goes with the rejection of marriage to kin, and the rule that wives should only be taken from areas outside the husband's village or local territory. This ideology stems from the Hindu principle of kanya daan, the gift of a virgin. It means a gift to a Brahman which never can be repaid as that which the donor receives in return is merit. Since the bride takers symbolise Brahmans, they are regarded as perpetually superior to the bride-givers even when the marriage is between peers. No bride-taker will ever willingly give a bride to a group which has previously been its bride-giver, as to do so would be to reverse their status positions. This means that the north Indian bride is married into a strange household far away from her natal family and that interaction between her kin and her husband's is minimal.

In south India the picture is very different. The ideal is marriage between social equals who are preferably also kinfolk, and within the village and locality of the young couple. The average south Indian bride moves into a household which often consists of relatives she has known all her life, and which is within walking distance of her natal one.

In north India the only way the wife in the average orthodox Hindu family can achieve any status in the eyes of her husband's kin-group is by bearing sons. The birth of a girl is a disaster. Therefore her husband and his kin will want to keep on trying for a boy, and she will collude in this because only through sons can she prove and redeem herself. The result is a high birth rate, in spite of the high mortality of neglected female infants, and a high death rate of women compared to that of men.

In the South boy children are desired more than are girls but girls are not unwanted. At least one girl in a family is considered to be a blessing, and I came across a number of couples who were determined to 'keep on trying' for a girl. Girls, I was often told, are auspicious. For every Chamarajnagar taluk respondent who said, "What's the use of having girls, they will only get married," there were others who said girls were more likely to care for their parents in old age, were better behaved than boys, more reliable, etc.

So, while the status of women in south India is not particularly high per se, it is a good deal higher than it is in the North, and this has an effect on the birth rate in the South, which is notably lower than it is in the North. Furthermore, women may inherit property, they don't marry at quite such an early age (though early enough), child mortality and the ratio of female to male child mortality is lower, and female literacy figures are higher for the South. In fact, as the demographer Tim Dyson has it, behind these contrasting estimates of female worth lies another concept, that of female autonomy, "the capacity to manipulate one's own personal environment". In fact the first thing to strike the traveller from North to South is that there are far more women to be seen about in the streets and fields in the South.

The same contrasts are apparent within the caste system. In Chamarajnagar, as in other parts of India, there is no sharp division between the high and low castes, but a gradual, intensely disputed continuum between the Brahmans at the top and the untouchables at the bottom. But as far as the status of women is concerned, a pronounced divergence is revealed between high and low-caste ideals. Professor M.N. Srinivas, himself a Mysorean, confirms that the relationship between men and women in the low castes is much more egalitarian, and that when low castes, or members of low castes try to move up in the caste hierarchy by adopting Brahmanic customs, one of the first consequences is the lowering of the status and restriction of the liberty of the women in their households.

Among the Chamarajnagar low castes I found that both sexes could divorce each other; that both sexes could marry again after divorce or being widowed; that women could go out at will and unaccompanied, that daughters' weddings cost no more than those of sons; that the birth of girls was even welcomed; and that there was no very strong concern with questions of female subordination or the equation of male 'honour' with the 'purity' of female family members. Among the orthodox higher castes, though, these easy-going usages were reversed. Women were more or less restricted to the house, according to the degree of conservatism of the household head; had no right to re-marry after widowhood or to divorce; could not eat until their husbands had eaten, however late they might come home; and in general were expected to treat their husbands as minor deities. Tim Dyson and Mick Moore summed it up thus: The more closely members of a south Indian high caste adhere to Brahmanic principles, the more their culture resembles that of north Indian high castes in its denigration and subordination of its female members.

I found, of course, that these differences between high and low-caste cultures were far from sharply defined, because they were complicated and confused by the influences of Westernisation, modernisation, urbanisation, education, in fact the subtle shift from caste to class values. Chamarajnagar men with a Western-type education often wanted educated wives. Educated couples — the new elite — had high aspirations for daughters as well as sons. It is true that low-caste parents were sometimes anxious to take advantage of the Government's 'protective legislation' to educate daughters as well as (in two cases, rather than) sons. But on the whole their poverty compelled them to put their children of both sexes to work as soon as possible to contribute to the meagre family income. On the other hand it was obvious to me that Westernisation was in the process of improving the lot of an increasing number of high-caste women in Chamarajnagar, one of many reasons being that the trappings of the new elitism included well-educated and at least relatively emancipated wives and daughters.

As the economist Robert Cassen has pointed out, 'The prominence of women in professional and public life may mislead foreigners into thinking that India is unusually liberal in its treatment of women, whereas on the contrary women in India, apart from the emancipated few, are as oppressed as anywhere in the world.' The historian A.N. Altekar has suggested that the standing of Indian women has deteriorated steadily since the Vedic age, when they enjoyed virtual equality with men. Certainly the laws of the

Brahman Manu, who lived about two thousand years ago, passed sentence on all women for the felony of not being men. Condemned to perpetual tutelage, first under the father, then the husband and then the son, they were also forbidden to study the Vedas, presumably to prevent them from getting subversive ideas. And in the past, the high-caste widow's position as an inauspicious appendage, shaven-headed and shunned, could only be avoided by pre-deceasing her spouse, (for which every good wife was supposed to pray, and probably did, in view of the alternatives) or being burned alive on his funeral pyre. But here again a divergence between north and south Indian culture is revealed. In south India views on the female sex exhibit an ambivalence which seems to spring from a mixture of contrary cultures, and indeed evidence for a past matrilineal tradition, is observable in many areas. Dual images in binary opposition abound: the potent and the vulnerable; the pure and the impure; the auspicious married mother associated with the sacred cow, and the intrinsically dangerous temptress. The concept of sakti the power or energy of the universe, is an important aspect of south Indian Hinduism. Sakti is sacred female power, since here the female and male principles are the reverse of the yin/yang duo: female is active and male is passive. So, the argument goes, because of her sacred powers the female must be kept under male control and her chastity well guarded.

The population study I undertook in Chamarajnagar taluk clearly revealed that female fertility there, as elsewhere, was governed by a number of factors, the most important of which was the relative autonomy of the wife in any given family. Other salient influences were the family's economic and educational position. But these had an indirect effect. The causal chain worked something like this. If a family inherited or acquired affluence it had a choice of routes to prestige: the traditional and orthodox caste route involving 'pure' customs, or the Western class route involving the adoption of 'modern' customs. If it chose the latter it entered the ranks of the new élite and educated its female members. Thus a rise in economic status could lead to female education and the graduate women I interviewed, especially those whose qualifications had led to lucrative and prestigious jobs, had no intention of having many children. Along with self-respect and self-determination, they had acquired control of their own fertility.

Thus the financial state of a married couple was an indirect determinant of fertility. If it led to the adoption of a 'modern' lifestyle, it affected the wife because she would either be educated or have educated daughters. My statistics showed that education had a kind of cumulative effect. Women with secondary education wanted graduate daughters, and so, apparently, did their husbands. Wives with higher education obviously started childbearing later, knew about modern forms of contraception, and so controlled the number of their pregnancies.

Education only affected fertility because it led to the relative autonomy of wives who traditionally had had no control over their fertility, since this was the prerogative of the husband and his parents. Where the autonomy of women, including the right to choose how many children they would have, was traditionally recognised by their caste / community, neither affluence nor education were relevant to the situation, since these factors had no effect on female status in an already egalitarian society. This was the case with the Sholiga tribe, who had fewer children per couple than any of the other castes in my survey. Both sexes were illiterate and when asked their views on the value of education, were prone to point out that literacy was unnecessary when you lived in the jungle. Economic and educational components were still involved in the tribal situation, but of a different kind. Sholiga women declared that they were not subordinate to the men because their contribution to family and tribe subsistence was equal. Both sexes gathered foodstuffs and other forest produce in the jungle, and both sexes worked in a somewhat slapdash manner at the hoe cultivation of ragi which supplied the grain staple in their podus. And the knowledge which was vital to their welfare, of how to survive in the jungle, they had learned from childhood. Furthermore, as a Sholiga father put it indignantly, "To teach your children good manners you don't have to be able to read and write."

It has all too often been observed by anthropologists that whereas among 'primitive' tribes living in (and on) the wilderness, women enjoy a high degree of independence and freedom from male domination, once they settle and turn to cultivation and animal husbandry, their influence and freedom diminishes. One suspects that the same state of affairs would arise with the Sholigas unless they become recipients of some new and imaginative development programme which would seek to preserve those elements of their culture which would benefit the population planners as well as Indian society as a whole. The results of my Chamarajnagar research showed that Indian planners have much to learn from tribes such as the Sholigas. But so far all they have tried to do is to incorporate them into 'the wider society'. There seems to be no advantage in this for anyone, least of all the Sholigas, since their traditional customs and attitudes are more valuable to the State in its struggle against over-population than are the observances of the society with which it is planned to integrate them.

This is not to say that literacy should be withheld from Sholigas and other hill tribes, but that it should not be allowed to take the place of their ancient knowledge, skills and attitudes. Many of the 'settled' Sholigas I met knew little or nothing about the wild land on the fringes of which they still lived, and yet had nothing with which to replace it but the precarious husbandry of the average Karnataka peasant. On the other hand I noticed that Sholiga women when 'settled' still sturdily cultivated their own fields, which some said their daughters would inherit, so there

is hope that orthodox Hindu ideology concerning Woman's Place will pass them by and that if and when the tribe acquires literacy, the women will be there learning alongside the men.

www.ingramcontent.com/pod-product-compliance
Lightning Source LLC
Chambersburg PA
CBHW061443150726
47987CB00001B/316